SUZIE SMILED...
THE NEW WAVE

BRITISH
HEAVY
METAL

Published in 2006 by
INDEPENDENT MUSIC PRESS
Independent Music Press is an imprint of I.M. P. Publishing Limited
This Work is Copyright © I. M. P. Publishing Ltd 2005

Suzie Smiled: The New Wave Of British Heavy Metal
by John Tucker

British Library Cataloguing-in-Publication Data.
A catalogue for this book is available from The British Library.

ISBN 0-9549704-7-0

Every effort has been made to contact and credit correctly the photographers
whose work has been used in this book – however a few were unobtainable.
The publishers would be grateful if those concerned would contact
Independent Music Press.

Cover Design by Fresh Lemon.
Edited by Martin Roach.

Printed in the UK.

INDEPENDENT MUSIC PRESS
P.O. Box 69,
Church Stretton, Shropshire
SY6 6WZ

Visit us on the web at: www.impbooks.com

For a free catalogue, e-mail us at: info@impbooks.com
Fax: 01694 720049

SUZIE SMILED...
THE NEW WAVE OF
BRITISH HEAVY METAL

by

John Tucker

Independent Music Press

I'd like to thank all the editors and contributors who've allowed me to reproduce extracts from their work.
If I couldn't find you to ask, it wasn't for the want of trying.

All photographs © John Tucker except Bitches Sin and Shiva (photographers unknown - photos supplied from the bands' archives) and Sharalee - The Bitches Sin Girl by Ian McDonald.
Cover photo - Wayne Renshaw of Savage, February 1984.

CONTENTS

ACKNOWLEDGEMENTS

This is a book about the New Wave Of British Heavy Metal, but perhaps it's more about the musicians and their stories. I am indebted to the following people who gave their time so freely to contribute to this book. So, in nothing more than band/organisation alphabetical order, my sincere thanx go to:

Mike Ellis of Aragorn
Tony Dolan of Atomkraft
Mick Moore of Avenger
Ian Toomey and Pete Toomey of Bitches Sin (not forgetting Sharalee)
Blaze Bailey of Blaze
Brian Ross and Jim Sieroto of Blitzkrieg
Tom Doherty of Communique Records
Sean Harris and Brian Tatler of Diamond Head
Denise Dufort and Jackie Chambers of Girlschool
John Mortimer (spelled it right this time!) and Ron Levine of Holocaust
Sean Hetherington of Intense
Paul Di'Anno of Iron Maiden
Garry Pepperd of Jaguar
Jon Craven of Liquid Sky
Lemmy and Mikkey Dee of Motörhead
John Gallagher of Raven
Geoff Gillespie of Sabre, Snowblind and Majestic Rock Records
(not forgetting Ade at Majestic)
Steve Hammonds and Jon Richards at Sanctuary Records
Sean Taylor and Russ Tippens of Satan
Biff Byford of Saxon
Andy Skuse and Chris Logan of Shiva
Garry Phillips of Soldier
Mark Sutcliffe and Dave Crawte of Trespass
Jess Cox and Robb Weir of Tygers Of Pan Tang
Montalo of Witchfynde

In addition, I would like to sincerely thank Sean Harris for summing it all up in his introduction to this book and the old gang, affectionately known as The Zoo from days gone by – that's Chris (lead guitar),

Dave (manager of Castle Records/drums), John (rhythm guitars), Steve (not a band member but the cleverest guy I know) and Peter (whom I've known for so long I think we're actually clones) – for many years of discussions/heated debates/full blown arguments over things as seemingly trivial as the best track on the first Iron Maiden album or whether Girl's 'Hollywood Tease' was better than 'My Number' (it's 'Prowler', by the way, and 'My Number' is the better song by far). I'd also like to thank my metal mayhem partner-in-crime Steven Bowler, who wrote to ask one day if he could review Blitzkrieg's *A Time Of Changes* LP for a magazine and ended up a close collaborator and great friend.

Finally, *Suzie Smiled...* is respectfully dedicated to Lia, without whom none of this would be worthwhile, and to the memory of my father, who taught me that music isn't a matter of life and death – it's much more important than that.

John Tucker
October 2005

INTRODUCTION

I became aware of the New Wave Of British Heavy Metal when the phrase was coined in reaction to the voice of a new metal underground. Bands everywhere were doing their own thing in an attempt to be seen or heard in the arena of memory. For me, personally, that consisted of a few priceless moments: having to use the chip shop next door to the venue to get changed into our spandex – "Would you like 'em battered, luv?"; playing Reading as surprise special guests to a gob-smacked audience of 30,000 at the height of our powers; witnessing the mighty AC/DC in full flight from the side of the stage at Newcastle Mayfair; sharing a scotch with Bon Scott; and playing to an audience of twelve in Sheffield – four of whom were Def Leppard checking out the talent (well, there was a lot of it about).

This was the Eighties, metal and denim and riots in the streets, the era of the metal punks in a land of myths and heroes, making the music of their time. There we were, at the beginning of modern metal, laying the foundation stone, sowing the seed of the great bands of tomorrow. A golden age in my opinion that was, unfortunately, without a suitable title, appellation or acronym. The 'New Wave Of British Heavy Metal' or 'NWOBHM' or 'Newobhim' (phew!) though apt, never quite rolled off the tongue like punk, new wave or good old rock 'n' roll, somehow meaning one had to eclipse it or outgrow it to receive international recognition; and although some did, most didn't. So by '83 the flame was flickering, and that was it; the boom days were over. Lacking the support of a modern infrastructure for networking, unable to break the grip of a pre-MTV radio-play dominated America or stimulate an ambivalent Europe, the movement found its lifeblood ebbing away. Caught between the past and the future, stranded in a moment when the nail of destiny was hammered into history.

The missive that was the New Wave Of British Heavy Metal was thus both a message sent by the bands and gladly received by the fans as a contract between them. A deal made between the flesh of freedom and imagination and the spirit of brutal honesty. That is why the heart still beats and will always do so, hidden but alive, secretive yet much sought after. A time of innocence and innovation for good and for bad; here was a diamond-hard melting pot with attitude and a do-it-yourself mentality that still resonates today. Maybe that's why my own kids, and some of their friends too, have a genuine affection for 'Dad's Music' – 'Am I Evil' being a particular favourite which may yet, it seems, become the national anthem of some future republic or undiscovered country! Wow! How Wagnerian!

I hope that with these few words about those 'happy days' I have been able to conjure up something of its Zeitgeist, a sense of the nature of the beast that still rides the silver skies. So do try and find what truth is out there; maybe here in this book is the beginning of a more perfect understanding.

In the words of the time scrawled on the wall of numerous sweaty dressing rooms behind so many stages:

"'AVE A GOOD 'UN, LUV ANGELWITCH!"

Sean Harris
The Original Voice of Diamond Head
September 2004

CHAPTER ONE

DENIM AND LEATHER — 1979

"Where were you in '79 when the dam began to burst?..."

'Denim & Leather' by Saxon (p) 1981

IN THE BEGINNING

The New Wave Of British Heavy Metal began for me on December 10, 1979 at a nightclub called Routes, in Exeter, Devon. At the time I was at school, about six months or so away from my A-Levels and whatever was to come next in the Big Wide World. I was considering journalism, or something using languages, but spent most of my time planning on being a rock 'n' roll star. I had a fledgling collection of traditional rock/metal records – Deep Purple, Bad Company, Led Zeppelin, AC/DC, you know the sort of thing, and was vaguely aware of new bands making waves (no pun intended) elsewhere in Britain – almost anywhere, in fact, except my sleepy home town of Torquay – but not having the cash to buy the music papers, all the info I got was second-hand. My introduction to the NWOBHM came when a bunch of friends invited me to squeeze in the back of an already over-crowded car to see a 'happening' new band. Fittingly enough, the band that kick-started the NWOBHM for me was Iron Maiden.

It was a great night. No-one, band included, realised that the club ran a teenage disco till 10pm so we all ended up in the pub across the road. Iron Maiden, back to a four-piece after parting company with Tony Parsons, were amazed that we had come so far (well, they seemed to think it was a long way) to see them without any of us having yet heard the band's mail order debut *Soundhouse Tapes* EPWe in turn were amazed by vocalist Paul Di'Anno's pork pie hat. These were times when different music factions not only didn't mix but actually hated each other with a vengeance; at Saxon gigs, Biff Byford routinely led chants of "we hate the mods" – and we did, actually – so a metal singer with Two-Tone accoutrements just didn't compute. But what a show! I had never seen a gig with that much energy and excitement, and I didn't even know any of the songs, hadn't even heard the band till they kicked into their opening number.

It would be an overstatement to say that this was a life-changing experience because, as I've said, I'd already begun to amass a collection of more mainstream rock/metal albums and singles, but it did start my hunger – quite literally in fact, as I began to pocket my school dinner money and spend it on *Sounds* and as many self-pressed singles as were advertised in its back pages. For that reason alone, though, I have always had a soft spot for Iron Maiden. Like many fans, I thought they lost the plot somewhere along the way, although that all changed again with the release of *Virtual XI* in 1998 which moved them near the top of my 'Essential Listening' list once more.

By the time I had left school just over six months later, a number of NWOBHM bands had reached the provinces. Def Leppard, Saxon, Sledgehammer, Girl... Okay, so if you lived in London you could probably have seen all these bands in one week, but I was in Hicksville, south Devon, where Monty Python's *Life Of Brian* had been banned (naturally), the local press had led the outcry over a record shop window displaying the Sex Pistols' *Never Mind The Bollocks* LP, and where I was routinely hassled by the police for the lesser-known misdemeanours of either being out of doors with long hair after the hours of daylight or wearing a denim jacket in a built-up area. All of a sudden I felt that this was something or somewhere I *belonged*. As Geoff Gillespie of Sabre says later on, it was "something personal to us." Rock fans in general were much derided, but all of a sudden there seemed to be an instant extended family of people to talk to or share a beer with. Dave, one of the clan, was the drummer of Tarsus and the manager of a flea-pit record store called Castle Records, and he began to turn the shop into a heavy metal emporium so the independently-released records became easier to come by. (You know how sometimes you push open the door of a record shop and get a feeling of dread – crap music, uninterested sales assistants, that sort of thing? At Castle Records it was not unusual to have to force the door open against the sheer shock waves of, say, 'Breaking The Law', being played at ear-splitting volume and all six-foot-four of Dave standing on the counter, hair flailing, tennis racket – no spelling mistake – in hand. As heavy metal grew in importance, Dave went on to become one of the suppliers of the *Melody Maker* weekly heavy metal chart, which meant that any band we came across could get instant publicity in a national music paper; eventually, of course, Castle Records went bust.)

As for me, in October 1980 I went to Swansea University – not a hotbed of metal at the time; in fact, it was probably home to the biggest faction of twelve-year-old gobby skinheads in the universe, which did make life difficult from time to time. However, three years and one completely useless degree later, I ended up in London where I wrote or contributed to a number of fanzines and magazines worldwide, and indulged my NWOBHM tendencies by writing Neat Records' in-house freebie magazine *Lead Weight* (named after the label's first ever compilation; label boss Dave Wood's title suggestion had been – ever helpfully – *Scrap Metal*). Woodsy always maintained that rival label Heavy Metal Records' *Rock Star* magazine was put out as a direct result of us creating *Lead Weight*, and maybe it was, but then in the great scheme of things, does it really matter?

Ah, daze gone by. This is not a nostalgia trip by an ageing rocker, but a personalised account of the NWOBHM; personalised by me, by other fans and by the bands that were its lifeblood. It is *not* an encyclopaedic A-Z of the New Wave Of British Heavy Metal; that's already been done and if that's what you are looking for, pick up a copy of Malc Macmillan's excellent *The New Wave Of British Heavy Metal Encyclopaedia*. Above all, it is a thank you to the hundreds of bands (Macmillan lists over 500, from Arc Lane to Zorro) who made those years of the early Eighties so musically enjoyable. Meantime, I have attempted to get all the facts right, but in trying to pull together stories that are up to 25 years old there are bound to be a few inaccuracies (hey, can you remember what you were doing 25 years ago?). Just treat them as bum notes, crank it up, and enjoy.

WHO THE HELL IS SUZIE?

Not only did Saxon and Tygers Of Pan Tang share a stage on the *Wheels Of Steel* tour in 1980, they also seem to have shared an infatuation with ladies named Suzie. 'Suzie Smiled' is a song from the Tygers' debut album *Wild Cat*, and was also issued as their third single (albeit in slightly edited form) in August 1980 with a brutal cover version of ZZ Top's 'Tush' on the flipside. 'Suzie Hold On' appeared on Saxon's *Wheels Of Steel* and was also issued as a single one month after the Tygers' 7", coupled with a live version of 'Judgement Day' on the flip and a back-to-front photo of the band on the picture sleeve.

So, who the hell was Suzie Tyger?

"Suzie was a friend," recalls Jess Cox, the original Tygers Of Pan Tang vocalist. "The thing is with Newcastle, and I should imagine it's probably the same for a lot of other cities, but particularly Newcastle being 300 miles away, there's this thing that you've only made it if you're in London and back then Newcastle wasn't a particularly great place to be. I'd only been to London a few times, but I'd seen the other side of things, wasn't under the impression that the streets were paved with gold, you know. And there was this girl who wanted to go down to London and see the bright lights, thought it would be great, but when she got there it wasn't so great after all, and eventually she came back. But she was very upset about the whole thing, it was a very bad experience for her. She was happy to be back. But she did say that to me – 'Yeah, I'm coming home,' and she smiled, and the song more or less came from there. A true story…"

And Suzie Saxon? "It's a true story. It's loosely about a girl we knew who had cancer and who died later," says Saxon's singer Biff Byford. "It's loosely based on that. That's the inspiration behind the song, a friend who died of a brain tumour. It's like a tribute to her."

LOOKING BACK...

Looking forwards, 25 years seems almost an eternity. In retrospect, it doesn't seem that long at all. But as you look back you realise just how much can change over a quarter of a century. The start of the NWOBHM pretty much coincided with the beginning of Margaret Thatcher's premiership as the Conservatives ousted the Labour Government on

May 4, 1979, swapping one period of industrial unrest and economic chaos for another. The wreck of the Titanic would not be discovered for another year, and there was still a complete set of Beatles alive and kicking (John Lennon being murdered in December 1980). Cashpoint machines (or ATMs to use the now accepted phrase that no-one had heard back then) dispensed £1 notes, as the £1 coin didn't come in until 1983. Credit cards were the preserve of the well-off, and the hoi-polloi paid for things by cash or cheque; the concept of the debit card didn't even exist. England's World Cup victory didn't seem that long ago, Prince Charles was still a bachelor and Ronald Reagan hadn't yet commenced either his first term in the White House or his single-handed attempt to provoke World War III. The Falklands conflict was yet to come, as was the collapse of the Iron Curtain, the fall of the Berlin Wall, two Gulf Wars, and Take That.

In that 25 years, there have also been a number of innovations as technology has advanced at an alarming rate. The following things that are pretty commonplace these days are things that the average British metal fan wouldn't have had in the early days of the NWOBHM; ah, let's hear it for the good old days!

VIDEOS

Video cassette recorders were almost mythical beasts in 1979. As they became more popular the price came down and they grew more compact (early jobs were expensive, top-loading machines about the size of a small fridge/freezer), but back in those days they were very much luxury items, with two formats (anyone remember Betamax?) vying for market supremacy. Pre-recorded video cassettes cost about £30.00 each (at a time when an album was about a fiver), which is just one reason why Holocaust's live video in 1981 was an adventurous but possibly none-too-smart way of publicising the band, as at the time almost no-one got to see it.

MTV

Hard though it may seem now, in 1979 there were just three terrestrial TV channels in the UK – no cable, satellite or digital. Channel 4 came on stream, amidst howls of anguish from *The Daily Mail* about the porn and debauchery it screened (ie *The Tube* and *Brookside*) in November 1982. MTV? Forget it!

A JOB

Although this isn't a book on politics, it's a fact that a new government with a blinkered, dogmatic belief in the free market economy led to massive rises in unemployment in the early Eighties. From 1.5 million unemployed in April 1980, the total rose to 1.9 million (the highest since 1936) by July 1980, hit 2.5 million in April 1981 and reached a new record – 3,224,715 – in February 1983. The government finally realised that it had to do something about the spiralling levels of unemployment; the solution it hit upon entailed changing the way the figures were calculated, reducing the reported total quite considerably at the stroke of a pen. It was difficult to get a decent job, especially in manufacturing towns where unemployment was exponential. Sport was one way to get off the dole queue; another was to become a musician.

A DEDICATED MUSIC MAGAZINE

Pre-*Kerrang!*, *Metal Hammer*, *Classic Rock* et al, music news, record reviews and tour dates came from the weekly music papers. The main contender was *Sounds*, a paper which tried to appear nonchalant – dismissive, even – towards heavy metal but produced more and more features as the editorial staff realised that metal was one of the main reasons the paper sold; look at any of the annual Readers' Polls and you'll see that it was largely rock/metal fans that bought *Sounds* and kept its journalists in employment (either that or it was only the metal fans who could be bothered to vote). *Melody Maker* came across as more of a musicians' paper, the one to buy if you were looking to form or join a band; *Record Mirror* was a bit of a joke; and *NME* was far too highbrow to consider heavy metal as a musical form.

    Kerrang! appeared for the first time in June 1981 bearing the by-line "*Sounds Heavy Metal Special*: the only one [of the weekly music papers] that doesn't sneer at the world of the headbanger. We cover the scene with enthusiasm…" The first issue was pretty much an experiment ("if this issue sells well enough, *Kerrang!* could well start to appear on your news stands on a regular basis") and was written almost entirely by Geoff Barton who had been championing rock and metal in *Sounds* for years.

    To be honest, *Kerrang!* was, from the start, pretty much a comic. From its childish name (an onomatopoeic reference to a power chord being struck – for those who still ask – originally used in *Sounds* in a feature on Rainbow and spelled *Kerr-aaannnngg!!*), poor layout and almost amateurish writing, the whole thing looked cheap, and many people (myself included) thought it would damage the much-derided world of heavy metal even more. Still, the first issue did feature amongst others Black Axe (eventually snapped up and then stifled by Chrysalis Records), and what was to become a regular feature entitled 'Armed & Ready', in which new bands could introduce themselves (although in the first issue it was a bit late to be 'introducing' the likes of Diamond Head, Raven, Venom and Bitches Sin). However, it was good to have a metal magazine on the streets, no matter how 'Mickey Mouse', and besides, it sold out very quickly.

Issue 2 followed in August, and *Kerrang!* soon went fortnightly, then weekly. At first it was written by the usual *Sounds* crew, who were happy to pretend they liked the metal scene, then established fanzine writers like the late, great Paul Miller came on board. For emerging NWOBHM bands, a dedicated magazine was a real shot in the arm, and once it went weekly, *Kerrang!* became the first port of call for tour dates and information on forthcoming releases. A number of its writers soon thought themselves bigger than the bands they covered (Geoff Barton noted in *Classic Rock* in January 2004 that "an old colleague of mine on *Kerrang!* used to claim that, because he was, ahem, such a highly regarded rock commentator, if he gave a new album a top 'KKKKK' ('Kolossal') review it would boost sales of that release by 5,000 copies" although its album reviews pretty much tended to follow the herd. Through a number of Dr Who style rebirths, it has long outlived the music weekly that launched it, and is now one of the biggest selling weekly music magazines. Unfortunately though, it appeared to turn its back on classic British metal many years ago, ridiculing it for no longer being 'relevant.' In turn, a spoof T-shirt spotted for sale at the 2004 Bloodstock festival lampooned the magazine's logo with the words *"Kerrap!!... Remember The 1980s... RIP – Overlooking Real British Metal... Every Wednesday"*

MOBILE PHONES

You have got to be joking! You want to make a phone call, go in a urine-drenched phone box with 10p like everyone else (if you can turf out the people either sheltering from the rain or having a shag). Early mobile phones came as handsets attached to boxes the size of airline pilots' flight cases that had to be plugged into the mains. Ringing up your mates and trying to hold one of those up in the air at an Iron Maiden gig when they burst into 'Run To The Hills' would induce a hernia.

HOME COMPUTERS

No. Look, a basic scientific calculator cost over £40, and people still used slide rules (ask your dad). What you could get was the innovative new Sinclair ZX81; my brother had one, and I still don't know what it really did. If you want to get a feel for late Seventies computers, watch sci-fi movies from the period and marvel at the walls of flashing lights and rolling tape spools.

CDS

This was the era of the 12" LP (that's 'Long Player'), 7" and 12" singles and EPs ('Extended Players'), with the odd 10" record lobbed in here and there. Good old vinyl: easy to damage, not so convenient to carry around, and don't forget to change your stylus every 1,000 hours of playing; and cassettes as well – supposedly hassle-free and less trouble. The late Seventies' idea of a Walkman was to cart around a stereo cassette player (aka Boom Box, Brixton Briefcase) the size of two large bags of oven chips until the batteries ran down or the tape got snarled up inside the machine (about four plays, either way). That said though, you've got to admit that a record sleeve (especially a gatefold) is much better – much more impressive – than a CD insert, and it was also great fun collecting singles in picture sleeves or pressed on coloured vinyl.

OVEN CHIPS

What's an oven chip?

THE MUSIC SCENE

Musically, there was a post-punk void, and a number of different scenes were evolving, jockeying for position to be the Next Big Thing. Steve, another of the clan and a person with a wide taste in music and a Witchfynde obsession, remembers it much better than I do.

"1979 to 1984? Musically these were interesting times... but to be honest, looking back on the British music that came out of that era, I don't think the NWOBHM was the most exciting. So, what did we have? There was the immediate post-punk movement; who can we rope into that one? Let's visit the steel town of Sheffield: while some would be getting their rocks off, others would be listening to the likes of the Human

League or Cabaret Voltaire, or perhaps visiting The Factory across the South Yorkshire moors – Joy Division, A Certain Ratio. Up in Leeds, at least they had some merciful release, as 1980 saw the first single from the Sisters Of Mercy (whose Wayne Hussey would soon leave and form the even bigger goth rockers, The Mission). What about down South? We'll fight them on the beaches? *Quadrophenia* and all that, a mod revival with Secret Affair, Merton Parkas, Q-Tips et al, sired by The Jam and then of course the Two-Tone phenomenon.

The early Eighties also saw a rise in surf music and garage psychedelia – the Barracudas, Miles Over Matter, the Mood Six. Maybe this was just a London thing. And wasn't this where the Futurists movement came in with Spandau Ballet, Human League (again), and some former heavy rock band (allegedly) called Duran Duran? This was also the time that the seeds of the gothic scene emerged with clubs like The Batcave and Alice In Wonderland. 1981 saw 'Mission Terminated' from Throbbing Gristle giving birth to a new industrial movement.

About now came the start of the modern dance scene: with the death of Ian Curtis, Joy Division became New Order, Chris and Cosey emerged from Throbbing Gristle; Cabaret Voltaire also moved in this direction, Soft Cell had their first remix album, 23 Skidoo brought in the funk...

One thing about the New Wave Of British Heavy Metal that made it different though was that it wasn't localised – bands were pretty much cropping up anywhere and everywhere, as we well remember..."

A TALE OF THREE CITIES

This book is not about Iron Maiden or Def Leppard or Saxon. The Big Three filled stadia all over the world, shifted shedloads of records and at one time almost lived on the set of *Top Of The Pops*, but there's been plenty enough written about them already. This is a book about the lesser-known bands of the NWOBHM. That said, without The Big Three, musically things might have been very different indeed; without them, and more importantly, without the media coverage they attracted, there might not have been a NWOBHM. A particular debt is therefore owed to a bunch of East Enders called Iron Maiden.

It all started – at least from the perspective of the press coverage that was to follow – when the young Iron Maiden took a copy of their demo to Neal Kay, the DJ of Bandwagon Heavy Metal Soundhouse in north London. Kay liked it a lot: "For a start it was a pretty together demo... and musically it was staggering. It was the melody plus the power that impressed me," he told Garry Bushell in *Running Free, The Official Story Of Iron Maiden*.

"It was really weird watching all these kids headbanging to us."

The demo, which ended up being known as *The Soundhouse Tapes*, was recorded on December 30, 1978 and featured four songs – 'Iron Maiden', 'Prowler', 'Invasion' and 'Strange World'. Unbeknown to the band, both 'Prowler' and 'Iron Maiden' swiftly became Soundhouse favourites, and they were quite surprised to see 'Prowler' in the heavy metal chart Kay submitted to *Sounds* in February 1979, which the DJ had based on dance floor requests. Consequently, bassist Steve Harris and singer Paul Di'Anno decided to go to the Soundhouse and check it out for themselves. According to Bushell, Harris commented: "No-one knew who we were, we were just two other 'eadbangers standing in the bar drinking. When 'Prowler' came on a big shout went up. It was really weird watching all these kids headbanging to us."

Thereafter, 1979 was a bit of a rollercoaster for Iron Maiden. By the end of the year they'd played almost every club in the UK. In November they released the self-pressed *The Soundhouse Tapes*, a three–track 7" EP taken from the original demo tape ('Strange World' was the track omitted, not officially seeing the light of day until the release of the band's 1996 double compilation CD *Best Of The Beast*) and recorded a session for BBC Radio's *The Friday Rock Show* (featuring 'Iron Maiden', 'Running Free', 'Transylvania' and 'Sanctuary'); and in trade journal *Music Week*'s December 15 edition came the news that they had signed to EMI.

Whatever Santa brought them for Christmas, it wasn't a holiday. In 1980 Iron Maiden contributed not one but two songs to the EMI flagship compilation album *Metal For Muthas*. Then came the ensuing *Metal For Muthas* tour (supported by Praying Mantis and DJ'ed by old pal Neal Kay), the debut appearance on *Top Of The Pops* in February, an appearance as fourth 'Best New Band' in *Sounds'* Readers' Poll in March, the support slot on the Judas Priest UK Tour the same month, the debut album, an

April mini-tour, a full-blown May/June tour, the Reading Festival, a European tour with Kiss and, ultimately, global domination.

Meanwhile, 167 miles up the M1, things were happening in Sheffield. Def Leppard actually cut their debut single slightly earlier than Iron Maiden, but had the disadvantage of not being based in London. The *Def Leppard EP* (later better known as the *Getcha Rocks Off EP* when Phonogram re-pressed it) was recorded on November 25 and 26, 1978 for the princely sum of £148.50 and released on the band's own Bludgeon Riffola label in January 1979, firstly as a pressing of 1,000 with a second run of 15,000 coming later that year. However, it wasn't until June 1979 that *Sounds'* Geoff Barton journeyed up from London to check out the band that had mailed him the EP some six months previously. A glowing feature appeared in the June 16 issue and a BBC Radio One session ('Wasted', 'Answer To The Master', 'Sorrow Is A Woman' and the vault-languishing 'Glad I'm Alive') recorded on June 7 was aired two days after the paper came out. *Sounds* began plugging the band, as did Neal Kay who was friends with David Bates at Phonogram Records, one of several A&R people who were now watching the band with interest. On August 5, 1979, Def Leppard signed on the dotted line.

Phonogram wasted little time with their new act. The EP was re-issued in September, with the band going into the studio the same month to record four songs ('Wasted', 'Rock Brigade', 'Hello America' and 'Glad I'm Alive', *still* destined to remain in the vaults) with producer Nick Tauber. A single ('Wasted' b/w 'Hello America') became the band's first new release for the label; issued in November 1979, it reached Number 61 in the UK Singles Chart. In his book *Animal Instinct*, David Fricke notes that Nick Tauber claimed to have been under orders from Phonogram to "...tone down the guitar solos and accentuate the songhooks. In other words, to deliver a hit record." The producer also claims to have been under the impression that all four songs were to be used for a seven-inch EP, so they had to be kept short, snappy and to the point. Some observers were not impressed. Indeed, some thought the record was so bad that Phonogram's US corporate counterpart refused to issue it in America. Quoted in *Animal Instinct*, Phonogram's Cliff Burnstein said, "if we put this out here, we'll kill the band stone-dead before we've even started."

By the end of '79 though, Leppard had played a number of major venues including Hammersmith Odeon as support on two separate tours

(Sammy Hagar and AC/DC). The band went into the studios to record their debut album *On Through The Night*, this time with Judas Priest producer Tom Allom behind the desk; a taster single from the album (rather bizarrely a re-recording of 'Hello America', the flip of the previous 7" coupled with non-album cut 'Good Morning Freedom') appeared in February and made it to Number 45 in the Singles Chart. The album followed in March and peaked at Number 15. But the backlash had begun. *Sounds* reviewed the single in February 1980 and hated it. "This is so bland, so lightweight and so godawfully obvious," wrote Mick Middles. "Not a record to be proud of, and Sheffield must be blushing. Hello America, goodbye England. Goodbye Def Leppard." Geoff Barton slagged them off in a feature in *Sounds* entitled 'Def Or Glory' the following week, and then knifed the album. In *Sounds* on March 22, he rampaged about everything from the cover (truly awful admittedly, but probably nothing to do with the band) to the songs, the running order of the album, the production, the number of old songs, the vocals... Bizarrely, he still gave it a four-star review before concluding, "*On Through The Night* will undoubtedly be a successful album. I could go on a little more... but I think I've gone on enough. And in any case I feel in dire need of a vinyl pick-me-up. Vardis will do. So will the Tygers Of Pan Tang. Or Mythra. Or Girl. But not Def Leppard."

He who laughs last... as they say. Three months later *Sounds* carried a favourable report of the band supporting Pat Travers in Los Angeles and although the band still had to get through being pretty much bottled off at Reading that August, a short and disastrous tour in December, and the fact that it wasn't until December 1983 that they were able to sell out venues in the UK, things haven't turned out too bad for them in the end.

HOW DO I KNOW WHICH PRESSING MY DEF LEPPARD EP IS FROM?

Simple; the first 1,000 had a picture sleeve, a red label and the catalogue no. SRTS/78/CUS 232. The 15,000 pressing second run had a plain sleeve, a yellow label and the catalogue no. MSB 001. And if the first track is 'Getcha Rocks Off' rather than 'Ride Into The Sun', it's a Phonogram job full stop.

Obviously, bands didn't just form overnight. But whereas the first Iron Maiden gig took place in May 1976 and Def Leppard can be traced back to 1977, Barnsley's Big Teasers were well ahead of the pack, their earliest recording sessions taking place in 1975 when Biff Byford and Paul Quinn joined forces with Graham Oliver and Steve Dawson to become Son Of A Bitch, and ultimately Saxon.

"The band got together from two bands," recalls Biff Byford. "Myself and Paul Quinn were in a band called Coast and Graham Oliver and Steve Dawson were in a band called Sob; I think the name came from the Free album *Tons Of Sobs*. We'd lost our drummer and they'd lost a guitarist/singer, so we joined up with them. We didn't want to call ourselves Coast and we didn't want to call ourselves Sob so we came up with Son Of A Bitch.

Son Of A Bitch had quite a following, especially in the North-East and south Wales, and sent our demo tapes to all the record companies in England. Then one day we got a fucking reply! Two guys left EMI and went to join Carrere Records and they had our demo. They liked us and so we signed to Carrere. Meanwhile we'd signed to Trident Management, who used to manage Queen.

The first album *Saxon* sold about 15,000 copies in the UK, which isn't bad for an unknown band. We only had one more album on the deal, but our new management persuaded Carrere to put the money up for us to support Motörhead on the *Bomber* tour prior to the release of *Wheels Of Steel*. I mean, Motörhead were massive at this time, and Lemmy was really good, he'd say 'Buy their album, they're a great band' and then things started to go big [Lemmy recalls "they were great on that tour, fucking excellent"]. The album, I think, [eventually] went Top 10 in the UK and stayed in the charts for about six months, and I think it went double gold, which is over 250,000 records."

As Biff says, Saxon's 1979 self-titled debut album didn't exactly set the world on fire. It was only when follow-up album *Wheels Of Steel* almost literally exploded into everyone's consciousness that sales of the debut album picked up on the strength of its successor. The album opened a number of doors and in 1980 everything clicked into place. A BBC session recorded on January 23 and broadcast on *The Friday Rock Show* three weeks later revitalised three songs off the debut album ('Backs To The Wall', 'Stallions Of The Highway' and 'Still Fit To Boogie') and introduced 'Motorcycle Man' and '747 (Strangers In The Night)' from the forthcoming *Wheels Of Steel* LP, released in March. While the album was going stratospheric, peaking at Number 5 in the chart, the band were undertaking a gruelling UK tour (supported by Tygers Of Pan Tang) of smaller and lesser-known venues (eg. Torquay Town Hall!).

"After the Motörhead tour, we had a club tour lined up," continues Biff, "and it completely sold out in an hour or so. So we had to move everything to bigger venues. Then we had to play two nights everywhere, so the *Wheels Of Steel* tour ended up being massive. It was a good tour."

Saxon's third album *Strong Arm Of The Law* was released in November 1980 to be met by a five-star review in *Sounds* (earlier in the year, *Wheels Of Steel* had also picked up top honours). Garry Bushell summarised their meteoric rise to prominence in the last month of that explosive twelve months: "Within a year of national exposure, Saxon have scored two Top 20 albums, a Top 15 single, and have proved themselves not only to be the most impressive band to emerge from the hideously-named NWOBHM but also to be well on the way to promotion to world class steel star status."

RISE OF THE NWOBHM?

Sounds prided itself on being a *music* – not a heavy metal – paper, although the majority of the poll winners tended to be heavy metal bands. The 1979 Readers' Poll published in March 1980 (and so voted for at the tail end on 1979) was headed thus:

"HEAVY METAL UBER ALLES! At least that's the message of the *Sounds* Readers' Poll, the most prestigious test of public opinion in the whole history of the world... Are the results a true reflection of the music scene in 1979/80? Who knows – polls are always a law unto themselves. But one thing is certain – HM sure has the most *loyal* fans of all."

The results show the diversity of the 1979 music scene. 'Best Single' was won by Def Leppard's *Getcha Rocks Off EP*, with 'Overkill' and 'Bomber' (Motörhead), 'Since You Been Gone' (Rainbow) and 'Another Piece Of Meat' (Scorpions) rubbing shoulders with singles by Pink Floyd, Police, The Specials, The Jam and Tubeway Army.

Best albums included rock/metal offerings from Pink Floyd (*The Wall*), Led Zeppelin (*In Through The Out Door*), Judas Priest (*Unleashed In The East*), Rainbow (*Down To Earth*), UFO (*Strangers In The Night*), and finally AC/DC (*Highway To Hell*).

'Best New Band' again went to Def Leppard, with Iron Maiden, Samson and Saxon making up the NWOBHM contingent. The Specials, Madness, Gary Numan, Joy Division, Cockney Rejects and Secret Affair rounded off the Top 10.

The 'Best Band' category was won by Rush, by the way, with Led Zeppelin, Motörhead, Rainbow, AC/DC and Judas Priest alongside The Jam, Police, The Damned and The Stranglers in the Top 10. The 'Best Live Gig' was Led Zeppelin at Knebworth.

There must have been something about 1979/1980 that made it a fertile breeding ground for hard rock/heavy metal music. The NWOBHM notwithstanding, a number of bands were at the peak of their creative and/or commercial success at this time. AC/DC made their two greatest albums back to back in *Highway To Hell* and *Back In Black*. Prime-time Ozzy is every Black Sabbath fan's favourite line-up, but the band's 1980 LP *Heaven And Hell* is undoubtedly their most comprehensive, most cohesive album. With a new line-up and new direction, Rainbow's pay-off came with *Down To Earth*, complete with two hit singles, video appearances on *Top Of The Pops* and ultimately their one-off headliner at Castle Donington in August 1980 which paved the way for many years of ensuing Monsters Of Rock festivals. Bands formed by fellow ex-Deep Purple members also hit their artistic peak: David Coverdale's Whitesnake released *Ready An' Willing*, and Ian Gillan launched his self-titled band with *Mr Universe* and *Glory Road*. Honorary Brits Krokus from Switzerland put out *Metal Rendez-Vous*; Motörhead were riding high with *Bomber* and *Ace Of Spades*, Judas Priest stormed the charts with *British Steel*; Germany's greatest band Scorpions had their big UK break with *Lovedrive*; Magnum had been around for some time but only really got recognition (the first time around) when their *Live EP* was released in March 1980; UFO's live *Strangers In The Night*… And so the list goes on. The growing popularity of heavy metal at the time was what put these LPs and their respective singles in the UK charts, but the fact remains that although some of the bands are still recording now – a testament to their longevity – these are all great records which have never been bettered by the artistes concerned. And against this backdrop came the new heavy metal hopefuls of the NWOBHM.

THE CHICKEN AND THE EGG
(OR, WHAT EXACTLY WAS THE NWOBHM?)

"Recently, perhaps more through circumstances than desire, I've been making spasmodic dives into the wide, deep and surprisingly varied valley of heavy metal. It's such a loose term really, heavy metal. From stiff dressed–up dolls like Rob Halford to slick super (non) stars like Styx to the raw, hard, uncompromising music forces like Iron Maiden, Angel Witch and, for that matter, Witchfynde. Well, it's the small bands that interest me most. Springing up from unfashionable, obscure towns all over the country. Dark, sleepy towns that have been ignored or just forgotten by the trendy rat–race of the pace–setting big cities. In these places, in the local clubs, pubs and discos, heavy metal is thriving…"

So wrote Mick Middles in a *Sounds* feature on Witchfynde in August 1980. There is little doubt that there was a massive growth of interest in heavy metal as the Seventies waned, and no doubt this ball was set rolling by the NWOBHM; unless of course, it was the other way round and it was the sudden and massive interest in metal that kick–started the NWOBHM. It's the classic chicken–and–egg conundrum: was there a sudden explosion of heavy metal bands in 1978/79 that the press and record companies picked up on – a new wave of British heavy metal, if you will – or were the bands always there, plugging away but invisible to music hacks and record company executives until the media and A&R people were roused from their desks and fell over themselves to find their next cash cow? At this time there were still plenty of 'old guard' rock/metal bands touring and putting out great records – AC/DC, Judas Priest, Scorpions, UFO, Thin Lizzy – and plenty of younger (mainly) guys forming bands to emulate them. But at the same time, the music press was looking for something new to write about, and there was a proliferation of fads to choose from.

The NWOBHM is a term applied to what was, or was to become, one of the most exciting times in rock music since a chubby guy with a kiss curl sang 'Rock Around The Clock'. The punk era had supposedly blown away the rock dinosaurs, but once the smoke had cleared and punk had become the irrelevant, supercilious and bloated Elvis it had abhorred, not only were those self–same rock bands still there but so were their legions of fans – some old timers, some new blood. It seems that unlike a lot of music trends that do come and go – the ska revival, new romantics, disco, punk – heavy rock, heavy metal, hard rock (call it what you will) has the capacity to evolve and *survive*.

"What happens is that when you get a movement like the New Wave Of British Heavy Metal," comments Mark Sutcliffe of Trespass, "a big net is cast across the whole musical spectrum and the bands are... well, caught; we weren't trying to be part of the New Wave Of British Heavy Metal, we were just doing what we were doing at the time. There are metal bands out there now, jazz bands out there, blues bands out there, just doing what they do, and waiting for 'The Moment'..."

One of the big problems, though, was that journalists saw NWOBHM as a fad with a limited shelf-life, rather than a continuum of rock music, and a number of bands saw it that way too. As a result, several didn't want to be associated either with the NWOBHM or the term 'heavy metal' in general. Interviewed by Geoff Barton in *Sounds* in July 1980, Girl vocalist Phil Lewis typified this reluctance:

> ## "New groups seem to be popping up every five minutes formed by guys who aren't dedicated to the music but who think it's an easy way to make a fast buck..."

"You've created a monster. It's got totally out of hand. It's a bubble that's gonna burst any day now and it's something I'm not about to involve myself with. Lots of places we play we're billed as Girl, the heavy metal band and I hate that, it's just not true. It conjures up lots of nasty things in my mind. I'm just going to keep on playing the music I like, regardless. It's kind of heavy, but no way would I call it heavy metal. In the days of Deep Purple and Black Sabbath heavy metal was great, it was real basic, very exciting. But now there are so many weak bands, everything's been blown out of proportion. New groups seem to be popping up every five minutes formed by guys who aren't dedicated to the music but who think it's an easy way to make a fast buck..."

The trouble is, once you define something, you limit it. Another problem with trying to describe the NWOBHM is the thorny question of 'what in fact is heavy metal?', which could be a book in itself. The guys in the Deep Purple Appreciation Society would turn a violent shade of, well, purple to hear their band described as heavy metal, yet White Spirit were a true NWOBHM band that drew on influences from both Deep Purple and Uriah Heep.

In the first issue of *Kerrang!* in June 1981, Simon Sparkes of Black Axe, helpfully suggested:"Thing is though, we don't really play heavy metal, do we? And speaking personally, I wouldn't like us to be labelled an HM band. I'd say we were more 200mph heavy rock, and more influenced by American than British bands..." Bitches Sin's Ian Toomey remembers it thus,"at the time, we always saw ourselves more as a hard rock band than a heavy metal band.You remember those distinctions?" he laughs."Purple and Zeppelin were hard rock bands with melody and structure, and heavy metal was more your Sabbaths. Then, courtesy of the Americans, it all became heavy metal, and I think, thanks to them, we're now kind of stuck with just the one term. I think we can live with it, though!"

So, if the bands themselves can't define heavy metal, how exactly do you describe the NWOBHM? Various authors have had a go. In the introduction to *The Great Metal Discography*, M.C. Strong states, "another by-product of the [punk] revolution came in the form of the New Wave Of British Heavy Metal (NWOBHM), a D.I.Y. grassroots movement inspired by the success of Proto-Thrash Brit-Metallers Judas Priest." No, I don't think so; if nothing else, Judas Priest's big break came at the time of the NWOBHM, with the release of *British Steel* in 1980. Rob Halford's *Sad Wings Of Destiny*-era kaftan-wearing days certainly didn't inspire much apart from hysterical laughter.

Joel McIver, in his book *Justice For All:The Truth About Metallica,* claims that "the New Wave Of British Heavy Metal was crude, poorly produced and played by musicians with rudimentary talents, at least in its earliest years... NWOBHM bands such as Venom, Angel Witch, Tygers Of Pan Tang, Anvil and Saxon were hardly acknowledged for their virtuosity or the clarity of their sound, although Iron Maiden were a notable exception on both counts." No! Definitely not! And who, in NWOBHM terms, are Anvil? That's the trouble with something that's twenty-five-years old – there's so much misinformation going around that it's hard to tell fact from fiction. Ian Christe's otherwise interesting book *Sound Of The Beast – The Complete Headbanging History Of Heavy Metal* muddles through the NWOBHM although succinctly points out that "musically, the NWOBHM cut Seventies hard rock into punk-sized pieces, producing a highly focused form of guitar energy." Unfortunately, he then puts his feet – both of 'em – well and truly in it by continuing: "By 1980 the movement was fully realised, with hundreds of 45s in print and a handful of landmark long-players by Motörhead, Saxon, Iron Maiden and Judas Priest. Though they were still very much London acts on the rise, these bands would dominate heavy metal for the next decade…". To compound the error that Motörhead and Priest pre-date the NWOBHM, and that Saxon and Priest both had healthy motorway journeys to reach London, his NWOBHM discography features not only the aforementioned Kilminster- and Halford-fronted metal juggernauts but also (and most bizarrely) AC/DC.

The best definition I can find comes from the summer 1989 *Kerrang! NWOBHM A-Z 10 YEARS ON* supplement: "The NWOBHM was a nationwide ground-breaking phenomenon from which sprang such heavy metal legends as Iron Maiden, Def Leppard, Saxon and Diamond Head. The NWOBHM also influenced the early careers of many of today's thrash metal acts – Metallica in particular."

OK, now we're getting somewhere. In basic terms, the NWOBHM was a time and a place in the history of rock music, influenced by what came before and influencing what came after. The term 'New Wave Of British Heavy Metal' itself is attributed to Alan Lewis, editor of *Sounds* in 1979. Iron Maiden's success at the Bandwagon Heavy Metal Soundhouse rock club and in the heavy metal chart which the DJ Neal Kay submitted to *Sounds*, gave the world's first Shock Jock the idea to put together a tour "to show the music world that there was not only life in the old metal dog but that it had also spawned new pups with real teeth," wrote Garry Bushell in *Running Free*. "Alan Lewis at *Sounds* christened the whole to-do The New Wave Of British Heavy Metal and on a Tuesday night in May 1979, a somewhat wary Geoff Barton pulled on his best stack-heeled carpet slippers and headed off to the Music Machine for what was to prove the metal new wave's first public unveiling. Neal Kay had gone out on a limb and cobbled together a package of the Bandwagon's three most popular acts with himself DJ'ing the whole event… Later, Geoff wrote: 'I do definitely recall Maiden being the best band of the evening, infinitely preferable to the Sabs-worshipping Angel Witch and way ahead of Samson in the musical if not the presentation stakes.'"

So this is my view on the NWOBHM, as a spotty little record buyer of the time. Post punk there was a vacuum. There were loads of things going on musically, but there was no real Next Big Thing. And record companies do like the Next Big Thing. Meantime, the established rock/ metal acts, your AC/DCs, Judas Priests, Black Sabbaths, Led Zeppelins, they were all still doing big business gig-wise and selling a lot of records. Despite what anyone will ever tell you, heavy metal or hard rock or whatever you want to call it will always have a market. It might not always be selling squillions of records or be on *Top Of The Pops* or MTV, but it will always be around. Trust me on this.

So, against this backdrop of an existing, healthy scene came a lot of influential new bands. Iron Maiden were packing them out at the Soundhouse; Def Leppard's EP was getting substantial amounts of airplay on Radio One thanks to Tommy Vance and John Peel; and Saxon had been successfully touring for some time. All three bands worked hard and played hard, headlined small clubs in front of handfuls of people, got signed to a label and picked up prestigious support slots playing in front of even more people. As Lemmy says later, record companies "have to wait till someone's had a hit to tell them what's going on and what to copy; they're not very clever, you see..."

That said, even the most short-sighted A&R people and music journalists would eventually have been forced to wake up and smell the shredding guitar strings. Not because major record companies are nice places where musicians are befriended and talent is nurtured, but because major record companies want to make money – that's what they do; and journalists make money by selling papers about what is current and hip. And all of a sudden there was a buzz on the street about heavy metal, and that it might just be the Next Big Thing. So the search was on to locate and either sign up or write about heavy metal bands. Many of these existed already and were still slogging their guts out at places like the Frogs Arse pub in Huddersfield, regardless of the preceding punk years; some came together because the musicians happened to be at the age to form a band and would have formed a heavy metal band anyway because that was their drug of choice; some were more traditional hard rock acts who got lumped in because the press needs to have pigeonholes in which to put bands; some were established rock or metal bands who benefited from an increased number of potential fans and record sales as metal became popular once more; and some were musicians who had failed at their first attempt (maybe punks who missed the boat so grew their hair longer and added a couple of chords) or who just saw a chance to make some money, bought a couple of Sabbath LPs for inspiration and plugged in.

Quality control as ever came through natural selection, or survival of the fittest. At the end of the day, no matter what music you play, there is only space in the market for so many bands of your ilk because the majors only sign one or two such bands apiece. The flotsam and jetsam, the wannabies and the poseurs all fell by the wayside, or tried their hand at something else. The others – the bands that believed in themselves and in what they did, but were realistic enough to know they would have to go it alone – invested in themselves by recording and releasing material either through independent labels or by stumping up the money themselves. These are the heroes of *Suzie Smiled*.

So, as 1979 progressed there was an upsurge in the number of bands playing heavy metal, a massive rise in the number of column inches written about them, and hefty record company chequebooks being waved around aplenty. The New Wave Of British Heavy Metal – in early *Sounds* articles it was abbreviated to NWoBHM but as the term became more popular the 'o' got promoted to a capital – had arrived, and stayed around for quite some time, certainly long enough to raise awareness of, and interest in, heavy metal worldwide. And this is why the NWOBHM is so important, because it spawned almost everything metal for the next decade. It threw the spotlight on metal as a music – no, let's go all the way – as an art form, and this was something the American and European bands who came afterwards were able to capitalise upon. The NWOBHM had already set the stage, so to speak, and directly influenced the next generation of heavy metal bands – in fairly crude terms without the likes of (oh, I don't know) Savage, Diamond Head and Angel Witch, just to pick three bands at random, there'd be no Metallica, Megadeth or Mercyful Fate.

So don't get too hooked up on defining the NWOBHM. It's just six words to try and pigeonhole a few years, hundreds of bands and thousands of records. To my mind it was just a great time to be listening to heavy metal music.

By the way, in 1981 *Sounds* noted that "the NWOBHM phenomenon has yielded four distinct categories of band:

original but tuneless;

original;

unoriginal but undisputedly fun/clever at what they do; and

unoriginal, tiresome, predictable, disposable as a Bic shaver."

I don't know if that helps at all...[†]

[†] The point of this exposition was to put the Tygers Of Pan Tang in the fourth category!

NAMING NAMES

Choosing a name for a band is not an easy thing to do. In the summer of 1980 I joined a band. We only ever had two songs of any note of our own. The first was an instrumental blues piece, the stunningly originally-titled 'Blues In A', which was written before I'd joined. I added a lyric and 'Nothing To Lose' was born, the title being a deliberate throwback to the Girlschool anti-sexism song 'Not For Sale' on their debut album and the lyrics themselves being complete early Eighties sexist rubbish ("as the sun is rising I'll do all the driving but baby you'll know how to steer"); in my defence, at the time I was a bit of a tosser. At the rehearsal where the finished song came into being we played it for 48 minutes straight, eventually terminating it with a drum solo. By my reckoning, we'd only have to play it twice with an encore of 'Wheels Of Steel' (one of the old chestnuts we'd warm up to) for a full headlining set.

The other song was brought in virtually complete by guitarist Chris, inspired by and named after the film *Driller Killer*. "I'm not going to show you my pecker/I'm going to get out my Black and Decker," ran one line. Never, never let your guitarist write lyrics; that's the reason God gave them manual dexterity, to prevent them from mangling the English language.

I don't bring this up because we were any good – we weren't; as you might have guessed, we were terrible! – but because every Thursday we would scan through *Sounds* and, more likely than not, find that another band with our name was one step ahead of us, either by playing live or releasing a single. So it was back to the drawing board, and the pub, to come up with yet another name. Medusa and Grenade were two names that I remember which came and went. We were not, contrary to drummer Dave's recollection, ever called Bludengutz (insert a smattering of umlauts wherever you feel fit), but we did end our days as Tarsus, a name I personally quite liked. The difficulty is coming up with something unique which befits a metal band yet which isn't too, well, crap really.

So, how did the bands come up with their names? I asked Garry Pepperd of Jaguar if they picked that name because it was descriptive of their proto-speed metal approach, or whether the music evolved to match the name. "As any band will tell you, it's really, really difficult to pick a name. It's mind-numbing; you end up looking round the room, you know, 'light bulb' or 'how about lamp shade?,' whatever. The times I've done this, just trying to pick a name. So, we picked Jaguar, as I recall, and agreed between us, and then we ditched it. We just weren't happy with it. But whilst we were still Jaguar we'd entered this *Melody Maker* 'Battle Of The Bands' thing as Jaguar – you know, sent this tape off and never thought any more about it until we got a letter back saying, 'Congratulations, you've made it to the South West regional finals' as Jaguar. So we were kind of stuck with it. We didn't like it but felt we were now press-ganged into it so we just stuck with it, you know, by accident really. It's alright, I suppose, but... Well, it doesn't really matter any more, does it! And it's a name of the time. I suspect that had we changed names we would have ended up with something worse!"

"'Raven' was literally picked out of a hat and was the one everyone hated the least."

As for everybody else, Garry Phillips recalls that "the name Soldier is from the track of the same name by the Groundhogs on the *Thank Christ for the Bomb* album. We're asked a lot about the name, I think, because it probably doesn't 'sound' very heavy metal (you know, there's nothing black magic or death about it) but there is very little in our lyrics about the 'darker side'. It's not that we're religious fanatics or anything – it's just that most metal bands seem to write about that sort of stuff and we like to be a bit different."

"'Raven' was literally picked out of a hat and was the one everyone hated the least," says John Gallagher. "Its pretty good in that it implies a lot but it's not like being labelled 'Iron Testicle' or whatever!"

"Our name came straight from a book, a Michael Moorcock sci-fi novel," is how Robb Weir remembers Tygers Of Pan Tang getting their rather unusual moniker. "Rocky the bassist was big into these types of book and came up with the name and it just stuck."

"It was my idea to use the name Diamond Head," notes Brian Tatler. "I had a poster of the 1975 album *Diamond Head* by Phil Manzanera and I cut the name out and stuck it on my wall and said 'that's the name'. Sean Harris wanted to change it to Wolf or Cobra or something but we reverted back to Diamond Head and it stuck."

"The name of the band came about from a guy who was our manager at the time, I think it was him who thought it would be a good idea to call us Girlschool with one 's'... It was the B-side of Paul McCartney's song 'Mull Of Kintyre'," admits Denise Dufort. [I guess I should have asked them how come their manager liked Paul McCartney!]

"The others had picked that out before Chris Logan and I joined," recalls Andy Skuse of Shiva. "I'm not honestly sure if they really knew who or what Shiva was. Once they knew all about the Hindu religious aspect of the name they decided to stick with it anyway as it kind of matched with our aim to do and to be something a little more unusual."

"We weren't Tolkein disciples, it was just a name," says Mike Ellis, on the decision to call their band Aragorn. "Jon Hull had read the book and liked it and thought it would be a good band name. I've never read it, and frankly, I thought the movie was a load of over-CGI'd pants!"

"I honestly don't know where the name came from," admits Mark Sutcliffe from Trespass "It may have been my brother Paul's Genesis album, you know? I'm pretty sure it came from that. Maybe a bit of *The Lord's Prayer* as well? It's a word that's not used in that sense very much, you know, to trespass against someone – what that means anyway I don't exactly know! – but I reckon it came from the cover of the Genesis album. We just liked the word. We were called Track Four before that; we did our first gig as Track Four at our school, where Richard our bass playing Geography teacher was teaching at the time, so thank God we changed the name! Someone drew a picture of us for the poster, which might have been me. I can't remember now, but whoever did it made us all the same height, which clearly wasn't fucking true, and put Richard's fucking woolly hat on!"

Sabre's Geoff Gillespie took what's probably the easiest option: "I came up with the name, but I am damned if I can remember how or why after all this time. In my time playing in bands over the years, I must have spent six months in total sitting around debating the relative merits of various names. Not this time; it was Sabre or nothing at all!"

On Satan, Brian Ross told me back in 1984, "it's not all death and doom, we're the exact opposite of Mercyful Fate, Venom and the others. They're into this Satanic thing, whereas to us it's just a name. After all, what else can a heavy metal band be called?" And Blitzkrieg? "Jez Gillman, our manager, came up with the name. At that time, we were still going out as Split Image, playing covers in pubs and clubs to pay the bills and finance demos and the single, come to that. Sarah Aldwinckle, the Split Image singer, was still around and we did some gigs with her or we split the set. We worked this way for a while until we had enough material with maybe one or two covers for a full set. Meanwhile, we were struggling to come up with a new name. We kicked around a few ideas, Thunder was one I remember; Ian Jones suggested The Priest, which was pretty stupid. Highway Stars was another. Then one day Jez came into rehearsal and said, 'the band's name is Blitzkrieg!' And we all looked at him and Jim Sirotto said, 'what the hell's that?' We obviously knew it was German and war-related, but Jez reckoned it meant something like 'lightning war' or 'very fast attack,' and we thought, 'yeah, what a great name.' I personally still think Satan is the ultimate name for a heavy metal band, but failing that, Blitzkrieg'll do!"

LARS ULRICH HAS GOT MY PARALEX EP

You must have guessed that Lars Ulrich would crop up eventually. He is well known for his knowledge of and interest in the NWOBHM, and how a lot of this came about is excellently described in Joel McIver's biography *Justice For All; The Truth About Metallica*. But just as telling are Ulrich's handwritten gig notes as reproduced in the booklet to their 1998 covers CD *Garage Inc*. From these you can see just how much the NWOBHM influenced the band. For example, Metallica played two sets in one night supporting Saxon at the Whisky A Go Go on March 27, 1982; the first set featured Diamond Head's 'Helpless' and 'The Prince', and Savage's 'Let It Loose' together with three originals, the second added a third Diamond Head song ('Sucking My Love'). In fact, for their first gig a couple of weeks earlier at Radio City, Anaheim, the nine-song set included 'Blitzkrieg', 'Helpless', 'Let It Loose', 'Sucking My Love', 'Am I Evil?', 'The Prince' and Sweet Savage's 'Killing Time' – all played as self-penned compositions. Metallica were also big fans of Trespass, but much to the chagrin of Suffolk's finest (and to the detriment of their bank balance) the Bay Area Noise Boys never recorded a Trespass song.

One famous NWOBHM cover to be recorded for their *$5.98 EP: Garage Days Re-Revisited*, Metallica's back-to-basics first release following the death of Cliff Burton, was Holocaust's 'The Small Hours'. "They had a little bit of cheese factor to them, but they also had some stuff that was really weighty," noted Ulrich in the *Garage Inc.* booklet notes. In an interview on the Holocaust website, John Mortimer says of the Metallica version of his song: "it made me feel like a million dollars! I remember putting the EP on and suddenly getting the terrible apprehension that they were going to take the piss out of the song. What freaked me out the most was hearing James Hetfield singing lyrics that I remember writing in my old bedroom! I liked their version then and I still do."

It's also interesting to note that according to those booklet notes, songs also considered for the *$5.98 EP* included Gaskin's 'I'm No Fool' and a track by the name of 'Silver Lightning' [sic] from the Paralex *Travelling Man EP* (both 'I'm No Fool' and 'White Lightning', to give it its proper title, were included in the Geoff Barton/Lars Ulrich *New Wave Of British Heavy Metal '79 Revisited* compilation album in 1990). In a rundown of NWOBHM favourites entitled 'Encyclopedia Metallica' in *Raw* Magazine, Ulrich told Malcolm Dome that Paralex were "one of the best of the obscure bands. We actually came close to covering 'White Lightning' (from their Reddingtons Rare Records three-track EP, released on green vinyl!). The sound quality on the record is a bit rough, but the songs still stand up today."

Now personally, I don't get it. As I've already said, most of my early NWOBHM stuff came from Castle Records in Torquay, where the manager Dave would get five or six copies of everything he could and then we would all go home happy and trade notes at the pub on Saturday night. Everyone loved this one Paralex 12" EP, but it left me colder than a cloudy day in Milton Keynes. 'White Lightning' is by far the strongest of the three cuts on offer, with 'Travelling Man' and 'Black Widow' being fairly standard metal-by-numbers compositions. The playing is competent, the lyrics are truly awful, and the vocals… Well, they're not good. It was therefore quite reassuring to read in *The New Wave Of British Heavy Metal Encyclopedia* that author Malc Macmillan wasn't that turned on by it either: "It seemed to strike precisely the right chord with both the local and national metal communities, rendering the three-tracker as one of the very first bona fide collectables of the period. Even to this day, however, the sheer reverence afforded to this EP by NWOBHM aficionados is quite baffling, and, to be brutally honest, I completely fail to see what's supposedly so fantastic about it." You and me both, mate. Macmillan singles out vocalist Phil Ayling (with his "tragically apt" surname) as the main fly in the Paralex ointment and goes on to add that "it's quite an achievement for someone to sing out of tune so consistently (the statistical probability of hitting the right note every now and again is actually pretty high)." Given the above, Lars' obsession with the *Travelling Man EP* has always surprised me.

So, where is all this leading? Well, back in the Eighties I used to write for the American magazine *Metal Rendez-Vous*. One day in 1986 or so I received a letter from head honcho John Strednansky saying that he wanted to get Lars Ulrich a copy of the *Travelling Man EP*, to replace one the drummer had sold to bankroll the band's early days/had stolen from him/eaten one day after a night out (delete as applicable). Now it just so happened that Steve was dismantling his collection, and I think the deal was done for a paltry £10.00 including the cost of postage to California. So Lars, if you ever read this, and are feeling at a loss as to what to do with your squillions, I reckon you owe Steve at least another tenner!

CHAPTER TWO

HEAVY METAL MANIA — 1979 TO 1980

"Where is the power, where is the glory?
Heavy metal is my story..." –

'Heavy Metal Mania' by Holocaust (p) 1980

SO, WHERE WERE YOU IN '79 WHEN THE DAM BEGAN TO BURST?

" I couldn't begin to relate what a great time it was and do it justice. I was 17, drumming, recording, gigging, doing interviews, signing autographs, I mean, what more could a teenage lad ask for? I think the supports we did were the highlights; crashing into Ian Gillan in a corridor and him picking me up, playing on Nico McBrain's drum kit during a sound-check (he was such a nice bloke), jostling with Ian Paice to get to the bar, liquid lunches with Raven, having Cozy Powell say, 'Hello, mate! How are you?' when we met for the third time. The more I think about it, the more I realise what a fucking great time it was..." Aragorn's drummer Mike Ellis remembers those early days with obvious relish. "In 1979 I was actually still at school! I'd been gigging with local bands since I was 13 and as my compulsory tenure as a student was drawing to a close, I was considering what path I might take. I'd been

45

playing for a guy called Arthur Kadmon who'd recently left Ludus and we tried out for a number of record companies, including the fledgling Two-Tone ska label. I stayed on at school until I was 17, mainly to avoid being press-ganged into working for one of the local engineering companies and in early 1980 I placed an ad in Melody Maker. I got a call from Chris Dunne, we arranged to meet and the following week I was driving into the hills of Wildboarclough for my first rehearsal."

So, what exactly was everyone else doing in 1979?

"The Tygers were up and running in 1978, so it's fair to say that we were there from the very start," notes Robb Weir. "By '79 the Tygers were rocking hard in the UK in just about every venue that would have us, playing with the likes of Iron Maiden, Def Leppard and Saxon. Such a great time to be around, you know? It's only when you look back now you realise just how big the NWOBHM really was and how influential it was."

"1979? Wow...I was six years old back then, right?" laughs Raven's John Gallagher. "I believe we'd lost our drummer Sean Taylor, who later played with Satan, and earlier that year the guy we'd started the band with, Paul Bowden, had left... It's a little murky now but I think Rob Hunter joined us at the end of 1979. And I remember walking home after a New Year's party just *knowing* the New Year was gonna be special!"

"Ah, 1979..." recalls Sabre's Geoff Gillespie, "soon-to-be Sabre drummer Allan Angold and I were playing in a Motörhead–ish three-piece called Switchback. We were nearly signed to GTO Records who loved the demo but took one look at the band photos – with hair halfway down our backs! – and decided we weren't a punk band! C'est la vie..."

"A bit before our time," laughs Ian Toomey. "We formed Bitches Sin in April 1980. In '79 I was doing my degree and playing in a local band, and I think Pete had just quit school!"

"Yeah, I was going to college, getting drunk, listening to the NWOBHM."

"In 1979 we recorded our first single 'Shoot Out The Lights' and played about 20 gigs around the Midlands getting our shit together, and, of course, doing lots of songwriting," recalls Brian Tatler of Diamond Head. "To be honest, I don't remember thinking it was the start of something big; for a start the single was on the Happy Face label and even a naïve teenager could tell that it was not going to be in the charts! I guess we picked that song as our first single because we all felt it was a good catchy chorus, and it was short enough to fit on a single – most of our songs were much too long!"

"I was 18, I was at college, and I was spending most of my evenings getting in the Colston Hall for nothing!" admits Jaguar's Garry Peppard. "I virtually lived at the Colston Hall and the Granary Club. That was when Jaguar was born, I guess. Yeah, I was going to college, getting drunk, listening to the NWOBHM; Maiden were just popping up, Saxon too. Having said that, I think UFO were my favourite band at the time. And I was still listening to some punk too but getting into the NWOBHM because at that time I was a massive *Sounds* fan. I was well into it, rushed out every week to buy it. And from that I gobbled up the NWOBHM."

Backstage at the self-same Colston Hall in Bristol in October 2003, I asked Motörhead's Lemmy what he remembered about 1979, the NWOBHM and whether Motörhead had been an influence.

"1979 was so busy it's almost impossible to remember what was happening. We were rushed around by the record company, who were trying to get the maximum out of their investment, and it shows in *Bomber*, which wasn't as good as *Overkill*. There were a couple of duff tracks on there; it's OK, but not as good as *Overkill*. But it did better than *Overkill*, but that's on the strength of popularity.

We came along quite a bit before the NWOBHM, so it didn't do us any good but was great for Iron Maiden and Saxon and the others. But there's no question about whether we influenced some of the bands because they said so themselves, didn't they? I don't hear it in them, but you don't hear the Everly Brothers in our music and I was influenced by them. We were aware of it because you had Iron Maiden at the Soundhouse and Saxon were on the '79 tour and that's where it all started really. So yeah, we were aware of it, but I don't know that we were aware of the scope of it, or that title… But then I was also interested in the punk thing; we came along at the same time as the punk thing so we used to feel as akin to the punks as we did to the NWOBHM bands.

But that said, for example, I'd never heard of Phil Campbell's band Persian Risk before he joined. He just wrote and said that was the band he was in. Apparently he didn't tell them he was going for an audition with us, just said he was going to see a man about a dog, except he was carrying his guitar case which must have looked a bit fucking obvious!

And I didn't know much about Warfare till Wurzel produced their second album [*Metal Anarchy*, released in 1985]. He was a lot more involved in that than me, I just went up to Wallsend [Tyne & Wear, home of Neat Records and their Impulse Studios] a few times. They were all right, a bit raw though. And I do like singing drummers, but you don't get 'em that often. I should imagine it's bloody hard work, especially the way he used to play them!

Tell you what though, back then all of a sudden everything was heavy metal. We were heavy metal, Journey were heavy metal, Hawkwind were heavy metal. Very strange. There have been a couple of attempts to create a second NWOBHM, but that'll never work, in fact that's the kiss of fucking death. The bands they pick are always the wrong ones, and besides, you can't create something; there's no substitute for paying your dues. That's the trouble with this *Pop Idol* shit – you can't have three judges with their preconceptions and prejudices. You have to know what's going on in the street. I talk to the people on the street more than most bands, and I know what they like; I always knew what they liked 'cos I always played what they liked – without deviating too much from what I liked!"

THE SPREAD OF THE NWOBHM

As mentioned earlier, the term New Wave Of British Heavy Metal was the brainwave of *Sounds'* editor Alan Lewis, and was specifically coined as a response to Neal Kay's three band bill at the Music Machine on May 8, 1979. Twenty five years later, in January 2004, Geoff Barton, the journalist despatched that fateful night, revisited the gig in *Classic Rock* magazine:

"It was a critical moment in the chronicles of rock; the creation of the New Wave Of British Heavy Metal, almost 25 years ago. Three bands – Angel Witch, Iron Maiden and Samson – making a dazzling re-emergence after years of punk-rock oppression, doing an embattled Iwo Jima-style flag-raising thing in a crepuscular old ballroom at the bottom end of Camden High Street.

At least that's how it should have been. But if truth be told, the birth of the NWOBHM was actually something of a troubled, forceps delivery… If Angel Witch ever had a finest hour, this was probably it, because they received a more positive response than Iron Maiden, the second act on the bill. Amazing, but true. The evening concluded with

Samson – pre-Bruce Dickinson, and replete with drummer Thunderstick in misguided Cambridge Rapist-type hood. More exploding bombs than Dresden successfully disguised the fact that this was workaday blues rock led by Paul Samson's tortuous guitar..."

Despite such recollections of that gig in 1979, the next year – and a lot of the following decade, come to that – really belonged to Iron Maiden whose intensive touring helped spread the NWOBHM across the country. Torquay is pretty far-flung (there are some who argue it hasn't been flung far enough), but within six or so months of Iron Maiden laying waste to Routes Niteclub in Exeter in December 1979, a number of bands had played within striking distance.

First up, in the February of 1980, the hot young Def Leppard turned up at Routes. Unlike the Iron Maiden gig, this time there was a support band too – real value for money – in the shape of Witchfynde. In a feature in *Sounds* in August 1980, vocalist Steve Bridges recalled the way it happened: "We had a phone call three days before the tour saying 'Will you do it?' Then we were waiting for a phone call on the Monday night. On Tuesday we were on. On Wednesday we had to be in Aberdeen, it was so quick. We had to pack our jobs in and everything. The day before we went, we were rushing round trying to get all the necessary gear together to go on tour. Crazy! We didn't know Leppard before the tour but apparently they liked the idea of having a complete Northern tour. We really owe everything to that, it put the name around. There were 40 dates and the receptions were generally very good. Better up North but in London all they seem to be interested in was Iron Maiden."

"It was pretty much just like that," confirms guitarist Montalo "We used to play a little pub in the Peak District, a great rock pub right in the middle of nowhere. At that time I don't think Def Leppard had done many gigs at all. Occasionally some of them would come to this place and they saw us there. In fact, I think there was a nasty fight there one night and Leppard stepped in and sorted it out, which was nice. Then they took off and asked us to come on the tour, which was the ideal opportunity for us. The tour also brought forward our LP's release, as obviously the record company wanted to capitalise on it.

We'd been playing together for years and had been getting gigs pretty easily. We started off, to be fair, as a covers band and made good money and used that to finance the recording of the *Give 'Em Hell* album. We originally recorded it with the idea of selling it ourselves, similar to what

Def Leppard had done with their EP. In fact, Def Leppard were very influential in the business respect. The whole NWOBHM thing, the whole do-it-yourself ethos... To me, that's the definition of the NWOBHM – that you've no need to rely on getting the record deal: get out there and do it yourself. So we went to Fairview Studios in Hull, the same studio Def Leppard used, and recorded an album's worth of material and so when we signed to Rondelet Records the record was already recorded and ready to go.

The Def Leppard tour involved quite a lot of money but the record company thought it was worth it. It really did happen very quickly. We got the call and it was almost a matter of just packing the bags and going straight up to Aberdeen in a van. It was quite a learning experience too; we learned from their professionalism, their energy and enthusiasm and the whole business thing they'd got around them. But on the stagecraft side, well, we'd go on and do our show and they'd be looking on from the side of the stage, and then they'd go on and look really unsure of themselves. But after a few shows they were a lot better, and seemed to do what we'd just been doing! It's a shame that in interviews now, Joe Elliott slags us off, yet we were very respectful and grateful to them. It was a great tour though, excellent crowds, and straight on the back of it the promoters wanted us out in our own right."

Montalo on the Witchfynde set list from the 1980 Def Leppard Tour:

"I've been speaking to the rest of the band, but set lists from over twenty years ago... That's not easy! On the Leppard tour we remember playing most of the *Give 'Em Hell* album with the exception of 'Unto The Ages Of The Ages'. We also included 'Tetelestai' and 'Wake Up Screaming'. Sorry, but that's the best I can do at present! We do have tapes somewhere recorded off the desk on the Def Leppard tour at Grimsby Town Hall but goodness knows where they are."

The quartet that was Witchfynde actually came together in 1975 and turned professional in 1980 when they took on the Def Leppard tour. The name had no significant meaning and was according to their own press something "just made up by the four original members of the band." They started well enough, and with the buzz still in their ears from the Def Leppard tour their debut album *Give 'Em Hell* was released in May 1980. "An unpretentious, enjoyably independent album," noted Geoff Barton, giving *Give 'Em Hell* a credible three-and-a-half stars in *Sounds*.

Having finally reached the stage of being professional musicians, it was a blow when bass player Andro Coulton left ("he had more personal problems than Marjorie Proops..." the other members noted in a fan club newsletter), although he was quickly and successfully replaced by Pete 'Thud' Surgey. At Coulton's last gig, Steve Bridges also announced his intention to leave but was persuaded to stay until the end of 1980, to complete album and touring commitments. He actually left in October and Chalky White, whose previous band had supported Witchfynde, took over. Their second album *Stagefright* was released on November 1, 1980, and not long after they recorded an excellent session for the BBC *Friday Rock Show*, featuring three golden oldies ('Getting Heavy', 'Give 'Em Hell' and 'Moon Magic') and one new song, 'Belfast', which has only ever seen the light of day on *The Friday Rock Show* compilation LP. However, the backlash was soon to follow.

"Naff clothes, naff songs, naff presentation..." claimed Carolyn Spence in *Sounds* in March 1981. "I don't believe this band do anything right. The heavy metal genre is one that imposes fairly rigid rules on its exponents, but that's surely no excuse for the excessive grossness of the likes of these lads." This is the same gig that the set list below was taken from, and Steve who was there on the night remembers it as a very different show to what you'd imagine from Ms Spence's scribblings. "She was also backstage before the gig at Walsall Town Hall. Montalo had written out a setlist for her on my pad so I asked him if he'd do the same for me. I don't think it was really her thing though as I remember her spending most of the time talking about seeing Spandau Ballet!"

WITCHFYNDE, WALSALL TOWN HALL, JANUARY 31, 1981:

'Stagefright'; 'Ready To Roll'; 'Getting' Heavy'; 'Big Deal'*; 'In The Stars'; 'Dead In Heaven'; 'Moon Magic'; 'Wake Up Screaming'; 'Tetelestai'; 'Give 'Em Hell'; 'Over The Top'; 'Pay Now, Love Later'*

* not actually played on the night

The review of their excellent third album *Cloak And Dagger* was no more favourable: "There's something so second-hand about it: riff, drums, shriek, end of track, riff, drums, shriek again... My favourite track was 'Fra Diabolo'. It is 20 seconds long," wrote Tibet in *Sounds* in November 1983.

Given the enmity shown by the UK press, I was surprised when Montalo told me, that he "never paid any attention to reviews, to be honest. In fact, we're quite an insular band. In terms of music, I like to listen to guitar players, Satriani, Blackmore... I listen to anything really and I'm not terribly bothered about what it is, as long as it's a well-written song. I've also got all sorts of strange music I've picked up over the years which influences me. I try to keep away from the general rock music scene as I don't want to be influenced by it. And to be honest I'm probably the most insular of us all. I spend a lot of time by myself and like to lose myself in the middle of nowhere. You won't get me in clubs or in the middle of the city. So, you see, I really am not that bothered about what critics say; it is, after all, only their opinion.

I tend to think we're quite a subtle band – if we went blatant full out with all the imagery, the press would either love us or hate us, simple as that. But we're quite subtle, and they can't make up their minds about us. I can understand why they didn't like some of what we did, but again, so much of it is down to press, promotion, production... A good song is a good song, but with a different production it can become a great song. There's no point regretting things but I wish Rondelet would have let us go to EMI when they were offered it after *Give 'Em Hell* came out."

Back on stage at Exeter, Witchfynde live gave the Maiden gig a couple of months earlier a run for its money. I can't remember much about headliners Def Leppard to be honest – they played well, but in those days I didn't take notes and the only real image I still have in my head is of Pete Willis, looking (a) very small and (b) scared witless! But they were nice enough guys and appeared genuinely astounded that Steve had transcribed the lyrics to the three songs on their *Getcha Rocks Off EP*, and patiently poured over his draft, making the necessary handwritten corrections. On the night, Witchfynde were more together and more confident on stage than the youngsters they were supporting; the crowd demanded an encore, an event which they said hadn't happened so far on the tour, so they reprised 'Give 'Em Hell'.

A few weeks later, *Metal For Muthas* faves Sledgehammer played at Routes. No support band this time round, and not much of a crowd either to be honest, but the added attraction of (unbeknown to us at the time) band leader Mike Cooke striking up a conversation in the pub opposite and asking what time we reckoned the band would go on, was quite a novelty. Sledgehammer were the first band I reviewed, my long-hand scribbles torn Julie Burchill-style from an A4 pad and posted to *Sounds*. Toe-curlingly embarrassing it might seem now – needless to say, after a couple of days sitting by the phone I realised that the editor was never going to call back – but the review is an honest reflection of the gig:

"First suspicions about the band's popularity this far from London were confirmed on arrival at the venue (Routes, Exeter). No milling metal mob in sight. In fact, no-one in sight. The usually-heaving pub opposite was also pretty much empty, apart from the archetypal one-man-and-his-dog and another bloke who, catching sight of us, came over and asked what time the venue opened, when the band usually came on and so forth. This was slightly more promising, being as it was Mike Cooke, Sledgehammer's guitarist, vocalist, writer and producer. The ensuing conversation revealed that he was somewhat worried about the local audience and the reception they would receive. Having been told that a South-West audience is probably the best in Britain, he hopefully went back to the venue confidence restored. Meantime, I regretted my words as the nightclub's doors were thrown open and about twenty people wandered in. By showtime – there was no support act – the crowd had grown to about 100, with about half at stage front and the others hanging back in the security of the bar. The bulk of the 55 minute set was unfamiliar, save for 'Feel Good' and the penultimate number 'Oxford City Hoedown' when all the stops were pulled out, and then, *sans* introduction, Cooke's effects board went into overdrive for a superb rendition of 'Sledgehammer' – tighter than the 7" and a vast improvement on the puny *Metal For Muthas* version.

SLEDGEHAMMER SET LIST – ROUTES, EXETER APRIL 16, 1980:

'I Don't Know Where I Am'; 'Troubleshooter'; 'Perfumed Garden'; 'I Don't Like Your Face'; 'Feel Good'; 'Food And Sex Mad'; 'Oxford City Hoedown'; 'Sledgehammer'; 'Over The Top 1914' // 'Blowjob'; 'Randy Robots' // 'Sledgehammer'

"Cooke later said that the band had not expected to be called back for an encore, but they most certainly were. The audience, which by this time sounded like an import from Madison Square Gardens, wanted more and got two for starters – one dedicated to inflation and Margaret Thatcher called 'Blowjob', and 'Randy Robots'. The band said their goodbyes, and that, theoretically, was that. But still the crowd wanted more. After what seemed like an eternity, Mike Cooke returned alone and held the audience spellbound with a stunning array of effects before plunging into 'Sledgehammer' one more time, his two band-mates caught on the hop and running to take their places. The song proper had barely started when two or three ambitious muthas took to the pretty sparse stage – to be followed by the rest of the floor crowd. The stage was packed, movement was impossible, backing vocals were shared by as many people as could crowd around the mikes – and the band loved it. When the protracted version of the song was finally over, the band could not leave the stage for a sea of autograph books, single sleeves, T-shirts and pound notes to be signed. The band said they were truly amazed by the reaction, and hoped to return."

"An exploding smoke bomb lit up the stage like exploding smoke bombs are prone to do."

The official version was printed in *Sounds* after Garry Bushell had caught up with the "three piece Bucks-based bulldozer" at their April gig at The Marquee:

"An exploding smoke bomb lit up the stage like exploding smoke bombs are prone to do, revealing the trio led by chest-and-crucifix-flashing guitar man Mike Cooke kicking off with the gutsy boogie 'I Dunno Where I Am'… 'Food And Sex Mad', although pretty penetrating lyrically, was only OK according to my notebook. Aw, but then the band underwent a Hulk-like transformation, changing from a fair-to-middling rock band to what the experts call a 'ravaging mutha' of a band. 'Oxford City Hoedown' exploded at a Motörhead pace. Then Gerry [Sherwin – bass] leapt on the amps while Mike created oceans of feedback for the mighty 'Sledgehammer'… and then finally the set closer 'Over The Top 1914' topped the lot with its machine-gun guitar, ferocious pace, dual vocals and angry lyrics. Encores come round thrice with the silly 'Blowjob', the raging 'Randy Robots' and finally 'Sledgehammer' itself just one more time, and I certainly didn't need any convincing that this band are going places."

Unfortunately, despite masses of talent, some great songs and an impressive appearance at the Reading Festival in 1980, Sledgehammer were just one of so many bands destined never to fulfil their potential. As for me, well, "oceans of feedback" is a turn of phrase that marks the obvious difference between a pro like Bushell and an amateur still at school!

April also saw the return of Iron Maiden to Devon, this time to Plymouth. Another brilliant gig; Maiden were now back to a five-piece with new recruit Dennis Stratton on second guitar. They shuffled on stage, Paul Di'Anno casually said: "Sa fing called 'Prowler'" (or words to that effect) and all hell broke out. I do remember that Steve Harris cocked up during 'Iron Maiden', which I don't suppose happened that often. Back in Exeter, lipstick 'n' glamour boys Girl (supported by Broken Home) strutted their stuff at Routes. The band now may be viewed as less than the sum of its parts, but back then the *Sheer Greed* album was pretty much a masterpiece and certainly not a metal-by-numbers LP, displaying in its grooves a strong diversity of both material and class. 'My Number', the song released as a taster for the album (a clear vinyl one-sided seven-incher retailing for 55p!) blew me away because it was so different. In fact, the weakest link on the album was the Kiss cover and live favourite 'Do You Love Me?'. 'Strawberries', 'Passing Clouds', 'Take Me Dancing': taken one at a time they don't appear to be heavy metal songs, but *Sheer Greed* is most certainly a heavy metal album *par excellence* (no matter what the band thought) and one that has nicely ridden the waves of time. And their *Top Of The Pops* performance to promote 'Hollywood Tease' was stunning!

I liked Girl a lot, both onstage that night and through their career. Most of their reviews concentrated on a perceived attitude problem and vocalist Phil Lewis' flirtation with actress Britt Eckland. But the Girl I saw were out there amongst the crowd before the show, quite happy to chat and sign stuff for an eternity after it. Their problem was though that with the make-up and name, they appeared too lightweight for the tough metal boys (several guys I knew wouldn't touch 'em with a bargepole), and live they were too heavy for the girlies.

Meanwhile, Torquay Town Hall itself got into the act, hosting both the Saxon *Wheels Of Steel* tour (supported by the ultra cool Tygers Of Pan Tang) and frankly old school Budgie supported by new boogie hopefuls Vardis. This final gig took place the night before my final exam at school; unfortunately it was an oral exam, so I had to respond to questions asked in Russian which I couldn't really hear because I was acutely deaf!

The coverage provided by *Sounds* no doubt helped support the spread of the NWOBHM, but help also came from DJ Tommy Vance, his producer Tony Wilson and BBC Radio One's *The Friday Rock Show*.

Not content with just playing the latest 'n' greatest releases, *The Friday Rock Show* also became famous for airing sessions of bands recorded exclusively for Radio One at the BBC's Maida Vale studios, and these sessions, produced by Tony Wilson, often sounded better than the bands' own commercially-available releases. Commenting on the BBC session version of Samson's 'Take It Like A Man', John (another of the clan and Tarsus' rhythm guitarist) added "…if only Tony Wilson had produced their *Head On* LP, they could have gone on to be as big as Iron Maiden…"

Recording a session for *The Friday Rock Show* was not only a good way to spread the word about your band, but also brought with it a degree of prestige, membership of an elite club of bands deemed worthy of such an honour. And besides, it was fun, as Shiva's Andy Skuse recalls:

"The Friday Rock Show session went out twice on air and was great to do. It had to have a "live" feel so was a pretty straight recording of us bashing away in a huge room with just a few extras added on to fill it out in the solo passages. We were all pretty excited about being on Radio One, although I don't remember how it came about. Our manager Ken Lintern must have arranged it with the BBC; I certainly don't recall having anything to do with it. We knew there wouldn't be much leeway for overdubs, some obviously, but not a lot, so we just chose four songs that were good to do live. Tony Wilson was a cool guy to work with and got a good sound very quickly, and he put in some good touches. We were a bit miffed not to see Tommy Vance though, I guess we'd expected him to be hanging around but he didn't show. At least I don't think he did, I was so engrossed with the superb mixing desk that Geddy Lee could have come in and I wouldn't have noticed!

You don't get that long to work on each track; they were basically bashed out as if we were gigging and once we were happy that the notes were in the right places that was it. Pretty much a one-take situation. It was much faster and much more 'live' than recording the album. We were only there for the day, after all.

We were all pretty tired by the end of the day and I'm sure that John had a sore throat, which I think you can hear on some of the high notes – he could usually hit 'em with no trouble! We were all pleased with the way things went but really wanted to get home for some kip, so much so that I left my Ampeg head in the studio. I had to borrow John's car and drive straight back to London to fetch it as we had a gig the next night. I couldn't do a gig on any other amp, it wouldn't have sounded right with the Ricky!

Anyway, doing all the driving for the tour and to the session and then another return trip to London left me hallucinating from lack of sleep!"

With all this going on, it came as no surprise that all of a sudden, bands were springing up everywhere. That said, forming a band is relatively straightforward, as John Mortimer of Holocaust discovered. "Putting Holocaust together was no problem, but keeping it together later on was an entirely different matter! But you've got to remember that when I started badgering everyone at school to get instruments together in order to form a heavy metal band, there was no NWOBHM; punk was the 'happening' music of the day. My own personal heavy metal mania began when I was 13 in 1976, and by the time I was 15 I decided that I just had to get an electric guitar. In our year at school there was a real movement of heavy rock fans and it was a fertile ground for band formations. The absence of live gigs was irrelevant to us then; we just loved to go round to each other's houses of an evening and headbang all night to Black Sabbath, AC/DC, Budgie, Blue Oyster Cult, Rush, Lynyrd Skynyrd, Scorpions, Led Zeppelin, Motörhead and the like. Albums were loaned and exchanged within our little collective. Man, it was the meaning of life!! So anyway, because so many people at school were into heavy music and wanted to make a reactionary – but at the same time progressive – statement against the punk movement, it was relatively easy to get a band together; the hard bit was saving pocket money for instruments!"

"It was pretty simple for us really," recalls Tygers Of Pan Tang guitarist Robb Weir. "I just placed an advert in a local university for a bass player and a drummer. Rocky replied and said he knew a drummer, that was Brian, and that was that. We advertised for a singer and Jess Cox was the second guy that came along. The rest, as they say, is history!"

"Drummer Allan Angold and I realised that Switchback wasn't going anywhere," remembers Geoff Gillespie of Sabre, "so we decided that we wanted to form something with a little more substance. We started advertising in *Melody Maker* and we came across two guitarists in North London – Kilburn and Tottenham, to be precise – who were looking for a rhythm section. We got together, chatted, jammed…and that was that! They were so different in style; Alan Beschi was basically a jazz player who had to 'learn down' to play hard rock and was very precise in his playing. Nick Fusco, on the other hand, was a naturally gifted player who made his guitar scream at times – always going for that one extra note that seemed to be just out of reach. Watching those two on a good night was always a highlight for me."

"We must have got together about 1979, at a guess," Jaguar's Garry Pepperd reckons. "It was just me and Jeff Cox at first. We were at college together where we met and we found we had a common interest in music. We started messing around really for a while, and so Jaguar was an extension of what Jeff and I had been doing – a 'proper' band, really. It all started to come together when drummer Chris Lovell joined. Chris was about 16 at the time, and although he wasn't big on technique he was big on energy and even at 16 he could make one hell of a racket! We were well impressed – you know, double bass kit, the works – and we thought, 'Yeah, brilliant!' Then the three of us spent quite a while working on songs before we even got a singer in. So it all started from just being college friends really; then one thing led to another, as it inevitably does…"

THE 1980 FESTIVALS

Appearing at a festival is a great way to improve your fan-base – or get bottled off, depending on how well you do – and in 1980 there were a number of events giving substantial breaks to the up-and-coming NWOBHM bands. The earliest gathering of the clans up to this point was the Heavy Metal Barndance at Stafford Bingley Hall in July 1980, when Motörhead were joined by Saxon, Girlschool, Angel Witch, Vardis, Mythra and White Spirit.

"That was the biggest thing we'd headlined up to then,' recalls Lemmy, "and then Port Vale came afterwards." Saxon had supported Motörhead on the *Bomber* tour and Girlschool had done the honours on the *Overkill* tour and, in addition, as Headgirl the two bands would go on to record the successful *St Valentine's Day Massacre EP.* "The best band we ever took out was Girlschool,' reckons Lemmy. "They were great, fucking excellent in fact. It was great to see girls playing heavy music, 'cos girls just don't seem to do it very often. We took them out on tour when no-one else was interested and got them signed to our label. They were very good, and we had our only Top 5 hit with them – and they had their only Top 5 hit with us," he adds, laughing.

To get a feel for the Heavy Metal Barndance, this extract from *Sounds* in August 1980 shows what Mick Middles thought about the bands:

"White Spirit are hammering through their set and I'm outside arguing about the absence of my name on the guest list; Vardis finish in a roaring triumphant climax brought about by sheer hard work and a ferocious desire to prove themselves; Mythra live to fight another day, while bearing a certain dullness due mainly to their lack of confidence; Angel Witch are, for many, the first major band of the evening... they push simple melody into a corner and cruelly batter it to death; four girls named Girlschool who stand every chance of becoming the first major all-female rock band in the entire history of rock 'n' roll... a brisk breath of fresh air in a world where dumb masculinity is the norm. Girlschool play one of the hardest, unmoving and completely mind-shattering sets I've ever seen from a band so new to the scene. Without any measure of doubt they are the best band on show; Saxon breed boredom... they are nothing but crafty hard rock caricatures... pure imitations and unlike the hilarious Witchfynde they contain not a hint of much-needed humour; Motörhead... awful, distorted beyond belief, only entertaining in a perverse fashion..."

"I remember how big the place was and how hot it was on stage. I think the stage was really high too," recollects Girlschool's drummer Denise Dufort. "I was really nervous too; there were so many people there. But we were all so young and excited, which is probably why I can't remember much about the other bands there on the day. I know it was a major event not just for Motörhead fans but for the band themselves. They'd been invited to appear at both the Reading and Castle Donington festivals but declined both in favour of their own 'Over The Top Heavy Metal Brain Damage Party' at Stafford's Bingley Hall. Impressive list of bands too. Motörhead brought the gig to a spectacular climax with Lemmy taking a ride in the nose of the *Bomber* rig. Then a trumpet fanfare, the National Anthem and the presentation of silver discs for sales of *Bomber* to Lemmy, Eddie and Phil by a fake Queen made the gig more memorable for all of us. And, of course, there was that funny little plane they flew across the hall before they came on. The highlight of that time was touring with them, because it gave us our first taste of big audiences and big theatres. It's funny though; we were scared to meet Motörhead for the first time because we'd seen so many photos of them and they looked really scary; we didn't know that they'd turn out to be such nice guys and that we'd still be good friends to this day."

It's not just Mick Middles who was impressed by Girlschool. *Record Mirror's* Malcolm Dome described their Bingley Hall appearance as "positive proof that Girlschool are not only the most successful all-woman group in the history of rock but every inch the equals of Saxon, Iron Maidens of this world and are, probably, the *most significant* outfit to have emerged from the new era of British HM."

Girlschool did extremely well in terms of press coverage in their early days, even getting a better review for their debut single for Bronze Records 'Emergency' than Iron Maiden's 'Running Free', released and reviewed in the same week. "Really?" Denise sounded genuinely surprised when I reminded her of the fact: "Which of our singles was that again?!"

GIRLSCHOOL 'EMERGENCY' (BRONZE)

It's a widely held belief that in those fields of endeavour normally associated with the male of the species, women must be not just as good but much better than the male companion if they are going to succeed. With girls doing pretty well in pop generally at the moment, heavy metal is probably the last bastion of all-male élitism, and 'Emergency' presents a pretty indisputable challenge. It certainly sounds like they've benefited (if that's the right word) from their tour with Motörhead because this is as good as anything I've heard recently from Lemmy & Co, with the added advantage of voices in place of the Black & Decker finishing sander for the vocals. It's all incredibly corny, of course, but then that's the whole attraction of heavy metal.

IRON MAIDEN 'RUNNING FREE' (EMI)

So this is the future of HM. I would have thought they'd try a little harder to come up with something catchy and original (within the confines of this very confining genre) for a single but what have we here? Nothing but cliché after cliché after cliché without, in my opinion, the spark that separates people like Kiss and Nugent from the rest. I would have thought British heavy metal would have learnt its lesson by now but it seems not. Disappointing. Singles reviews by Tony Mitchell, Sounds, February 1980

From Denise's point of view, there was very much a NWOBHM scene in London. "It was great. We made a lot of friends with bands like Motörhead, Angel Witch, Praying Mantis. It was great to be able to see and check out new bands. It was a really great scene back then, and of course there were loads more places to play than there are now, especially in London. And, like I said, we had a brilliant time with Motörhead back then. We've never split up. I always have to tell people that in interviews. Everyone seems to think that we split up around 1988 or so but we never did. I think what's kept us together is the friendship in the band. We've had a few line-up changes but we've all become best friends; Tracey Lamb's a mate, Kelly's a great friend. We're all like sisters. I really do think that's what's kept us going after all these years. But then, it never crossed our minds back then that we'd still be doing this twenty-five years later.

"We may be a lot older but we're a lot better at playing our instruments!"

We used to just carry on from day to day, writing, rehearsing, recording and touring. Mind you, we're a lot better now; we sound a lot more professional than we did back then. We may be a lot older but we're a lot better at playing our instruments!"

Two other bands on the bill that day – Mythra and White Spirit (along with Fist, Raven and Tygers Of Pan Tang) – had recently been covered in a *Sounds'* feature *Are You Ready For The NENWOBHM?* in May 1980, an article lumping together a number of bands coming out of the North-East of England (hence the North-East New Wave). Centred around the growing Neat Records, with three of the named bands already signed to the label and Raven auditioning that day, the feature noted that Mythra were "not part of the Neat set-up but [were] at the forefront of the (if you insist) New Wave Of British Heavy Metal North East Division. It added that Geoff Barton had been so impressed with the band's *Death And Destiny EP* that he had called it "this year's *Getcha Rocks Off.*" Twenty-odd years later, in *Classic Rock*, Barton recalled this in a list of acts he had championed "but who everyone else considered to be unlistenable bollocks." Interestingly, he also pointed out that Lars Ulrich didn't want the band included on the *New Wave Of British Heavy Metal '79 Revisited* album the pair co-compiled in 1990, a bit bizarre given the fact that the *Death And Destiny EP* is a cracker.

In the meantime, White Spirit, Ravendale had noted, "are the craftsmen. The other bands speak in hushed tones about the Hartlepool-based quintet's musicianship. Until very recently a percentage of note-perfect covers were included in the set but now, with the advent of Neat and the 'Back To The Grind' single, these have been dispensed with. Like Fist, Spirit reckon they aren't a heavy metal band but if they're not then neither were Deep Purple, the combo they most resemble."

Hot on the heels of the Barn Dance came the first ever Monsters Of Rock festival at Castle Donington. Saxon was the sole band to represent the thriving domestic metal scene, alongside American hot young hopefuls Riot and Touch, Cannucks April Wine – who were only just making headway in the UK thanks to their exceedingly catchy 'I Like To Rock' single and the *Harder... Faster* LP from which it was drawn – and the established triumvirate of Judas Priest, Scorpions and Rainbow. Saxon, of course, immortalised the event in the song 'And The Bands Played On', which was released as a single in April 1981 and which reached Number 12 in the charts. Saxon's forty-five minutes of Donington fame were officially released on CD a few years back, and a cracking set it is too.

For *Sounds* at least, Saxon were one of the festival's highlights: "Saxon, who are fast becoming equal to or even better than Motörhead, gave Donington a very necessary kick in the lobotomy as a reminder that Festivals Are Fun and wrought some overdue changes among the slowly sinking audience. Saxon have no class. Far better, they do not pretend to have it... Saxon are entertaining because they really do enjoy themselves, because they don't 'give a shit' and because, unlike most of their contemporaries who have all the stage presence of a troupe of performing dogs, they have some wonderfully crude style. Musically, though I'm not so sure that music is the prime attraction in this case, things were not so hot with Saxon's supposed attempts at being the loudest band in existence sorely wrecked by patchy sound and the distinct impression that the drummer, Peter Gill, played the exact same beat throughout with the odd change of speed. Mind you, by the time they returned for a mighty encore of 'Machine Gun', Saxon had definitely deserved it, what with scattering the guts of 'Wheels Of Steel' all over the heads of the audience and bellowing a magnificent '747 (Strangers In The Night)' to the mistimed accompaniment of an East Midlands aeroplane."

The Big One back then was without doubt Reading, an unparalleled collection of rock and metal bands spread over three days in late August. The NWOBHM highlights below are taken from Geoff Barton and Robbi Millar's joint review in *Sounds* although be aware that sometimes it is very difficult to ascertain whether the journalists actually liked the bands or not (the validity of the music weekly sending Ms Millar – who didn't even like "HM garbage" – is questionable):

"NENWOBHM outfit White Sprirt shook off their 'Uriah Heep clones' tag with a perfectly-played set that at times almost reached pomp-rock proportions. Although the guitar was sadly inaudible for most of the time, the Spirits quickly won over the crowd. Exuding down-to-earth *When The Boat Comes In*-type appeal, the satin-clad Geordies were more impressive than any band that appeared on the *Muthas Pride EP* has a right to be. What Styx would have sounded like if they'd been British and made up of road menders instead of chartered accountants…

I must admit to being slightly disappointed with Samson. With such a strong image and several truly superb songs to their credit they really should have taken the festival by storm. But as it was an inexplicable failure to project coupled with an unsympathetic sound system contrived to make this a less than spectacular showing overall…

From here on in it was up, with Iron Maiden putting on the performance of their lives… The immensely partisan punters were with the band every step of the way – in fact, the audience's enthusiasm was so spontaneous and unforced I can't believe that Iron Maiden will remain anywhere but at the top, even after the Metal Revival has died its inevitable (and probably ignominious) death…"

"That was a great day," notes Iron Maiden's Paul Di'Anno. "We had arrived, and we were ready to take over the world of metal."

Back to the *Sounds* team, who "missed Praying Mantis and caught Angelwitch. A severe error of judgement. I can believe the Mantis' manager's claims of 'the band were fucking great' – could have done with some melody at that point – but I couldn't believe the horror that assaulted all my senses at the sight of Angel Witch. 'Grooaahh!' yelled the biker contingent in appreciation as the three gross objects on stage proceeded to destroy the sunny atmosphere with all the delicacy of a bull elephant practising trampoline in Fortnum and Masons."

Robb Weir from Tygers Of Pan Tang remembers that, "everything seemed to move so fast. One minute we were doing local venues, and then we were on telly and playing Reading. It was the biggest gig we had done to that point, and also it was John Sykes' first gig with us. I can remember feeling nervous and excited and wanting to shit myself all at once! When we were approaching the stage, I could hear the roar of the crowd and the chants – 'Tygers! Tygers! Tygers!' We stood on the side of the stage and I have a photo of the lads and me with my fist clenched shouting 'Come on! Let's go out and rock the place, you fuckers!' I can't describe the feeling I felt, it was like someone had plugged me into the mains! The show went really well and we did two encores, even David Coverdale was at the side of the stage at one point with Bernie Marsden and Mickey Moody. We all had a bit of a crack afterwards!"

"How pleasant, then," the *Sounds'* overview noted about Tygers Of Pan Tang, "to find a band able to spark life into the ludicrous HM overkill line up without the assistance of a top bill placing. The Tygers played a set so riddled with cramped-up heavy rock clichés – right down to the machine-gun mikestand – and high energy music kicks that you'd have to be landed with the features of Ritchie Blackmore not to have smiled at it and by the time they'd gotten round to 'Wild Catz' acknowledgement was running higher than the sheer brute force in Jess Cox's vocals[1]. The same could not be said of Girl. Their problem lies deep in the fact that while the Men enjoy the music but can't stand the image, the Little Girls are the people who are boosting attendance at Girl parades. Therefore, it was a case of 'more cans than anyone else' and, although Philip Lewis had recovered his voice by the time it came to a hoarse rendition of 'Hollywood Tease', his temper was frayed sorely. Not the best section of the day, methinks...

Def Leppard were the third nice (well, OK) surprise in ten hours... I hear they copped some Party Sevens in painful places. They didn't deserve it..."

NWOBHM bands started to gain wider national exposure as bigger names like Ian Gillan (whose own career was no doubt invigorated by the upswing in interest in heavy metal) took them out as tour supports. Gillan's October 1980 *Glory Road* tour featured both White Spirit and Quartz and like most Gillan tours of the time, slogged through thirty or so venues all over Britain, thus giving both bands healthy exposure to new fans. White Spirit in particular were well-received, having had a fair slice of coverage in *Sounds* in particular and copping a three-star album review the same month, although Barton unfairly claimed that "away from the immediacy of the moment [referring to his previous glowing review of the band at Reading] and in the cold light of debut album day, it's sad to discover deficiencies arising... Much as I enjoy this album, there's scarcely a note, riff or vocal phrase that hasn't been borrowed from elsewhere." Quartz, on the other hand, were pretty solid riffers in the Sabbath-style and "an enigma I can't really fathom," claimed one *Sounds* writer.

My personal favourite tour came at the end of the 1980 with the mixed bag coupling of Girlschool, Angel Witch and openers Tank, who didn't even feature on the posters. The brainchild of Algy Ward, formerly of The Damned, Tank shared some of Motörhead's connections and had material produced by Eddie Clarke, which is possibly how they got the gig in the first place. Tank's early days saw them doing Motörhead without the subtleties, from Ward's "Wakey Wakey!!" opening to their bludgeoning set closer. I liked them later in their career, when they started writing well-crafted songs, but on the night at Cardiff Top Rank I couldn't wait for them to finish. Plus, to my rather blinkered way of thinking back then, they were just punks who'd jumped ship. That said, the crowd on the night at Cardiff Top Rank loved 'em to bits. Girlschool were crowning a defining year and went on to headline a night at Reading in 1981. Angel Witch were pretty much on the way up too, although a headliner gig at The Lyceum in London with Vardis, Geddes Axe and Raven in May 1981 pretty much marked the end of the original incarnation of the band; a shame, because all I can remember about them on that night is an average show and the three band members looking real girls' blouses kitted out in glowing white robes.

Angel Witch were probably one of the hardest working bands of the early days of the NWOBHM and as a result had built up a loyal following; but the music writers of the day remained adamant that, no matter how popular they became, they were to remain the critics' fall guys. Hated at Reading, and described in another *Sounds* review as "a dreadful punky paraody of Sabbath... Kevin Heybourne, a guitar player *par excellence* true, but a singer with a flat thin and wimpishly vain voice..." Angel Witch on vinyl fared no better:

"Not as godawful as I'd been led to believe..." the *Sounds* review damned the 'Sweet Danger' single with faint praise (adding "comes in exciting black sleeves for fans of The Devil"). "Metal for muckrakers. The flip contains a tribute to Vincent Price's immortal (not to say immoral) 'Dr Phibes' character. He had half a face, when all was revealed. When all is revealed about Angel Witch, they'll probably be found to have half a brain. Between them," ran the *Sounds* review of 'Loser'.

"GREAT, FABULOUS, I *really* like it! I am of course referring to the *ending* of this appalling piece of vinyl..." was how Paul Suter reviewed the band's self-titled debut album.

All of which is a great shame, really. As I said, they had a large and loyal following, and the final line-up of the early days, when guitarist and vocalist Kevin Heybourne was complemented by the solid bass work of Kevin Riddles and the talented Dave Dufort (brother of Girlschool skinbeater Denise) on drums, was generally a joy to see and listen to.

> ## *"It's sad now when I go back home and drive past a boarded-up venue or a pub that's now a McDonald's that we played a blinding gig at."*

After the split, Riddles and Dufort moved on to form Tytan, and despite flirting with a few other ventures (including a band called Blind Fury with vocalist Lou Taylor which did nothing aside from giving Taylor a name to take with him when he joined Satan), Heybourne eventually reformed Angel Witch. Several times, in fact. Having chatted at various venues over the years, I would love to have interviewed him but, depending on whom you ask, he is either living in one of four different cities across the globe which makes the task rather difficult, or dead, which makes it even harder.†

BANDS' VIEWS ON THE NWOBHM

A simple question which I put to some of the interviewees: "Did you feel there was, or that you were part of, a 'movement'"?

Mike Ellis of Aragorn: "In my mind, the term was applied as a convenient term of reference to distinguish bands from the more established acts; it was a Bartonism that stuck! We didn't really feel we were part of anything until we were 'told' we were part of it, so to speak. We felt more kindred with Manchester metal bands and no-one really made a point of saying 'we are part of the NWOBHM' – we were just playing music we loved in our own style. There was a huge metal scene in Manchester at the time and loads of venues would have metal bands

---

† Jess Cox, of course, never sang 'Wild Catz' as the song was a showcase for Robb Weir

playing every weekend; it's sad now when I go back home and drive past a boarded-up venue or a pub that's now a McDonald's that we played a blinding gig at."

Ian Toomey of Bitches Sin: "Well, it was interesting to see a lot of good bands get noticed and to get attention for British metal. But as far as I am concerned, we just happened to appear at that time. We are very different to the other NWOBHM bands – Bitches Sin was always a heavy metal band that set out to be original."

John Gallagher of Raven: "Naaah, it was just a blanket term given to all the bands that were 'suddenly' popular. I don't think any of the bands thought they were part of a movement per se. The best thing about all the first tier bands was they were all different!"

John Mortimer of Holocaust: "We were a bit isolated from the rest of the New Wave Of British Heavy Metal. We went to all the gigs when the English bands came up to Scotland and there were loads of metal fans around, but let's just say, Edinburgh was not Sheffield, Birmingham, London, or even Barnsley!"

Garry Phillips of Soldier: "There was definitely a feeling of being part of a movement although Soldier didn't really think of ourselves as NWOBHM until we got caught up in it; I guess you could say that all the new heavy rock bands at that time were involved in it whether consciously or not. But it was great when from time to time we came across each other on the road!"

Geoff Gillespie of Sabre: "Damn right we felt part of a larger scene! And following our two appearances in *Kerrang!'s* 'Armed & Ready' section we got letters from all over the world. The New Wave Of British Heavy Metal gave us *our* punk rock, something personal to us. I had actually enjoyed an awful lot of punk – especially Generation X and The Clash – but I had also been chased and attacked at punk gigs. Now, this was *ours*."

Andy Skuse of Shiva: "I guess we did feel part of a movement, although we never aimed to be in this or that particular pigeon hole but we were obviously doing the same sort of thing that a lot of the New Wave Of British Heavy Metal bands were doing. However, we always wanted to be a bit more out-on-a-limb and not conform to the stereotype metal image too closely."

Garry Pepperd of Jaguar: "We basically did our own thing. There's never been, I don't think, a Metal scene in the South-West; I mean, Bristol's not like London, Birmingham, Newcastle… When we were around back then there were a few metal bands, and some that came after us like Onslaught, but only the odd one or two. No, I can't say we were ever part of anything. We were just out on our own. We did have a bit of an affinity with Raven, I must admit, because they were top lads and such a great band. I still think their first couple of albums are superb – *Rock Until You Drop* is a great record. And they were the most energetic band I ever saw. They were fantastic. But I always thought we were out on our own. A lot of people round here didn't even know we were a local band. We just happened to be based here but there was no local scene – unless there was one and we weren't invited! As for the NWOBHM, I don't know…"

Montalo of Witchfynde: "We'd been playing since the mid-Seventies, but what the NWOBHM meant to us was this thing of doing it yourself. We'd been demoing songs and waiting for a label, and then we heard about Def Leppard and their do-it-yourself approach. And the punk thing; you know, there was raw energy, and although I don't want to be disrespectful, they might not have been expert at playing their instruments, but at least they were out there doing it. So we thought that's what we'd do – record an album with a view to putting it out ourselves, and that to me was what the NWOBHM was all about. That, and the under-produced – not in a disrespectful way – the under-produced sound, just the basics, which suited us because that was our approach."

Brian Ross of Blitzkrieg: "The New Wave Of British Heavy Metal was a breath of fresh air. There'd been the glam rock thing in the early Seventies, then the punk thing, which to me was really the start of the New Wave Of British Heavy Metal, where people were saying they'd had enough of disco shit and wanted to have fun, make some noise. It wouldn't have happened without punk, or at least it would have taken a lot longer. It was on the back of the punk thing that enabled bands like us to do what we wanted. We were just playing heavy rock in the mould of Deep Purple, Black Sabbath, Led Zeppelin etc, and we looked at the way Judas Priest were doing things and decided that that was the way we wanted to go. It was a very special time."

Paul Di'Anno, Iron Maiden: "Part of a movement? No, we weren't part of it; we were it, and I was the voice of it."

DENISE DUFORT ON GIRLSCHOOL'S SUPPORT BANDS

Girlschool were seemingly forever on the road, and unsurprisingly took out a number of NWOBHM bands as their tour supports. I wondered how many Denise could remember...

"Oh, there was Jaguar. I really liked them and got on really well with them. Funnily enough, I did their lights at every gig on the tour as they didn't have anyone to do it. They were really impressed, and I was too because I was actually very good at it!

Then there was Raven. They were a great bunch, really nice guys. They split up didn't they, or moved to New York or something?" When I confirmed that they are still pretty hard working and are indeed based in New York, she added, "Well, tell them Girlschool said 'Hi!'"

'Boy, do I remember touring with Girlschool!" laughs Raven's John Gallagher in response. "It was 1982 and our first full tour in the UK. Girlschool's people were really good to us and we got on well with the girls. Jeez, they could put away the drink! It was a warm summer and we had a blast. We were supporting the *Wiped Out* album and, well, we were rather insane, just for a change! On the last gig – Glasgow – Mark and I got up and jammed on 'Johnny B. Goode' with them which was a lot of fun. They had some great songs. 'Future Flash' was my fave, especially as we had the comedy of watching their pyro guy trying to sneak his gear onto the front of the stage during the taped intro to the song. Pyro was usually not allowed, but he always got away with it!"

But back to Denise, and AIIZ. "Ah, I remember them really well, largely because I went out with Simon Wright, their drummer, for a while. He's with Dio now; even though he's my ex-boyfriend he still rang me up when Dio supported Alice Cooper and put us all on the guest list at Wembley. And Kim used to go out with guitarist Gary Owens. They were a really good band. He was a great drummer though; I always knew he'd go places. When we were still going out he auditioned for AC/DC – although he didn't know exactly who he was auditioning for when he went for it. And AC/DC were like my all-time favourite band, and still are. And he phoned me up and said, 'You'll never guess who I've just joined!' We went out to a posh restaurant that night to meet up with the band and wives and girlfriends and it was like, 'This is fantastic; I'm in a posh restaurant and I'm surrounded by AC/DC!'

Angel Witch was another great band. I'm still in touch with Kevin Heybourne through my brother who was in the band. I think he's in France, or Belgium. We went out with them and Tank on the same bill, but that was when Dave Hogg was still their drummer. That was a good tour. And Tank were really good too on that tour. They had the same label and management as us."

I was curious to know if she remembered Atomkraft. "The name rings a bell but I don't remember them. I can't place them at all. It's hard to remember the one-offs, whereas when you're on tour... I mean, the *Hit And Run* tour with AIIZ was a seven-week tour. And the Angel Witch tour was quite long as well... Well, it certainly seemed it at the time!"

"We supported Girlschool at a one-off gig at Newcastle University either at the end of '86 or very early '87," says Atomkraft's Tony Dolan. "It was She and the girls, with us sandwiched between. We'd actually just recorded our cover of 'Demolition Boyz' and I took them a cassette copy, which I presented to them. They were great, of course, and they said we were a great band and that they thought we were gonna be massive and certainly the next big thing! Denise and Kim said I reminded them of Lemmy from the back, as I had my mike almost to the ceiling in those days like the Kilminster! I remember Kim saying to me at the end of the gig that she noticed on our set list a track called 'Foliage' and she asked me what it was about. I began to explain to her what foliage is and she stopped me saying, 'I know what fucking foliage is! What the fuck is the song about?' to which I replied, 'I have no fucking idea!' I did, of course; I wrote the bloody thing! But it was much easier and funnier to give that answer, and we all just laughed!

They were great to be around and it was a storming show for us and for them. Me and the vocalist Ian Swift hung around with them after the show and had a bevvie or two. Then they went to their tour bus. They were due to play London the day after at the Clarendon Ballroom. I said they had to listen to the tape of 'Demolition Boyz' and that I may make the show. They said I should come down which I did, but when I got to the Ballroom no-one was there and after quite a while I began to feel self-conscious about just turning up; I thought that they've probably had so many support bands, although they were really cool, they probably forgot me and Atomkraft as soon as they'd left Newcastle. But I was wrong; as I walked round the block for the tenth time, I heard, 'TONYYY!' and turned around to see Kim and Denise hanging out of their bus window as they pulled up.

I went in with them for their sound-check and Kim was fantastic, introducing me to everyone who hadn't been in Newcastle. The girls told me they thought our version of 'Demolition Boyz' was amazing and wanted to do it with us as a single. I was blown away! Shame it never came off; it would have rocked! They played a blinder that night and I was even approached by some fans who'd seen Atomkraft at Hammersmith Odeon on the Longest Day gig with Agent Steel and Nuclear Assault and thought we – and especially my bass playing – were great. I left the show early as I was staying with a friend and never saw the girls again. Big shame; it had been a rather special three days!

In fact, as I now remember, I did actually see the girls again in a professional way, when myself, Mantas and Abaddon as Venom played St. Petersburg outside the Winter Palace in 1991 or something. It was a festival in Russia with UFO, Magnum, Asia and Girlschool, as well as the Sweet and us! I didn't make myself known to them as I looked kind of different and so they never knew it was me. I don't know why I didn't. Just shy, I guess."

FORGIVE US OUR TRESPASSES

"I got my first guitar about '77," begins Mark Sutcliffe of Trespass. "I started fairly late, sort of 16, 17. Then I kept on at my brother Paul to get a drum kit 'cos at that time he was banging on pots and pans and using the front of our gas fire as a cymbal – bet the neighbours loved that! And our cousin Rick played bass, so there were three Sutcliffes in the band at that time. Then we moved across town where there was a music shop and that's where we met Dave, who'd somehow managed to blag himself a job at the music shop doing bugger all but playing guitars all day. I don't think he'd been playing all that long, but had ended up in a band called Black Maria."

"I could play 'Caroline' and a couple of other Quo songs!" laughs Dave Crawte. "Then I met Mark. I must have had some sort of natural ability, because Mark came along and taught me how to really play…"

"So we met with Dave," continues Mark, "and kind of cannibalised the band he was in, so, there's me, Paul and Dave, and a friend of his, Nick, who came from a really well-to-do family in town. They had a big medieval hall where we could go and rehearse. Then Nick, being the son of a very wealthy barrister, decided he had other fish to fry and we got our geography teacher Richard Penny in on bass guitar…"

"'This isn't going anywhere,' so I stood up and said, 'Look Richard, we can't say 'cunt' in front of you!'"

"He'd been in bands before. He was only thirty at the time but we sacked him for being too old!"

"Well, we used that as an excuse," adds Dave. "We were sitting round in Mark's front room when we had to sack him and he came round. He knew. He always used to wear this woolly hat…"

"But that wasn't the reason we sacked him!" cuts in Mark.

"…and he took this bloody woolly hat off and he's scrunching it up – I remember it so well – he was scrunching this woolly hat up out of nerves, and we were sort of saying, 'Look…'…"

"I was 'umming' and 'ahhing'," concedes Mark, "and Dave…"

"I said, 'Look, you're our Geography teacher, Richard, you're too old,' and he said 'I'm not too old,'…"

"He wasn't really…" Mark chips in.

"…and I thought, 'This isn't going anywhere,' so I stood up and said, 'Look Richard, we can't say 'cunt' in front of you!'"

"Some rock 'n' roll band, eh?" adds Mark.

"Didn't we ask him to shave his beard off too?" laughs Dave, mischievously.

"We did our first gig in March '79, recorded 'One Of These Days' in October '79, so that's how green we were," notes Mark. "We'd never played live before that year. And suddenly our single is being played at The Bandwagon and places like that. Maiden and Leppard were that little bit older than us, and were a little more established and ready for the movement than we were; we were probably just a little bit too late. And they had experienced management. Experienced management is everything."

"We had a local manager and he had his own label," says Dave. "So when we started getting interest – and we were getting interest from all the record companies – he just wanted a deal for himself rather than a deal for us."

"I mean," adds Mark, "this was post-punk, the year of indie labels and the best thing would have been for him to get his label attached to EMI or someone, and you can't blame him for trying it."

"We were universally hated by all the bands around here," says Mark, switching topics. "They'd all been playing Eagles' covers for years then suddenly we come along – braanngg!! – and we've got a single in the heavy metal chart and are down in London doing the Marquee club! We were pilloried by all the other bands around here!"

"A lot of bands liked to kick the jukebox when our single came on!" adds Dave "We just used to hope the needle would jump back to the start! But they'd been trying for years and years and hadn't got anywhere and we came along and the first thing we do ends up Number 3 in the heavy metal chart. So they hated us; it's only human nature, to be honest.

There weren't any other bands like us around here anyway. Suffolk is such a musical backwater. I don't know why, but maybe our isolation actually almost helped us, because we were able to develop. It's a bit like those isolated islands where you get weird mutated forms of life coming up, like pygmy elephants and stuff like that! That's what we were like! The beauty of it was that things were happening for us, and it was being generated by the music – there was no bullshit, no hype; people just liked the record. We were quite different, I really think we were. Perhaps if we had moved to London it might have been better. We never really considered the independent labels, like Neat. I guess Neat was more of a Northern thing at that time. It's one of the weird things that even Barnsley seems closer to London than East Anglia does. This is a bloody backwater. We were very naïve young men. I honestly believe that with a decent producer we could have put an album together, sort of 1980, which would have been very good. A major label may have taken up the finished product. But besides, back then, just the idea of having the 'forty five' was pretty amazing. 'One Of These Days' was being played in almost all the rock clubs in the country, almost oblivious to us, John Peel was playing it, Tommy Vance was playing it …"

"We'd pick up *Sounds*," adds Dave, "and see 'One Of These Days' in the heavy metal charts, and there we were, back in East Anglia…"

"…dipping sheep!" laughs Mark.

"Totally oblivious, I was going to say, to what was going on. Then suddenly we'd read *Sounds*, and it was Number 3 in the charts. I guess one of the reasons we were happy to leave our management in charge was because things looked like they were going really well. It's not like things weren't happening."

"Anyway, so Richard went," continues Mark, and this is post 'One Of These Days', and we got a guy called Cris Linscott in. Cris joined first on bass, then Steve Mills on vocals subsequently. The thing is, Trespass wouldn't have been Trespass without the people that were in it, you know, no matter how good or bad they were."

"Well, all the original Trespass stuff was totally innocent, natural," adds Dave. "There wasn't any influence from outside except for influences from the bands we liked. So we started off with Mark singing, then Neal Kay said 'you're an absolutely brilliant band, you're going to go somewhere BUT you've got to get a vocalist.' We were only 19 or so, so we thought 'OK, Neal Kay says we've got to get one, so we've got to get one!'"

"We didn't have a bloody telephone, that's how backward we are around here!" interjects Mark. "I got a message from my aunt who lived quarter of a mile up the road that this guy Neal Kay was on the phone so I had to run to my aunt's to answer the bloody phone," he laughs.

"That was the first mistake we made, listening to Neal Kay," laughs Dave. "Steve's vocals weren't that good!"

"He had balls the size of coconuts! He couldn't give a toss!" adds Mark.

"Yeah, he wasn't very pretty and he wasn't the greatest singer, but he had balls of steel!"

"The band he was in before, they had flashpots filled with magnesium powder, and he'd just smoke a cigarette and chuck it in. Boom! Burn all his fucking hair off! I mean, to be in a band then; it's all so slick now, but then it was a bit rough! Steve came from up near Birmingham somewhere, and he was living in Camden at the time and of course to us he was pretty switched on, well, compared to us anyone was switched on! Anyway, it wasn't so much that I wanted to sing, but I wanted to keep control of the way the band progressed. And I wanted to find a singer that I could really work with, otherwise you can play guitar all fucking day, but you've got to make songs people can identify with. Getting the right singer is so important because whoever's doing that is the focal point as well. Well, he hated that as well."

"Then came the *Metal For Muthas ll* album," says Dave, "which again was rather weird. Maiden had done the first one with two tracks, and EMI were very interested in us."

"There's more to the business than just music," cuts in Mark, "and they did catch us on the hop, it has to be said. My brother's got a theory that there's only room at the top for two really big bands in any particular type of music: Stones and the Beatles, Oasis and Blur; and of course Def Leppard and Iron Maiden were the only two bands who came out of the New Wave Of British Heavy Metal who are still around to pack out stadiums now. There aren't any others; maybe Saxon I suppose, but by that time Saxon were already fairly long in the tooth. They were a good band, and they really rocked the scene... Anyway, Rob Eckland joined post-*Metal For Muthas II*; it was a real tight join..."

"Rush was a big influence for us, as were Thin Lizzy and UFO as well, and if you think back to then, they were the acceptable face of rock and metal. And although we were embraced by the New Wave Of British Heavy Metal, we were never really a metal band. The heavier stuff probably came a little later on as we picked up influences from other people. Steve Mills wouldn't have been the singer though. I think we would have got someone else or I would have done it myself. We did the Radio One Session with Steve and producer Tony Wilson said, 'you do it yourself, you go and sing'..."

"That was another bloody singer catastrophe, wasn't it...?"

"Get the feeling it's like Spinal Tap's drummers?" laughs Mark.

"Cos when we came to record the BBC session Steve had the worst cold ever and you can really hear it..."

"Yeah, particularly on 'Snotchild'" deadpans Mark. "So we'd done the *Metal For Muthas II* album and the BBC session with Steve and nothing was happening, so we decided to record a second single. 'Live It Up' is on the Radio One session, so we'd had that song for quite a while. We started getting a lot of interest from Chrysalis Records, which is a label I liked because of UFO and it turned out that this guy who worked in the publishing division thought 'Live It Up' might be good for Michael Schenker to do. And we were asked not to release this single; you know, hold on to it for a bit longer."

"Otherwise it would have followed 'One Of These Days' almost immediately," adds Dave.

"But we held onto it, and if Michael Schenker had done it we wouldn't be sitting here now!" laughs Mark. "But he didn't, he wanted to write his own tunes, grow a beard, that sort of thing! By the time we got round to recording it as a single we'd got rid of Steve Mills; in fact that was after the gig where a major record company had come to see us and said 'ditch the singer' so we ditched the singer, again, as you do... I regret that now."

Dave takes up the story. "This is where Chrysalis come in. This guy from Chrysalis, it turned out that he was more interested in getting the song for Schenker than signing us, but of course we were convinced they wanted us. We got another singer in, Rob Eckland, because they wanted us to. Eventually we managed to get them along to see us in Leeds, and they came along and our new singer had the worst cold you could possibly imagine. He was a lovely guy from Liverpool, he had David Coverdale hair and quite an interesting voice, bit undeveloped, but very interesting Coverdale/Glenn Hughes type voice. But anyway, it was one of those nights when everything went wrong! On this night, the big night when Chrysalis were here to see us, Rob's nose was streaming and he was running off after every song to blow his nose..."

"I kept telling him to wipe it on his fucking sleeve; 'Don't keep going off the fucking stage!'" cuts in Mark.

"Because I've got no 'O's or 'A's' because I could have done, but I'd rather play fucking guitar instead."

"Also, we used to use pyro and the first number our main roadie John, he knew what he was doing, but poor old John... halfway through the first song after the pyro had gone off to start the set, he went out to fill up one of the pyros but didn't turn it off. He almost blew his fucking head off. It was only the fact that he wore glasses that saved his eyesight. He burned all his hair off. So halfway through the first song we see John crawling off-stage with his face black and his hands burned..."

"But being professionals we didn't miss a beat! But the smell of burnt roadie wafts across the stage to the record company's collective nostrils, and that was that, that was Chrysalis," notes Mark. "So we decided to record a third single, the *Bright Lights EP*. Another new member, too, in bass player Bob [Irving], who unfortunately committed suicide. A bit of a blow..."

"...but he had left," adds Dave, "we'd got rid of him before them; that wasn't the reason he committed suicide, at least I hope it wasn't!"

"But," continues Mark, "the *Bright Lights EP* is an interesting mix of stuff, because 'Bright Lights' is a fairly unique sort of song. Geoff Barton described it as Joe Jackson-esque because of the riff, but then we had 'The

Duel' which we still do because it really rocks and 'Man And Machine' which is one of Dave's riffs, both on the flip. But we were still looking for a direction, even that far in, although it was only, what, '81? I remember writing 'Bright Lights' on an acoustic guitar, sat out in the garden on a fantastic sunny day. I just came out with the riff. It's just about me, that song; 'because I've got no 'O's or 'A's' because I could have done, but I'd rather play fucking guitar instead. We recorded it in the wrong studio really. It's one Cliff Richard used occasionally which was its claim to fame – fucking brilliant! – 'Congratulations!' The in-house producer did mix it as a different, interesting song, but it's not metal. It was pretty much a live take. I mean, that's how we used to record in those days. We literally went in and played – all our stuff is like that. Of course that tape got out – everything gets out! – and we started getting letters from one Lars Ulrich, who's actually in the Fan Club, and then suddenly he's with fucking Metallica, you know, a superstar! We did get to meet him eventually though and had a chat."

"It was at The Marquee," adds Dave. "We used to go down there to see bands and try and filter our way into the scene, and then one night – probably another reason why people hated us! – we were in there and Lars and the whole of Metallica walk in and, of course, everyone in the whole place is staring at them. They then find out that Trespass are in so – Metallica who'd done Donington and who were huge – all they wanted to do was talk to us which we did for ages, just James and Lars talking to us as if we were the superstars and they were reciting lyrics of our songs…"

"'We used to jam your stuff all the time, man,'" cuts in Mark in a false American accent. "SO RECORD ONE! RECORD ONE NOW!"

"Why they never recorded one of our songs is another great Trespass mystery," laments Dave.

"Ah, they couldn't work out the chords!" Mark fires back. "No, 'Bright Lights' was the swan-song really; to be honest, I think we'd taken it as far as we could by then. My father passed away completely out of the blue, very young, mid-forties, and I think that probably put the lid on us, to be honest. We did carry on for a bit longer after that…"

"One of the reasons why Mark's Dad's death more or less split the band was because he was so involved right from the start," adds Dave. "It was he who pushed you, didn't he? He wanted you to do it, to make it, so much. He drove us to gigs, he used to do everything for us. And Paul took it really bad, obviously Mark did as well, but Paul took it really badly.

And we just stopped, didn't we? Me and Mark went into business, we started our own little video business, recording weddings and stuff like that, we got ourselves a little office in Sudbury and after about three days of trying to take it seriously…"

"The way to make music is to pour your heart out and let everybody step on it."

"Out came the guitars," laughs Mark. "But we've always been frustrated at not getting an album deal in the early days. I think we were conscious of trying to produce something deliberately marketable; and that's not the way to make music. The way to make music is to pour your heart out and let everybody step on it," he laughs, "and ignore 'the business'. Perhaps we represent what it was all about really, because what happens is that when you get a movement like the New Wave Of British Heavy Metal a big net is cast across the whole musical spectrum and the bands are…well, caught; we weren't trying to be part of the New Wave Of British Heavy Metal, we were just doing it at the time. There are metal bands out there now, jazz bands out there, blues bands out there, just doing what they do, and waiting for The Moment… Bands like The Darkness, well, that's why there's something not quite real about it. They're great players, the guys have got a hell of a lot of talent, but there's something – and it cuts across music in general – that's so bloody fabricated. It's not real any more. The last metal band I really liked was Alice In Chains, I really thought they had something and I loved the vocals; it's a shame the whole drugs thing has come into it. The *Head* album, which we recorded in 1993, was heavily influenced by Alice In Chains, and there's a bit of Metallica in there as well. I always feel we are legitimately able to rip Metallica off because, after all, they wouldn't be quite the same band as they are without hearing us…"

"They'd probably be better!" laughs Dave.

"Yeah, they wouldn't do so many slow intros! But, my biggest regret in Trespass is that we didn't stick to our guns. No matter what happens, when you've got something you believe in, you must stick to your guns. That would be my advice to any young band. If you've got something, no matter what happens, stick to it."

THE PREMATURE DEATH OF THE NWOBHM

The *Sounds* Readers' Poll for 1980 (ie voted for and published in early 1981) confirmed the growing strength of heavy metal as a musical force amongst an otherwise eclectic bunch of music genres. The 'Best New Bands' category included Girlschool, Saxon, Angel Witch and Iron Maiden (at Numbers 2, 5, 7 and 8 respectively). The New Wave Of British Heavy Metal itself came second in the 'Bore' category, sandwiched between The Police at Number 1 and rival paper *New Musical Express*!

With all this going on, *Sounds* seemed keen to own the New Wave Of British Heavy Metal – both the term and the movement – and began to invent spin-offs; for example, there was the Old Wave Of British Heavy Metal and the North East New Wave Of British Heavy Metal (targeted, as mentioned earlier, at the thriving North-East of England scene and in particular the goings-on at Tyne & Wear-based Neat Records). And then, just when things were getting interesting, they tried to kill it off.

As a fan reading *Sounds*, at the time it looked like sour grapes; and re-reading the clippings once again it still does. EMI's *Metal For Muthas* compliation LP appeared – without any input from anyone else at *Sounds*. The album largely featured unique recordings of songs rather than currently available versions but was unfairly panned at the time of release.

Eventually, and, it has to be said, rather unexpectedly, in his joint review of the *New Electric Warriors* and *Metal Explosion* compilation albums in *Sounds* in October 1980, Geoff Barton wrote the NWOBHM's obituary:

"Sadly but inevitably, the movement known as the New Wave Of British Heavy Metal – and that's positively the last time I use that term – has peaked and is currently and irrevocably locked into a slow downward spiral into ignominy…"

Yet the news of the NWOBHM's death was somewhat premature; there was plenty of life left in the young dog yet.

CHAPTER THREE

AXE CRAZY – 1981 TO 1982

*"Now I'm back I'm a dangerous force, fallen victim
to life's evil course, I'm a madman so watch out for me,
got my six-string, I've gone axe crazy..."* –

'Axe Crazy' by Jaguar (p) 1982

COMPILATION ALBUMS

I f 1979 to 1980 was the NWOBHM's childhood, then 1981 to 1982 was when it hit adolescence; the time when you think you know everything, certainly more than your parents, and you are free, wild, creative and expressive, yet still young enough to travel half-price on buses. Established bands were hitting their stride, younger bands were breaking through, and if the major record labels already had a token band or two on their books and weren't that interested in anyone else, the independents were quite happy to step in and make things happen at street level.

So why was Geoff Barton so keen to announce the death of the NWOBHM in October 1980? A lot of great music was being produced by great bands, although since the release of EMI's *Metal For Muthas* album in January 1980, his enthusiasm had been rather obviously waning.

Love them or hate them, compilation albums, like death and taxes, are a fact of life as record labels either show off their new signings, test the waters before committing to bands or recycle any old crap released countless times before. On the plus side, such albums are generally released at a budget price, although (particularly noticeable with the NWOBHM) in truly horrendous covers; I mean, when you look at the sleeve of *Metal For Muthas*, say, or *New Electric Warriors*, you have to wonder what were those people thinking?

Quick to realise the money-making potential of the NWOBHM, EMI Records were by far the fastest off the mark to issue the first of what was to be a flood of NWOBHM compilation albums. *Metal For Muthas* was to be the first of a trio of LPs, although the label lost interest and the final 'album' was no more than a 12" single entitled *Muthas Pride EP*. The aforementioned *Metal For Muthas* deserves closer inspection as it reveals much about the bands and the politics involved in the NWOBHM. *Metal For Muthas* was a useful promotional tool for the EMI's new signings, Iron Maiden, of which much was expected, although by the time the album was released guitarist Tony Parsons had left, to be replaced by the short-lived Dennis Stratton. In contrast to the other bands included, Maiden negotiated about the album in a tough, professional manner, demanding a couple of days' studio time, the inclusion of two songs and having the album's opening cut. "Our attitude was we do it our way or we won't do it at all," said manager Rod Smallwood in *Running Free*.

Neal Kay provided the sleeve notes, and everything but the Ethel The Frog's contribution ('Fight Back') is a version exclusive to the album. However, despite the fact that the NWOBHM was in its ascendancy, *Metal For Muthas* was not well received by *Sounds*. The LP was panned by Geoff Barton where it was given a two stars walloping: "from its shabby sword and sorcery orientated cover to its clumsily-written (not to say bigoted) sleevenotes, the album smacks to me of being a low-budget cash-in on the UK's much-vaunted metallic revival and, far from giving it a boost, cannot do it anything other than considerable harm. Apart from the two Iron Maiden tracks, *Metal For Muthas* is a bummer of the first order, a disgrace to all concerned with its compilation and will only delight sceptics of the NWOBHM, people who will doubtless chortle happily to themselves and use the LP as evidence for their case against the movement."

The fact remains that *Metal For Muthas* is an important album, and is also a great souvenir of the times. Of the eight bands on the record (that is, excluding Maiden), all went on to some degree of fame or fortune (Ethel The Frog, Samson and Angel Witch all had further dealings with EMI; Nutz – by no real stretch a NWOBHM band – went into a Rage, and Sledgehammer and EF Band did their own thing) aside from Toad The Wet Sprocket. Which is not surprising really. *Metal For Muthas* still raised hackles later in the year when Paul Suter, reviewing the *Brute Force* compilation for *Sounds*, referred to the sound on the record as 'a crock of shit' and went on: "I know of one band who had their finished tape de-produced to fit in with the overall quality on offer."

"EMI stood for 'Eavy Metal Innit'."

Meantime, EMI pushed on with *Metal For Muthas Volume II* (subtitled *Cut Loud*), released in May 1980. This time Suffolk's finest Trespass were in the driving seat, delivering two of their greatest songs and, to my mind, two of their greatest performances with 'One Of These Days' and 'Stormchild'. Most people recognised Krokus vocalist Marc Storace's vocals on the cut by Eazy Money (produced by Neal Kay) as Krokus were becoming one of the bands to listen to, and you could easily start a great argument by *insisting* that Robert Plant was the singer on Horsepower's 'She Gives Me Candy'. Xero delivered a muggy version of 'Cutting Loose' (the BBC Tony Wilson-produced version is far better), Jameson Raid were mis-titled The Raid, and White Spirit ('High Upon High') went on to MCA while Dark Star ('Lady Of Mars') and Chevy ('Chevy') were signed by Avatar.

The series ground to a halt with the much-maligned *Muthas Pride EP*, on the sleeve of which some wag in the Press and PR Department decided that EMI stood for 'Eavy Metal In'nit'. *Muthas Pride* is well worth having for the version of White Spirit's 'Red Skies' alone, which knocks spots off the version on their MCA album. Wildfire ('Wild Dogs') and Quartz ('Back In The Band') rock out quite nicely, and Baby Jane's self-titled effort may be a bit poppy, but it's fun. At the time of writing, it's unfortunate that whereas both albums have now had two official CD releases, the *Muthas Pride EP* is still languishing in a vault someplace. 'Red Skies' (and the ridiculous 'Eavy Metal In'nit') appeared on the CD re-issue of White Spirit's self-titled album in 2005 and 'Back In The Band' appeared on *Satan's Serenade – The Quartz Anthology* in 2004. Apparently it's about Ozzy Osbourne's return to the fold for Black Sabbath's *Never Say Die* LP; it's a shame it wasn't put out as a single as they could have written a B-side called 'Oh, He's Buggered Off Again'.

MCA weren't far behind EMI in recognising the value of the NWOBHM, and snapped up Tygers Of Pan Tang, Fist and White Spirit – Neat Records' first three signings – pretty much in one job lot. Strangely then, the label's first rock/metal compilation of the NWOBHM period – *Precious Metal* released in May 1980 – was an eclectic offering described by *Sounds* as "strictly OWOMAHM (that's Old Wave Of Mostly American Heavy Metal to you)." It continued: "The NWOBHM is without doubt the best thing that's ever happened to MCA. Not only has it inspired the label to invest in Neat's Tygers Of Pan Tang and Fist, thus updating its roster, but it's also given them a good reason to remind us of all the dross stashed away in the vaults. Take it from me, bands like Mythra and Vardis are taking over. Re-hashes like this are for the kids who don't understand." Personally, I don't think it's that bad an album, certainly worth more than the two stars awarded by reviewer Des Moines, but NWOBHM it certainly wasn't, with just the Tygers as-then-unreleased 'Don't Take Nothing' hinting that anything new was happening metal-wise.

MCA was determined not to make the same mistake twice, and the result was *Brute Force*, a NWOBHM treasure-trove, released in September 1980. "In 1980 we are witnessing a resurgence of talent so diverse that a situation akin to Liverpool '63 is again beginning to develop. Despite a dominance of bands from the north-east of England it is not however confined to one area of the country," dribbled the LP's sleeve notes. That said, *Brute Force* came with an embarrassingly awful cover shot, supposedly of a fist being waved about it a threatening manner. "To describe the front sleeve of *Brute Force* as laughable would be an understatement akin to putting World War Two on the level of a minor fracas... I've seen better sleeves on a waistcoat," wrote Paul Suter in his four-star review in *Sounds*. Diamond Head's 'It's Electric' and White Spirit's 'Back To The Grind' were familiar items, and Colin Towns' and Mick Underwood's contributions aren't NWOBHM at all, although the ever-growing popularity of Gillan at that time meant that two rare cuts from members of the band would ensure a few more record sales from that angle alone. Fist contributed 'Brain Damage', a trailer for (although not actually on) their debut album which MCA released a couple of months later. Raven dropped in the manic 'Let It Rip', Sledgehammer the weird and wonderful 'Fantasia' (later to appear as a B-side to 'Living In Dreams'), and Quartz added 'Can't Say No To You'; both White Spirit and Quartz were trekking around the UK on Gillan's *Glory Road* tour just after *Brute Force* was released. That just leaves Xero, Prowler, Cryer and May West, all of whom make healthy contributions to the album although unfortunately all four pretty much peaked at that point. "In five years time it will perhaps be of interest to look back on the artists included on this compilation," concluded Stuart Watson's sleeve notes; "there may be a surprise or two in store." Depends on how you like your surprises, really; by 1985 Raven were in America, Diamond Head were on life support and everyone else was either defunct or more underground than the Circle Line.

BBC Radio One's *The Friday Rock Show* was still very popular, so it was inevitable that sooner or later some of its studio session tracks would appear officially on vinyl, and *Metal Explosion* was the first such venture. Released in September 1980 and encased in one of the worst sleeves known to record buyers, it rounded up eight bands, each of them contributing one song. In Angel Witch, More, Praying Mantis and Samson, the album contained four of the heavyweight names on the scene, coupled with rising stars Trespass, the lesser-known Taurus and Money, and a one-off from Gillan, a new song ('If You Believe Me') supposedly played live on the programme by going on air direct to Gillan's studio. Despite the pedigree on the vinyl, *Sounds* still wasn't impressed.

The follow-up came in November 1981, with the less-than-imaginatively-titled *The Friday Rock Show*. Encased in one of the worst record sleeves etc, the album followed the same format of eight bands and eight songs. This time around, Black Axe's 'Edge Of The World' and Witchfynde's exclusive and haunting 'Belfast' made the record pretty much an essential purchase, and producer Tony Wilson breathed some real life into Xero's 'Cuttin' Loose', turning the sludgy song on *Metal For Muthas II* into a cracking album closer. Healthy contributions from Diamond Head, Sweet Savage, Last Flight, Demon and Spider, completed the line-up. Whereas a number of individual bands have been able to access their session material and add it to CD re-issues, trying to get these two albums out on CD, or any further compilations of BBC sessions is an almost Herculian task. Maybe one day...

It was *New Electric Warriors* that appears to have been the straw that broke the camel's back and gave Geoff Barton cause to pen his aforementioned NWOBHM obituary. Indie label Logo Records, boasting

Vardis and not much else, released this collection in September 1980. Its interest lies in the number of bands who were less than household names at the time and so gained a lot more publicity for their cause. That said, it is a very long LP, meaning that the running surface of the vinyl was compressed with a resulting loss of sound quality, added to which some pressings were incredibly thin – "don't do this at home, boys and girls," said Dave at Castle Records as he bent the album to touch opposite sides of its circumference together. Plus, the sleeve notes can only really be described as drivel.

"Don't do this at home, boys and girls."

It's only really the tail end of the album that makes it a dog, with Kosh and Race Against Time being completely missable. Unsurprisingly, neither got a record deal. Offsetting them though are Turbo's and Buffalo's opening pairing of 'Running' and 'Battle Torn Heroes', a new rendition of Vardis's well-known 'If I Were King', and personal favourite 'Holding Back Your Love' by Colossus. Jedediah Strut had the best name (although not the best track) on the album, and Dawnwatcher would have achieved a good deal more if the world had been a fairer place. British Steel re-issued the album on CD in 1997 which improved the sound quality no end, although still couldn't save those last two tracks.

But there was hope on the horizon. In May 1981 the *Lead Weight* compilation album released on cassette only (although European LP and Japanese CD copies followed in time) by Neat Records proved popular with the critics. Neat had established itself as the UK's leading independent HM label, but up to this point had restricted itself to singles. *Lead Weight* was its first stab at a 'long player,' albeit on tape. And the result? Well, *Lead Weight* is a fantastic collection of tracks, and although I will admit to having some affinity to Neat Records (eventually leading to me producing the label's in-house promotional magazine entitled – wait for it – *Lead Weight*), it is the best NWOBHM compilation bar none. Three of the eleven tracks (those by White Spirit, Aragorn and Axis) had been previously released as B-sides, but the rest were all new to commercial release at this time. Highlights? – too many to count really, but the running order of Side One, with Raven, Venom and Blitzkrieg hitting you square between the eyes while White Spirit and Axe (an early incarnation of Fist) give you a pause for breath and Aragorn round things off, takes some beating. And whereas a number of songs were re-recorded for later albums ('Inferno', 'Angel Dust' and 'S.S. Giro'), the versions on *Lead Weight* were much better than the renditions that followed. And on top of all that, Bitches Sin's 'Down The Road' is an energy-clad rollercoaster ride while the final track 'Soldiers Of War' by Satan's Empire shows that here was another band that really should have gone all the way instead of leaving a one-track legacy. To cap it all, *Lead Weight* came with a no-frills, sensible cover, and cost just £2.99.

The label's second compilation came out at the end of 1982. The *60 Minute Plus Heavy Metal Compilation* again came out as a cassette only, a little strange as by now Neat Records had established itself in the album market as well. Through *Kerrang!* it could be obtained for the princely sum of £1.25 (plus postage), and again at the time of release it was an album of primarily new material, personal favourites this time around being Goldsmith, formed by ex-Bitches Sin bassist Pez Hodder (whose only other known contribution to the NWOBHM was a single 'Life Is Killing Me'), Sabre's enigmatic 'Cry To The Wind' (another band whose three song legacy shows how little justice there is in the music business) and Hellanbach's storming 'All The Way' which again appeared on the band's debut album in a much weaker re-recorded form. A final compilation *Powertrax* was put together early in 1986, again on cassette. I presume it was a budget price release, but I don't know anyone who bought it; I gave shedloads of them away to anyone who wrote asking for a copy of *Lead Weight*. Very much the runt of the litter, it did have its moments in Atomkraft's 'Your Mentor', the lead track of a 12" single that was shelved when the band changed line-up and the demo version of 'The Power' by War Machine, a vastly superior version of the song that appeared on their *Unknown Soldier* LP. And whereas *60 Minute Plus...* kept with a simple cover, *Powertrax* reverted to compilation album-type, with a cover featuring a robotic DJ (at least, I presume that's what it's meant to be) as drawn by a three-year-old in a sack in a coal cellar at night.

Along with *Lead Weight* and *Metal For Muthas*, *Heavy Metal Heroes* is *the* must-have NWOBHM compilation – twelve tracks, all prime-time examples of what the movement was all about. Originally released in 1981, at the end of Heavy Metal Records' first year of operation, *Heavy Metal Heroes* was their first album, released originally in a plain red sleeve (a pressing of just 1,000), before inflicting yet another crap cover on the record-buying public. OK, so the sleeve was a turkey but inside was meat not stuffing, and although the label arguably always ran second-best to Neat Records, all the bands featured on the record went on to at least marginal success. It's an album of quality material, although as it features a number of demos recorded at different studios the sound balance comes and goes a bit. A successor, *Heavy Metal Heroes Volume II*, was released in December 1982. Although not as good musically (and not featuring as much exclusive material), it was a better-sounding item than its predecessor, and did feature a real belter in No Quarter's 'Power And The Key'. Elsewhere, Shiva's beautifully fragile 'En Cachent' and Witchfinder General's storming 'Paranoid'-esque 'Free Country' were lifted from their respective albums, and the other highlight has to be Mendes Prey's catchy 'What The Hell's Going On?' On the down side, Lionheart's contribution shows why they were strictly Third Division despite the fanfare with which they arrived on the scene, No Faith's cover of the Fleetwood Mac chestnut should have stayed roasting in the fire, and Jess Cox's contribution 'Devil's Triangle' about the Bermuda Triangle really should take a day trip there.

The final most notable release of the time was Guardian Records' *Roxcalibur*. Only a couple of thousand copies of the original LP were pressed which is why it was so damned hard to find at the time That said, *Roxcalibur* is an odd collection really, boasting fourteen tracks (seven bands each donating a pair) and, at almost 63 minutes, one hell of a running time for a good, old-fashioned vinyl LP. On the down side, Skitzofrenik and Unter Den Linden are more disposable than a Bic razor, although UDL (I'm reliably informed by Avenger's Mick Moore it means Under The Limetrees) did play a minor part in the Blitzkrieg/Avenger story. Marauder and Brands Hatch turn in some metal-by-numbers NWOBHM (not necessarily bad, just nothing inspiring), but Black Rose and Battleaxe both went on to put out a couple of respectable albums apiece. The jewel in *Roxcalibur's* crown is the pair of songs by Satan which, when added to their debut single 'Kiss Of Death' b/w 'Heads Will Roll' (all recorded at the same session), wrap up the recordings of the band's original line-up. OK, the songs sound dated now, but they do give a good indication of where Satan were headed, especially 'Oppression' with its twin-lead guitar intro and minute-and-a-half lead in to the first verse. I didn't mention the album sleeve, did I...

THE 'ZINE SCENE

Along with the do–it–yourself work ethic championed by many NWOBHM bands, another borrowing from the punk scene was the fanzine – cheap magazines written by fans and either xeroxed or churned out on the photocopier at the local print shop, work or the library. Probably the biggest and best in the UK was *Metal Forces*, which soon became a barometer of what was hot and what was not, and which was certainly better than *Kerrang!* for coverage of the metal scene in general. Starting off as a 'zine, although with a natty glossy cover and A4 format, and written like all 'zines by genuine fans, *Metal Forces* went on to make the transition to mainstream magazine before eventually being killed off. It also had the advantage of being linked by association to Shades, the import record store which opened in central London in 1983 and which soon became the place to go for not only the latest releases but also the current news 'n' gossip.

When Metallica's Cliff Burton was killed in 1986 it was the fanzine circle that spread the news with every writer getting the call then phoning two further people to pass it on. *Forearm Smash* was probably the best 'zine in terms of value for money, as Paul Miller – who later moved on to *Kerrang!* and was unfortunately also killed in a road accident a few years later – squeezed more words onto a page than you can get ants in a jam jar (on more than one occasion he called me lazy for the amount of blank space – which I called 'margins' – I'd leave on a page in my *Stack Attack!*). There were hundreds of 'zines, some good, some bad and some ugly, and many music journalists cut their teeth on these DIY publications before joining mainstream magazines.

"I'D DO ANYTHING TO GET IN THE CHARTS AND ON *TOP OF THE POPS*..."

At one time I used Tygers Of Pan Tang albums as a barometer of the NWOBHM. Their 1980 debut *Wild Cat* was as raw as they came, rough round the edges and all the better for it. April 1981's *Spellbound* was probably a better record (although the first will always be my personal favourite), polished, confident, self-assured – like a football team coming on for the second half knowing that they've got the game in the bag.

Seven months later came *Crazy Nights*; as the release date suggests, it sounds rushed, unfinished, uncared for; everyone is tired, but still The Business is demanding to be fed. By the time of the fourth album, released in August 1982, it was all over bar the shouting; *The Cage* is a nice record, a pleasant album, the sort you could take home and introduce to your parents; it was however just a couple of needles of inspiration lost in a haystack of indifference. Of course, there was also *The Wreck-Age* and *Burning In The Shade* (featuring just Brian Dick from the original band and second vocalist Jon Deverill), released by Music For Nations and Zebra Records respectively once MCA had given the band the royal order of the boot, but almost no-one bought them, so who cares?

> *"The truth is that if you're into banging your heads, and love the sound of loud and frantic guitars playing at breakneck speed, then you're onto a winner here."*

The NWOBHM was pretty much the same – an exciting build-up, a plateau of great music but with little further innovation, a slow decline as market forces stifle bands and a long, protracted fade to black. The unfortunate irony of my analogy is that in terms of the charts, *The Cage* actually did better than the rest, with the albums' chart placings being 18, 33, 51 and 13 respectively. Ah well, so much for theorising; the fact remains that 1980 was the metal Year Of The Tyger; a great album ("the truth is that if you're into banging your heads, and love the sound of loud and frantic guitars playing at breakneck speed, then you're onto a winner here," claimed Paul Suter in his August 1980 three-and-a-half star review in *Sounds*), a handful of singles with collectable B-sides, a blistering session on *The Friday Rock Show*, and an ever-increasing profile. John Sykes came in to boost the guitar sound (upping the cool quotient even further to a point where we mere mortals just couldn't compete); and then it all kind of unravelled.

By the end of 1980, original vocalist Jess Cox was out of the band. "We didn't feel happy with Jess and it wasn't working out at all," the others later told *Sounds* in November 1981. Wasting little time, he hooked up with ex-Iron Maiden guitarist Dennis Stratton and the pair formed Lionheart, dubbed in the January 10 issue of *Sounds* "the first NWOBHM supergroup." Additional guitar duties were to be handled by Steve Mann, who had auditioned for the Tygers at the same time as John Sykes. Cox upset his former colleagues by telling *Sounds* that "Sykes finally won the day because his hair was longer." Drummer Frank Noon (who had played on Def Leppard's *Getcha Rocks Off EP*) and bassist Rocky Newton finalised the line-up. The next week's *Sounds* reviewed Lionheart's live debut at The Marquee as "a storming success." Unfortunately, the future stretched to just seven days. A news feature in *Sounds* dated January 24 entitled "The Supergroup That Lasted A Week!" reported that "Cox's voice, it was felt, did not complement the harmony work of the rest of the band."

From such auspicious beginnings, Lionheart never fulfilled their early promise, releasing just one poor album and eventually ending in the mid-Eighties. Jess Cox returned to the North East and went back to being a lifeguard at Whitley Bay for a while until he was approached by Max Atom (of The Revillos) to do a song, 'Devil's Triangle', which ended up on *Heavy Metal Heroes Volume 2*. A solo career beckoned. The rather tasty 'Bridges' single emerged first on Neat Records, soon followed by an album entitled *Third Step*, which copped a four star review in *Sounds*, but which I thought was one of the worst albums of all time; to be fair, I only played it once, and now many years later would like to hear it again, but in those days at the beginning of 1984 money was tight, and I could just about afford one LP a week. I played it, I hated it, and luckily those nice people in Shades Records exchanged it for me. "It wasn't what I was expecting, I just let him get on with it," Neat's boss Dave Wood told me years later. "It's big in Japan, though!"

Back in the Tygers camp, Rob Weir, Rocky, Brian Dick and newbie John Sykes had been joined by Jon Deverill, vocalist with the then-unknown Cardiff-based band Persian Risk, who went on to supply Motörhead with Phil Campbell. The first blood of the new Tygers came in February 1981 with the single *Hellbound*, initial quantities of which came with a free 7" boasting two Jon Deverill audition songs. Far too heavy to make a significant impact in the charts, *Hellbound* was probably more a call to arms that a commercial release – someone at the record company exercising some forward-thinking for once. But when its March follow-up, the more chart-orientated *The Story So Far* made no headway whatsoever, alarm bells probably started to ring. The LP *Spellbound* came out in April and, despite a four-star thumbs up in *Sounds*, inexplicably stalled at Number 33 in the UK Album Charts, and another single *Don't Stop By* also came and went. Interviewed by *Sounds*, the band were asked if they'd consider a single written by an outsider, or a cover version. "I would," answered John Sykes. "I'd do anything to get in the charts and on *Top Of The Pops*."

MCA Records must have rubbed their hands in glee at the notion of such compliance, and rushed them straight back into the studio for the notoriously tricky album number three. "I was disappointed with the outcome of the third album *Crazy Nights*," says Robb Weir now; "it was poorly produced and the sounds of the instruments are shocking! There are some great songs on that album which never reached their full potential. Maybe in the future we will find time to do them some justice." *Crazy Nights* was poorer than the proverbial church mouse (a bit ironic being as the band used to rehearse in a church), and sounds like what it was – hurried and incomplete. Stuck out in a truly awful cover, its one redeeming feature was a freebie 12" single that came as a limited edition in a bid to get it to chart (the two slabs of vinyl were crammed into the album cover rather than creating a special gatefold sleeve). John Sykes later claimed in *Kerrang!* that *Crazy Nights* was so bad he didn't even own a copy.

Two more singles came and went and eventually the Tygers opted for the cover version, their exceptional take on 'Love Potion #9' probably now being their most famous song. It looked like they were back in business until John Sykes left and *The Cage* was cobbled together. Replacement guitarist Fred Purser contributed material, a couple of covers were worked up and an outside writer Steve Thompson was enlisted to help (anyone who wrote 'Paris By Air' and 'Letter From L.A.' for my band would get crossed straight off the Christmas card list). The more commercial material did get the band back in the charts once more, but it was all a bit too late really – the fat lady had not only sung but gone up to bed. "The lowest point for me was 1983 when the demise finally came about, and I couldn't do a damn thing about it," says Rob Weir. "There was actually a fifth album written, but because of the circumstances it never went any further."

As a footnote, Jess Cox, never one to give up easily, eventually re-activated the defunct Tygers Of Pan Tang with original guitarist Robb Weir under the name Tyger Tyger in 1986. One new song 'Small Town Flirt' appeared on the Neat album of early Tygers Of Pan Tang demos, *First Kill*, as a taster of things to come, but the band floundered fairly quickly.

First Kill was re-issued in 2004 on Metal Nation Records with four bonus tracks, and is pretty much an essential item in any NWOBHM collection. In *Classic Rock* Issue 69, Malcolm Dome noted that "these recordings are full of boy-scout enthusiasm... the desire to riff and burn cannot be denied, and hearing the first glimpses[†] of future classics 'Don't Touch Me There', 'Euthanasia' and 'Don't Take Nothing' fair brings a nostalgic tear close to the surface."

After the demise of Tyger Tyger, Cox went into business (first with Neat Records before forming Edgy Records and now running Metal Nation Records) although was involved once more with Tygers Of Pan Tang when he and Robb Weir performed a set of early Tygers material (together with later hit single 'Love Potion #9') at the Wacken festival in 1999. With the rest of the original band not involved, Blitzkrieg (who were also there) supplied a second guitarist Glenn S. Howes and bassist Gav Grey, and Chris Percy played drums. A storming success (check out the *Live At Wacken* CD), the gig inspired Robb Weir to put a new Tygers Of Pan Tang back together. Meanwhile, all four early Tygers Of Pan Tang albums (*Wild Cat, Spellbound, Crazy Nights* and *The Cage*) were re-issued by Edgy Records with bonus tracks, lyrics and band-written liner notes, and are well worth picking up. The *Wreck-Age* and *Burning In The Shade* have also been re-issued, and aren't.

THE RISE OF THE INDEPENDENT RECORD LABEL

Up until the punk rock revolution, the idea that anyone could pick up a guitar, form a band and release a record without the backing of an established record company was ludicrous. Musicians had to work long and hard at perfecting the craft and then work long and hard at perfecting an album. The punk ethos proved that anyone with a modicum of faith in themselves could bang out a single or LP, or even form a record company in their bedroom, and the new breed of metal musicians were keen to learn from their spiky-haired predecessors.

"That's one thing that we've got to thank punk for," says Mark Sutcliffe of Trespass. "If it hadn't been for punk, small labels wouldn't have been so widely used. 1980 was, in effect, the year of the indie label."

[†] Just as a matter of interest, has anyone else ever "heard a first glimpse"?

Bands knew that to make any headway they had to release something, and many of them were savvie enough to realise that, although a major label might just come a-knocking, the more likely route to fame and fortune – the Def Leppard and Iron Maiden route, more to the point – would be to release something themselves. For those who didn't want (or couldn't afford) to take such a risk, the other alternative was to get signed to a recognised independent label.

Hull-based Ebony Records was late to the game and always last in the field of the big three NWOBHM indie labels, forever trailing in the wake of both Neat and Heavy Metal Records; but that's not to dismiss its importance to the NWOBHM. Like Neat, it started life as an existing recording studio. Gaining a reputation for making metal bands sound like metal bands and marketing itself as both affordable and specialist, it was in use by both record companies and demo-making hopefuls.

From there the logical progression was to launch itself as a label. Starting with a compilation LP *Metal Fatigue* which introduced the world to Savage (and eight others who remain in the filing cabinet of obscurity), it swiftly built up a roster of influential bands (although its catalogue was by no means exclusively NWOBHM). Although Ebony Records later became more famous for its unheard of bands in sword 'n' sorcery covers and compilations of no-hopers entitled Metal Something – *Metal Warriors*, *Metal Maniaxe*, *Metal Plated*, *Metal Duck*; no, I made that last one up), in its formative years the label was responsible for some of the best releases of the NWOBHM, including LPs by Savage, Shy, a pair by Grim Reaper and three from Chateaux. The debut albums from Savage (*Loose 'N' Lethal*) and Shy (*Once Bitten...Twice Shy*) both copped nine-out-of-ten reviews in Issue 2 of *Metal Forces* magazine.

With Ebony eventually disappearing off the end of their own run-off groove and Neat selling itself lock, stock and back catalogue to the Sanctuary Records Group at the end of the Nineties, I'd assumed that Heavy Metal Records had also gone to the great second-hand vinyl store in the sky. But a conversation with label boss Paul Birch soon put me straight.

In March 1981, *Sounds* reviewed The Handsome Beasts' 'Breaker' (Heavy Metal 2), Buffalo's 'Battletorn Heroes' (Heavy Metal 3), Dragster's 'Ambitions' (Heavy Metal 4), Last Flight's 'Dance To The Music' (Heavy Metal 5) and Witchfinder General's 'Burning A Sinner' (Heavy Metal 6) in one job lot. "A label new to me, where's Heavy Metal 1? With each sleeve stamped 'Made In England', this lot have unearthed some startlingly good homegrown product... It's a good start for a new label who seem to know what they're doing and not just cashing in."[†] Not a bad start for a label set up, as urban legend has it, just because manager Paul Birch couldn't get a deal for his band.

"That's actually dead right," he confirms. "I was managing The Handsome Beasts and I couldn't get them signed to a label so I started Heavy Metal Records. We put out 'All Riot Now' and sold a couple of thousand units quite easily, which gave us the money, and perhaps more importantly, the confidence to put out a second single, again by The Handsome Beasts. And before we knew where we were, we'd got six singles out and started thinking about what was to be the *Heavy Metal Heroes* record. On advice from colleagues I took it to a trade fair in Cannes, where I was approached to take on albums by Cirith Ungol – who never really went anywhere – and Motley Crüe, who did! [that fell through]. The next year I was offered Accept's *Restless And Wild*, and that sold very well indeed. Their next one, *Balls To The Wall*, didn't do at all well, and I've never worked out why I wasn't offered that one following the success of *Restless And Wild*. But we diversified quite early on; Neat Records had a very good hold on the domestic market, but I think that Heavy Metal Records and then Music For Nations, and the competition between us, pretty much opened up the overseas market, and paved the way for the growth of the independent sector.

"Page Three models draped over gravestones on the covers."

We've never done what other labels did, you know, put out any old stuff. We worked hard to find the next decent release. Domestically, I would say that Witchfinder General was probably the big band for us. And there was all that stuff with Joanne Latham, you know, Page Three models draped over gravestones on the covers. There was a gore element to it, but in the Hammer Horror sort of way, very tongue–in–cheek."

[†] The label's first single was The Handsome Beasts' 'All Riot Now', reviewed by Sounds back in June 1980, although an unfortunate typo in the header re-named the band The Handsome Beats.

I had this debate with Paul Birch when I interviewed him back in 1983 and we didn't resolve it then or now. Both 1982's *Death Penalty* and 1983's *Friends Of Hell* are both very good NWOBHM releases and well worth checking out, but came in ridiculous sleeves featuring scantily-clad women covered in theatrical blood. To my mind, for every neutral fan who saw the albums in the racks and thought 'Ohh, sassy cover; nice tits, I think I'll check that out,' another ten thought 'cheap crap' and walked on by.

"It's a shame," he continues, "that a lot of great bands fell apart, slipped away, disappeared... It was a shame that the Soldier LP never came off, and I would have liked to have done the follow-up album to Magnum's *On A Storyteller's Night*. Grim Reaper was another one; they were on *Heavy Metal Heroes* and why we didn't do an album with them I'll never know. Wrathchild was one band that really stood the chance of major success. They weren't musically brilliant, but were young and dynamic. We had some US reps from RCA come over but it came to nothing.

Heavy Metal Records is very much alive. We decided as we grew and our interests diversified that it would be restrictive for Heavy Metal to be the parent company so we developed Revolver. But Heavy Metal is now a separate limited company, and only yesterday I was talking to someone about developing a separate website for it – heavymetal.com. After twenty years, what goes around comes around and we have signed Soldier to record that album. Sat by my desk here are masters of the two Witchfinder General albums and all the two-inch tapes which I want to go through with a view to gathering up all the singles and out-takes – if there are any – and put out a third and final album. What I want to do is get our heads back around the label and give fans what they want once more. It would be nice to go back, retrace our steps and make some of the old stuff available again at the same time as looking forwards and going ahead with some new music that redefines heavy metal for the 21st Century."

If Heavy Metal Records was about a band without a label, Neat Records started life as a label without an identity or direction. Owned by Dave Wood, a Geordie with a complete inability to mimic my West Country accent no matter how hard he tries, the original organisation revolved around Impulse Studios, a 16 track (later upgraded to 24) recording studio in an old theatre in Wallsend, Tyne & Wear. Based on these facilities, Wood decided to create his own record label. The first two releases were abject failures, so much so that even when I started writing

Bitches Sin

Shiva – spot the drummer!
(Photographer unknown)

Atomkraft's Tony Dolan at the Bristol Bierkeller, 1987

Dave Patten, Hellanbach, live at The Royal Standard, Walthamstow, October 1983

Brian Tatler, Diamond Head, live at The Marquee February 1984

Brian Ross of Blitzkrieg, promo shot circa 1991

Ian Swift, Avenger 2005 reformation tour supporting Y&T,
live at JBs, Dudley

Kevin Heybourne, Angel Witch 1984 reformation gig,
live at The Royal Standard, Walthamstow, June 1984

Tokyo Blade live at The Royal Standard, Walthamstow, December 1983

Raven's Mark and John Gallagher live at The Concrete Foundations
Forum, Burbank, California, September 1994

Girl's Phil Lewis at Routes, Exeter, May 1980

Saxon – the Crusader tour, February 1984

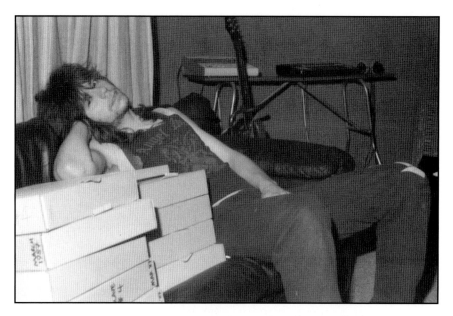

Satan's Russ Tippins, struggling to keep awake at the end of the sessions
for the Suspended Sentence album, April 1986

Ex-Iron Maiden singer Paul Di'Anno fronting Battlezone at the
Eindhoven Open Air Festival, October 1986

Wayne Renshaw of
Savage, live at The Royal
Standard, Walthamstow,
February 1984

Sheralee – the Bitches Sin girl; out-take photo from the
'Always Ready (For Love)' single
Photo: Ian McDonald

the label's in-house promotional magazine, *Lead Weight*, he refused to name them, and when he finally did talk about them it was on pain of death that the records' titles were revealed (the first was Motorway's 'All I Wanna Be Is Your Romeo', which conjures up a mental image of a large bucket of vomit, followed by Janie McKenzie's 'One And Only Girl', which Woodsy himself described as "a birthday present or something").

However, it was a chance sighting of Tygers Of Pan Tang that launched Neat Records as a – or possibly *the* – independent heavy metal label, and arguably made history. Without Neat Records, the future of heavy metal might have been very different indeed. "Back in '79 we were playing a gig at a local high school where Dave Wood's son attended," is the way Tygers guitarist Robb Weir remembers it. "David came along and saw us perform, liked what he saw and invited us to his recording studio to lay down some tracks. Out of those sessions we all agreed that 'Don't Touch Me There' was a great song for a single, so it was released and sold thousands! It was one of those things – when I wrote 'Don't Touch Me There' I must admit I had a good feeling about it, nothing you could put your finger on, but it just rocked! It's one of those feelings that sends goosebumps up your arm when you know it's right."

From that moment on, Neat had a direction. "I'd be lying if I didn't say we were surprised by the reaction to 'Don't Touch Me There' especially after its predecessors," Dave Wood once told me, "but we'd wanted to concentrate our efforts in one market and success with the Tygers showed us where our future lay." Fist's 'Name, Rank & Serial Number' and White Spirit's 'Backs To The Grind' followed, and the label began to develop its own fanbase. A deal was struck with MCA Records, and, in effect, it looked like the first three bands were sold on in one job lot. "We weren't big enough at that time to make things happen, and didn't have the resources to put out an album," explained Wood. "But the economics of what we do means that we initially press 1,000 copies of a single, but that's the minimum we need to sell to break even. What with overheads and things we need to sell at least 2,000 of each single to see a return." Some would argue MCA were more motivated by the cash potential of an instant heavy metal roster than any great plan to develop the bands long-term, and whereas the Tygers were indeed one of the top bands of the second echelon (as Lemmy always refers to it), despite touring widely and some early promotion by the label Fist and White Spirit managed just one album apiece before being unceremoniously dumped. A revamped Fist later re-appeared back on Neat's books, but White Spirit never really recovered from the double-whammy of being dropped and guitarist Janick Gers joining Gillan, and eventually evaporated.

However, within twelve months the next tranche of singles threw up a few new interesting acts in Raven, Venom, Blitzkrieg, Aragorn and Bitches Sin, with Raven and Venom going on to become the label's star attractions. Economies of scale were still important though. As much as possible was done in-house, sleeves tended to be cheap (although the fact that almost everything came in a picture bag made them more interesting to collect), and records were released in batches to reduce publicity costs, leading to some records being held up for some considerable time. Because of these delays, one of Neat's famous taglines – "bringing you tomorrow's music today" – was corrupted by one wag to "bringing you yesterday's music tomorrow"!

Neat's policy of releasing just singles was expanded in April 1981 with the release of the *Lead Weight* compilation. Marketed as an anniversary celebration of the label, *Lead Weight* was an eclectic collection of B-sides, newies and rarities, and copped a full-marks five-star review by Geoff Barton. From this, the decision to go for a full-length album wasn't that big a step, and it was Raven who released that all-important first LP for the label. In May 1981, I watched Raven open a four-band bill at London's Lyceum, warming things up for Geddes Axe (replacing the billed White Spirit), Vardis and Angel Witch. Although playing just a half-hour set, Raven were on marvellous form that night, and my one enduring memory is of Mark Gallagher playing a solo standing on one leg before keeling over – still playing – and the rest of the band not missing a beat.

"I don't remember that show too well now, I must admit," comments vocalist/bassist John. "We got on well with Angel Witch's bass player, I remember that much. I remember our next gig at The Lyceum better, as the main act had the power pulled on us 15 minutes into our set as we were going down a little too well!

We've been going since 1974 really. Mark and I were playing one classical guitar we'd got on holiday in Spain, decided we wanted to form a band and bugged Mam and Dad for an electric guitar and a bass for Christmas. With Paul Bowden, we went through a succession of drummers before playing our first show in December 1975 at our school. A great start: I remember falling down the stairs backstage before the show, Paul walking off the stage during the show, and us trashing the stage at the end – the start of a glorious tradition! We even used to smash gear up at rehearsals!! We eventually played pub gigs and Working Men's Clubs – a bloody good way to hone your craft and thicken your skin!

We played a gig in Newcastle and Tygers Of Pan Tang came to see us, and their manager said, 'How would you guys like to do a single?' and we jumped at the chance. We did a rough two-track demo of 3 songs – 'Don't Need Your Money', 'Wiped Out' and 'Let It Rip' – and Neat liked it so much that we did the single. 'Don't Need Your Money' had to be the single; it summed us up perfectly!

The whole time was a succession of highlights... Just to get to make a single... to make an album... and have people actually BUY it... and LIKE it... AND want more!!! For three kids out of Newcastle it was astounding; really amazing... And then we played Europe... Got to play with Motörhead, Whitesnake and Ozzy... Got to go to America... Yeah, there were low points (there still are!), like when we were told 'Your second album is straight in the Top 20' only to find out it most certainly was not!!... But being from Newcastle means you are usually pretty grounded, so we'd just grin and bear it; just smash up more guitars and imagine they were the people you'd really want to smash instead! As for regrets, well, you can play that game until the cows come home, but we should not have been swayed by what people told us around '86. We got led up the garden path a bit before we sussed out what was going on and figured to hell with them all and went back to playing music for us!

At the end of the day, we love what we do and no-one else does it quite the way we do. In many ways we were totally naïve when we started the band and slowly formed our own sound. It was a different era back then; we saw every band that came to town and just acted like sponges, taking it all in and learning from the best! And we played each and every gig like it was the most important gig you'll ever do. And, believe me, it is!"

"Despite numerous attempts to bring about the downfall of the NWOBHM – including a few, I'll admit, by yours truly," wrote Geoff Barton in *Sounds*, "late '81 finds the mega-movement probably in an even healthier state than in its Maiden/Leppard/Saxon heyday. Two factors have convinced me that this is so. First, the 'Armed And Ready" section of 'perhaps the loudest publication of all time' – our mayhemic monthly *Kerrang!*... and the second factor is, of course, this Raven album..."

Raven's debut album *Rock Until You Drop* was released on Neat in October 1981, and heralded a shift in direction for the label which now started to become more a vehicle for star acts (and thus a lot more viable commercially). A healthy five-star review from Barton included the comment that *"Rock Until You Drop* is the best LP to emerge out of the NWOBHM since Saxon's *Wheels Of Steel"* and the LP itself – complete with poster, lyric sheet, badges and autographs – really was a cracker, and sowed the seeds of the thrash movement to follow.

Meanwhile, of course, Neat's other real claim to fame was to break ground in another direction; enter Venom, and the origins of black metal. By the time they'd secured the label's second LP release with *Welcome To Hell* (yet another five-star review at the pen of Geoff Barton), Venom had already divided metal fans straight down the middle with 'In League With Satan'. You either liked 'em or hated 'em – there was no middle ground. Geoff Barton and Garry Bushell at *Sounds* hyped up the trio of Cronos, Mantas and Abaddon, although the mystique was spoiled as most people knew that Cronos was Conrad, who worked at Neat Records and the guy who drew Fist's fist on the sleeve of 'Name, Rank And Serial Number'. Venom didn't gig, which gave them a certain 'unknown' quality, but also meant that they couldn't be judged on the strength of their live performances. A feature in *Kerrang!* in September 1981 revealed Venom were actively rehearsing for a super-gig which would be a bomb-ridden spectacular, although nothing actually happened on the live front till the *Seven Dates Of Hell* tour in 1984.

"We didn't want to be any regular heavy metal band," Cronos more recently told author Martin Popoff. "Because, basically, Venom came out of the big back end of the punk explosion in England. And we've always been basic rock fans, Deep Purple and Led Zeppelin and bands like that, but the thing for me was bands like Sex Pistols and The Damned, the real hardcore element. I really wanted to combine the two... And we had to call it black metal because calling it heavy metal didn't describe it."

Like many Neat releases, *Welcome To Hell* suffered a number of delays, but eventually appeared early in 1982. It eventually turned up in my local HMV (I'd been bothering the staff about it for weeks), and the manager played me the two opening tracks then actually refused to sell it to me. How on earth it received a five-star review is anyone's guess, but it did strike a chord with many. Love it or hate it, *Welcome To Hell,* and its follow-up *Black Metal* (which again copped top marks in *Sounds*) inspired the whole black metal movement; which may or may not be a good thing, depending on your point of view.

Meanwhile, all was not well with Raven, despite their position – perceived or otherwise – as Neat's flagship band, and they were also copping bitchy comments from journalists and other bands that the rest of the roster was merely subsidising them. "Things were OK with Neat at first but as time went on it got, uh, confrontational," recalls John Gallagher. "It was very frustrating. We were living on about £30 a week and bugging the hell out of them to help us get out and play more, to basically get out and sell ourselves. It got soul destroying. Then in 1982 we got an offer to come to the States to play a festival and a few shows with Anvil, and this led to our relationship with Johnny Z. We came over again to tour the States in 1983 with Metallica as the opener, and after that we decided to come over again in 1984 and tour until we got a major deal. We pretty much uprooted everything; marriages went poof! We gambled everything as we knew we could do it."

"It was discovered that the planned massive pyrotechnic display would put audiences at risk in some of the smaller venues..."

With Raven out of the picture (although Neat licensed back the double live *Live At The Inferno* set from Johnny Z's Megaforce label) Venom became Neat's premier band, a position they maintained for the rest of the label's effective working life. I didn't see Venom's debut UK appearance at the final gig on the *Seven Dates Of Hell* European tour on June 1, 1984, preferring to catch and photograph the reformed Angel Witch instead. The 1985 *World Possession* tour was something I didn't want to miss though, and had even toyed with the idea of seeing several different nights of the ten–date UK trek for a hefty review in Neat's *Lead Weight* magazine. However, six of the dates were pulled "when it was discovered that the planned massive pyrotechnic display would put audiences at risk in some of the smaller venues..." I wrote in *Lead Weight*. Quoting Cronos, I continued: "We want to apologise to ticket holders in all the cancelled towns. However, I know that our fans understand that when Venom make a promise to spend £1,000 per show on fireworks we keep that promise. The pyros are an integral part of the show and we would rather cancel dates than compromise our show in any way whatsoever."

October 8, 1985 saw the band at Hammersmith Odeon with Chariot and Exodus in tow. "As the smoke began to clear the crowd went wild... The band opened with 'Too Loud (For The Crowd)' and immediately it was clear that tonight there would be no let-up as the trio's aural assault rocked the balcony..." I wrote in *Lead Weight*. I know that's a fact because after about 30 seconds my two companions were moaning so much about the noise that we actually retired to the balcony where we joined a couple of other people (it wasn't exactly a sell-out gig). I capitulated to the moaning and after about eight numbers we left. The rest of the review in that issue of *Lead Weight* I made up from the pyrotechnics cue-sheet!

A SOLDIER'S STORY

"The world seemed to be ready for a Soldier long player," noted Matthias Mader in his booklet notes to the British Steel CD *NWOBHM Metal Rarities Volume 3* in 1997. "The project title was *Infantrycide* – but Heavy Metal Records supremo Paul Birch, who vividly remembers the days they parked their huge fifty-seater bus in front of the recording studio, somehow didn't react. 'It was definitely a mistake not to record an album with Soldier and the same goes for Buffalo,'". So why didn't it happen for the Northants five-piece, given the quality of the one single they released in their lifetime?

"Soldier was formed by Ian Dick," recollects Garry Phillips, "the original members being Ian on guitar, Steve Garner on drums, Ram Tiwary on bass, and guitarist Al Cannam. I moved to Leicester with my then-girlfriend and saw an ad in the local music shop for a vocalist, so I went for the audition and was in, just like that. We recorded a demo, started gigging a few weeks later and built up quite a large local following and the rest, as they say, is history. Or so we thought. By the end of 1980 it was down to just Ian and me, so we had a long, hard think about what we wanted to do, brought in Steve Barlow on bass and Ian Astrop, and submitted a demo to Heavy Metal Records which led initially to 'Storm Of Steel' appearing on the *Heavy Metal Heroes* compilation. To be honest, the demo we sent to them had been re-recorded a couple of times and the version that appeared on the album was not, in my opinion, the best one.

We also had to pay £200 for the privilege of being included on the album but we saw it as a foot in the door and, anyway, that sort of thing seemed to be fairly common practice. But it was great when Paul Birch offered to do a single with us. By that time, Ian Astrop had left and Steve Taylor came in on drums, and we brought in another guitarist Nick Bicknell to beef up the live sound. We recorded 'Sheralee' [b/w 'Force'] in October 1981. Apart from the fact that the single was big in Italy, we didn't know it was as popular as it was and in fact we're only just finding that out now! The track was the property of Nick Bicknell who used to perform it in his band Alien Heat. We liked the song and liked Nick's guitar playing so we lured him into our ranks with the promise of releasing it as the single! The actual riff was inspired by the *Pearl and Dean* adverts at the movies, believe it or not, but I don't know where the lyric came from. 'Force' was inspired whilst watching the *Scanners* movie; you know, the one about people who develop massive mental powers and go about blowing people's heads up? Very messy!! I financed the recording of 'Sheralee' out of a payout from a motorbike accident, incidentally.

The down side of the single was when we found out that it was going to be released as part of a triple pack and not on its own, so it had to compete with Shiva's 'Rock Lives On' which was excellent and the Handsome Beast's 'Sweeties' which wasn't – sorry, guys! We then heard that it had got to Number 3 in the Italian Rock Charts – great!!! – but that Heavy Metal Records didn't have the mechanisms for collecting royalties abroad – bummer!! That seemed to be our relationship with Heavy Metal Records – lots of ups and downs. Then they offered us a deal for three albums with the chance of working with Martin Birch as producer but the other guys declined.

There were a few personality clashes appearing in the band; there had been a few offers made and withdrawn, we spent twenty out of thirty days touring in the bus and things started to get on top of us. Steve and I both left – they knew Steve was leaving but I announced it at a Christmas gig at the end of 1982 – and Soldier never really recovered after that. I know Paul Birch is still sorry we didn't record the album with him back then, but so was I! There's no regrets though; life's too short to spend regretting things. I guess personally I wish I had kept singing because it can be a bit of a struggle at times now I've got older and my vocal range isn't what it was. Now that we're back together I've joined a local blues band just to keep my voice up – otherwise I was finding one day's intensive singing a month at our rehearsals was killing me!

Actually there is one thing I regret – and I certainly don't want to do it again now that we are back together – is that we never sat down as a band to write songs. I like to write in the bog-standard way – verse, chorus, verse, chorus, break – but we'd all bring stuff in and some of it could get quite disjointed."

We had some good times though. I would say the best bits were supporting bands like Wishbone Ash and Budgie, the latter being the better of the two because they actually spoke to us! The first night we supported them was at Stirling University and their lighting rig didn't turn up so we lent them ours, and their road manager was a bit worried that we would take advantage and charge him loads of money for the service, as that was the usual practice with support bands. Lending them our gear broke the ice and they and their road crew really looked after us and we had a great time on the rest of the dates. As for the lowest point: how about going from Cumbria to London for a gig and finding out the venue was closed, having had the electricity cut off due to non-payment of the bill, and having no money to get to our next gig in Leeds. I had to blag money from the Social Security to get us there."

Before Soldier folded, in 1982, the final line-up of the band released a live eight-song cassette album called *Live Forces*. "I only thought we ever sold about fifty of the *Live Forces* tape," Garry reckons, "but everyone seems to have one! Anyway, I was speaking with Steve Barlow and he reckoned that because it was Nick Bicknall who compiled *Live Forces* from several different shows, he chose all the songs that he didn't fluff much guitar on. He used to play a Gibson Explorer, which used to go out of tune if you so much as looked at it – so much so I used to call it 'The Plank'!"

Having seen an advert in *Kerrang!* I wrote off for the tape, and received the following response (dated July 10 1983): "Thanx for the letter, sorry that we've took so long replying but I hoped to have some news for ya. Yes, we are the Soldier that was on *Heavy Metal Heroes* – but none of the members are now in the current line-up. We have found a new bass player + a vocalist and we have just done some recording for a single. Unfortunately I can't go into too much detail at the moment because everything is very much 'up in the air' with us at the moment. As soon as I have some concrete details I'll let you know. You're gonna luv the new band!! All the best, Nick Bicknell."

According to Garry now, "I think the single would have been 'Charlotte Russe' backed with 'Heartbreak Zone'; the bass player was ex-Gaskin Mark Mackenzie, and the vocalist was the guy who's now in LA Guns – Phil Lewis, that's his name."

Suffice to say though, despite the enthusiasm that had ebbed from Nick Bicknell's pen, that was the last I or anyone else heard from Soldier for twenty one years.

AIN'T LIFE A BITCH

In October 1980, I left both Torquay and my band Tarsus to go off to University and every time I came back home the guys in the gang were trying to play something different, some new lick or riff they'd picked up on. And one time, the object of their attention was the Toomey brothers' finger-knotting opening instrumental passage: Bitches Sin's 'Strangers On The Shore', an instant metal classic. A hard-working band with a desire to write great rock songs, Bitches Sin seemed to have everything going in their favour until one awful review set them back years and after a brief career they split in 1986. They reformed recently, as Ian Toomey elaborated.

"Both my brother Pete and I loved the Seventies' rock stuff – heavy rock as it was called back then – and did the old playing-records-in-the-bedroom stuff, but it was pretty boring just listening to records so we started to learn to play guitar. There really wasn't any band giving us what we wanted to hear. Sure, we had Led Zep, Sabbath, Purple, Blue Oyster Cult etc, but no band set out to hit you between the eyes with aggressive, hard, exciting music. If they did then all the songs sounded the same. And you know how on so many albums, you just like two or three songs? So we tried to find a band where we liked all their stuff, and as we couldn't we decided to form our own. So in April 1980 we formed Bitches Sin. We wanted to give metal fans original, exciting music that we would have bought ourselves. In my opinion, the NWOBHM tag doesn't really fit us, by the way; it just happened at the same time as we were releasing records. So Pete and I formed the band and Cocky Cockburn joined soon after. Then we got a bassist Pez Hodder and Billy Knowles on drums and that was Bitches Sin.

As for the name, Pete and I decided that very quickly one night after we had been out on the beer! There were no other alternatives! In those days, there'd been the glam thing, then punk, Page Three was kicking off, a lot of sleazy stuff was happening. Some bands had great names – Iron Maiden being one – others were quite ambivalent. We wanted a show-stopper; we wanted people to say 'OK, you've got a show-stopping name; what else you got?' and then back it up with good songs and good guitar work. And we weren't image conscious at all – one of the things about us is that any of our fans could be Ian or Pete Toomey sitting in their bedroom, playing records and learning to play guitar. Any of them could give it a shot. People like us for what we are, and for the songs we write and for the guitar work.

We did our first demo in a studio in Manchester. The whole thing – seven songs – was recorded in about 10 hours and is all live takes with just one overdub – the second guitar solo on 'Ice Angels'. All the rest is live in the studio. The title *Twelve Pounds And No Kinks* came from a call girl advert, and the sleazy title and cover fitted in with our name. On the strength of that demo we went to Neat's Impulse Studio and recorded the single 'Always Ready'. David Wood at Neat said he really liked the *Twelve Pounds And No Kinks* demo and invited us to do a single with Neat, but when we got there we found we'd have to re-record songs – because the quality of the demo 'wasn't good enough, wasn't of sufficient quality,' we were told. So we re-recorded 'Down The Road' and recorded two new songs, 'Always Ready (For Love)' and 'Sign Of The Times'. Our intention was that 'Down The Road' would be the single, but 'Always Ready' was eventually used, with 'Sign...' on the B-side. We were later asked if we would like to contribute 'Down The Road' to the *Lead Weight* compilation cassette, and that seemed like a good idea; the exposure would be useful, and the song was already recorded and doing nothing else, so we agreed.

It was a bit of a struggle as I was still doing my degree, and Pete and the others were in low paid jobs, apart from Pez who wasn't working at the time. We also did another song at Impulse – 'Strangers On The Shore' – later on, but Neat didn't feel that it fitted with their sound, which I find quite hilarious really! The same line-up of the band recorded another full-length demo *Your Place Or Mine* in June or July 1981, and we re-recorded 'Sign Of The Times' for it because we just didn't like the Neat version.

There was a bit of competition back then between Pete and I – we were both a lot younger after all – as to who was the best player, but we agreed that whoever had the best feel for the song did the solo for it. So sometimes one of us would be playing the lead right through rehearsals, but when it came to record it if it didn't sound right then the other would give it a go. We both admitted much later that when we did the solos the competition between us did provide an edge – 'Down The Road', for example, blisters along. Someone once said that when they heard it on *The Friday Rock Show* session they thought it was the first elements of the speed metal scene. But we weren't thinking about stuff like that. It was just a matter of bringing material to rehearsals and saying 'What do you think of this then?' As a band we do tend to analyse and be over-critical, because we want to be as original as we can. It's a bit harrowing though when you present your 'baby' to the rest of the band and wonder if they're going to tear it apart. The song 'Invaders' is perhaps a prime example. I wrote it and Frank did the lyrics but Pete and the rest of the band weren't too keen on it at first, and it was like 'Let's play it through to the end and see what you think' and, fortunately, once we'd worked it through, everyone liked it. There'd be nothing worse than putting something out and someone saying 'I'm sure that sounds like Judas Priest' or something.

Anyway, so we did the single for Neat and then submitted 'Strangers On The Shore' for the *Heavy Metal Heroes* LP, and then did the BBC session. After the single came out, I arranged to see *The Friday Rock Show* producer Tony Wilson. I remember I was quite apprehensive about it but after listening to a few songs he said he liked the material and would be in touch, and not long after we were invited to the BBC Maida Vale studios to record a session. Unfortunately, Pete and I drive ourselves very hard and that pace isn't for everyone, and by the time we arrived at the BBC studios in August 1981, we had a different line-up with Tony Tomkinson on vocals, Dave Newsham on bass and Tony Leece on drums.

Maida Vale doesn't look a great deal from the outside but inside it's a really large set-up. The studio had hard floors, a sloping ceiling, and was set up for ambient miking which suited us and our kind of music – gave it a very bouncy, very live feel. Also, surprisingly for those days, it was a digital studio, using those large old Philips discs. We were very pleased with the results, although the session was the only thing recorded by this line-up. It was all done in one day but we struggled for ages to get the set-up right as Tony had forgotten to tune his drums and he and I had an almighty row. If you listen to the drum track you'll hear how hard he's hitting the drums – probably instead of hitting me, I suspect! The other thing I remember about that session was that it was red hot in the studio, and Pete and I were swapping leads for 'Hold On To Love', stripped to the waist, dripping sweat... Lovely punchy sound though, and if you listen to 'Down The Road' from the session, it's probably the fastest we have ever played.

So, we'd had some very good European reviews, were voted best new band by Aardschok in Holland, the BBC session went down very well and Paul Birch at Heavy Metal Records wanted us to do an album, which was very much the right thing for us to do, to capitalise on the past 18 months of hard work. The album was recorded in April/May 1982, I think, but it was rushed. Both time and budget were tight and the production wasn't all it should have been. Other things were in place – like the Rodney Mathews sleeve for example – but it didn't go so well in the studio. There were some good things on *Predator*: 'Aardschok' and 'Haneka' were strong songs, but the production was weak, and some stuff just didn't work at all. That said, it had some good reviews and some average reviews – the *Kerrang!* review was three column inches of pure vitriol!"[†]

So, what do you do after a review like that in Kerrang!? You write a song called 'Ain't Life A Bitch'!

Sounds, incidentally, gave *Predator* a four-star review, noting it was "destined to stand them in good stead amongst their fellow practitioners..." and highlighted in particular both 'Loser' and 'Riding High'. But the damage was done. Ian though was more pragmatic than most.

So, what do you do after a review like that in *Kerrang!*? You write a song called 'Ain't Life A Bitch'! You have to take it on the chin and move

---

[†] "BITCHES SIN!! Aaaargh! Kerrang! That name – it's sooo heavy. They've just gotta be good. One problem – they aren't! In fact, Bitches Sin are useless, garbage material. They can't play, they can't play [sic], they can't sing, they can't produce and they sure as hell can't write a good song! I've heard the likes of 'Runaway' (yawn), 'Loser' (snore) and 'Riding High' (oh, the tedium) a hundred, nay a thousand times before and I've never been turned on to them. It's the same old beats, the same old ideas. God, it was hard to sit through this album, but I managed to and deserve a medal for it. If this is what Hëavy Metal's all about, then I'm a futurist! Oh, the shame! 'Fallen Star' is average for its harmony guitar, but that's the best I can do for you lads. Ain't life a bitch!" – Howard Johnson, *Kerrang!*, July 1982

on. Or give up. As I said, maybe there was some stuff that wasn't so good, but there was a lot of stuff that was. 'Ain't Life A Bitch' came up at the first rehearsal after we saw the review, after we'd mulled it over for a week. I got up on the stage at the little rehearsal place we used and started the riff, the drums kicked in and that was that! It eventually turned up on Roadrunner's *12 Commandments In Metal* compilation LP. It was one of those songs that just happened, and it scored high acclaim; like 'Strangers On The Shore' before it, when it appeared on *12 Commandments In Metal* it became one of the focal points of the LP

About this time we were starting to see the upsurge of American and European heavy metal – we'd started to write the *Invaders* album but with jobs, shift work etc, it took a good couple of years to write and record it and with more line-up changes by the time it came out it was 1986. *Invaders* was an album where I wanted to say, 'Okay, follow that!' and I think we achieved that; one review called it 'a classic moment in Eighties' metal.' I'm glad we got it out, it was well received and proved to be a classic metal album, but there were a lot of internal and external pressures back then and they ultimately caused us to call it a day. There were just so many of them. Combine them all together and something had to give and sadly it was the band. Everyone recognised that it was not a problem with the band or the music, but life can hit and hit hard sometimes, and so we quit, until now.

Bitches Sin has always been pretty much a holy grail for Pete and I. With *Invaders* we thought we'd got what we wanted, but we weren't really aware of what people thought of the band, or how highly people thought of the band. It's only really recently that we became aware of this – it was both interesting and revealing at the same time to find out how we were regarded as guitarists and how well the band was liked. There was a lot of bootlegging going on which supported our cult status, and gave us a grass roots following which we can now actually capitalise on."

Every Neat Records' single came in some kind of picture sleeve but inventiveness was not high on the priority list of whoever designed them. The early sleeves featured either drawings (Fist, Tygers Of Pan Tang, etc) or band photos – a live shot for Raven or Aragorn posed on a roundabout (the road version, not the children's park type)! Then came NEAT 09, Bitches Sin's 'Always Ready (For Love)' with its posed cover of an attractive model (scantily clad, naturally) and Flying V guitar. Looking at it now, the cover is nothing out of the ordinary, but back in 1981 it was quite a risqué cover shot. "To be fair," says Ian, "we wanted something that summed up the band, and we were trying to be as creative as possible – the name set the scene, the song title set the scene..."With another photo from the session being used on the cover of the band's *The First Temptation* CD, I asked the model Sharalee (not be to confused with the object of desire on the Soldier single 'Sheralee') how she ended up gracing the cover of that debut single.

"I had been working with a local photographer who Bitches Sin approached to shoot the cover of the single and he asked me if I'd do it. From there I met the band; they wanted to see if I was what they wanted, getting a local girl in fitted with their ideal. I'd already done some fashion and glamour work, and obviously I fitted in with their idea of the girl they wanted on the cover. I didn't know the band at that time; I'd not heard them but I had heard of them – they were local and they were doing quite well for themselves.

It was freezing in the studio, and I was quite nervous at first, especially with so many people hanging round. Most of them were shut out of the studio though, and I felt much more comfortable once I was in costume – it's like getting into character and becoming someone else.

I was really pleased with the results. Obviously I had to sign the rights away, but I would never sign anything off that I wasn't pleased with. I didn't have a lot to do with choosing the cover shot itself. Basically all the contact prints were put together and the boys chose the final shot, with the photographer helping, you know, advising on the technical side.

There were some strange repercussions after the session. Don't forget, this was a long time ago, and for a local girl in a small town the photos were quite raunchy, even though you'd think nothing of them now. I got recognised from the sleeve shot, and had some nice compliments; some were quite nice, you know, 'It's a brave thing to do,' although some called me the usual, you know, 'tart'. So it was a very mixed reaction. I actually got quite a lot of local publicity, even to the point of some creep calling me up. I certainly wasn't prepared for how the local people reacted. The local newspapers carried the story but didn't know who it was at first, then someone recognised me and they published my name. Then it got quite scary. The police actually tapped my phone because of some of the calls I was getting. It was quite a big deal at the time; but the band got quite a lot of publicity from it, and I went on to have a successful modelling career. I enjoyed doing it and am glad I did it. Someone actually came up to me in a pub a while back and asked if I was the model on the cover, so I'm still getting recognised, even now."

DANCING WITH FIRE

"Shiva are a very good band," noted Rab in a gig review in *Sounds* in June 1982. "You could call them a heavy metal band but they're not, at least not in the way I'd use the term. Guitarist John Hall seems possessed of real sensitivity... admirably supported by Andy Skuse on bass and the newly recruited Chris Logan on drums. Chris, especially, is an aggressive yet subtle player, adroit at sudden changes of pace and stabbing inflections. Shiva avoid the basic riffing and repetition of heavy metal in favour of real feeling for song structure and the ability to surprise..."

There were a number of bands I was hoping to include in this book. Some I just couldn't find, others either declined to get involved or never returned my calls. Shiva was a band I particularly wanted to talk to and, as I knew they were based in my adopted home town of Bristol, I wrote a letter to the local paper. A couple of days later I found a piece of paper stuck through my letter box with Chris Logan's name and his mobile phone number; neither of us have any idea who did this, but a big thank you goes out to whoever it was. A little after that I received a postcard from Andy Skuse. A legendary band, very different in sound and style from the majority of NWOBHM bands, Shiva's legacy at the time of the interview was just twelve songs – but what classic songs they are, finely crafted and performed by the trio of John Hall (guitars/vocals/keyboards), Andy Skuse (bass/vocals) and Chris Logan (drums/percussion).

"The origins of Shiva...?" muses Andy. "Well, by 1979 I'd been in various bands in the Bristol area, notably Mantiss and Red Shift, but I wanted a break and was all set to embark on a round-the-world trip. John had just come down to Bristol to join two mates who had set up a band here. He was a superb guitarist already but to my knowledge Shiva was the first real band he'd been in. I auditioned to complete the first Shiva line-up after I was put in touch with them by Ken Lintern who worked at one of the local management agencies. I'd had dealings with the agency from working in previous bands and Ken knew I was between bands at the time. That line-up was a four piece but only lasted a while, we did some gigs and made demo tapes but it wasn't really happening. John and I formed what we decided was the definitive Shiva line-up when the other two left and Chris Logan joined on drums. Chris was working in the area as a drummer; I remember that he was known to play in a band with Ken Lintern doing weddings and stuff like that on occasion – something of a waste of talent! Ken signed us up under his new Elephant Management agency along with Vice Squad, who were to gain some notoriety on the punk scene. We actually gigged together once and had a surprisingly good night considering that we came from opposite ends of the music scene! Headbangers pogo-ing and punks head-banging – great!"

"So I'm playing Top Ranks and stuff like that," says Chris, "and one day the keyboard player Ken says, 'Chris, the band I'm managing, their drummer's got an ear infection; can you help them out and do one gig with them?' So I thought I'd just do it, a one-off, you know, and I had an hour-and-a-half's rehearsal with them – this is the honest truth – an hour-and-a-half's rehearsal to go play the Talk Of The Abbey in Neath. I remember it as a fairly big club, and as I'm setting up I was thinking 'Where is everyone?', you know, and I walked back in a little later on and it's packed. To me, that gig lasted five minutes, I'll tell you that, five minutes, because my head was swimming. There was so much to remember, so many intricate parts to the music, and if you didn't know what was going on..." he laughs. "So, that was my first introduction to the band. As for the guy with the ear infection... well, I guess they liked my drumming! That would have been sometime in 1981."

"Elephant Management got us the record deal with Heavy Metal Records," recalls Andy. "We also had a lot of help from our friends Andy and Bill from Cave Studios in Bristol with demos and stuff. I'd had some previous experience of recording studios, contracts and all that stuff in the Seventies, but this was much more important to me as this time I felt we really had a chance to make it on our own merit, without 'help' from outside songwriters or session musicians, which is what they'd tried to do with Mantiss. We jumped at the chance of doing a single of course but wanted to get an album out most of all."

The first thing Heavy Metal Records put out was the 'Rock Lives On' b/w 'Sympathy' single. Although the A-side is quite different in NWOBHM terms, it isn't very strong compared to the rest of the band's work, and not at all representative of what Shiva went on to do (to be honest, I prefer to flip it over and play 'Sympathy').

"I agree completely," notes Andy. "This was a management decision as far as I can remember, the theory being that we should do something fairly 'commercial' to gain airplay. We insisted on 'Sympathy' for the flip side to show what we were really about. The release of the other single 'Angel Of Mons' was driven much more by the band than the management/record company and it did a lot better."

"Yeah," agrees Chris. "'Sympathy' is a better song, although I wasn't on that. They already had that, and wanted to concentrate the money we had on recording the album. It's an odd song, 'Rock Lives On', weird drum sound, which was Ken's idea. I like drums to sound like DRUMS, you know, but it was so stupidly catchy that it worked! And the vocoder as well; we were using a lot of effects in a scene that wasn't renowned for it, so people noticed it. Still don't like the drum sound though! It did fairly well in some European countries, I think, but tell the truth I didn't follow that side of things. I just loved the band and wanted to play."

"All three records were released within a fairly short time really during 1982," says Andy. "'Rock Lives On' in the spring, the follow-up single 'Angel Of Mons' in the summer and finally the *Firedance* album around the end of the year. The 'Angel Of Mons' tracks were exact copies of the tracks as they were to appear on the album, by the way."

"Instead of my gleaming chrome thirteen-piece kit there's this poxy piece of shit sat there!"

"There was also the BBC session on *The Friday Rock Show* which was fantastic," recalls Chris. "We went up to the Maida Vale studios and there's Howard Jones in one studio and... I can't remember if it was Eric Clapton or Jeff Beck in Number 3. Don't know if you've ever been there but they're huge. Every single one of them can hold an orchestra. We didn't take my full kit, just a smaller studio kit, and I'm not kidding, I set it up – five little drums and a couple of cymbals – and I looked out from the control room and instead of my gleaming chrome thirteen-piece kit there's this poxy piece of shit sat there! I remember trying to play this bloody thing... I mean, it came out well on the radio, they pumped it up nicely. I can remember it being bloody hard work though, playing this horrible thing. Tommy Vance was great though, as was Tony Wilson."

"It was hard work," says Andy. "Most of our time was spent gigging the club circuit, a lot of the time up in the North of England. This was all during the big miners' strike. People up there were looking to have a good time to forget the troubles and hopefully we gave it to them. At the time a lot of other NWOBHM bands either came from the North or were playing up there. The circuit was a good one and suited us more than the New Romantic stuff going on in the South. Having said that we always got a good reaction in London (The Marquee especially) and Wales."

"The highlight for me would have to be Birmingham Odeon with Michael Schenker," notes Chris "That was fantastic. It's very difficult when you're supporting major acts; you've really go to give it your all and you're not sure if you're going to have half the hall watching you or walking out! But with Schenker's lot it was about three-quarters full and we really pulled all the stops out and went for it and Bang!"

"Doing the gigs in general, that was always the best part for me," adds Andy. "Being on stage… We also got to meet a lot of great people, like the two who started the Shiva fan club and all the other amazing folks who would put us up for free, help out with the gear and turn up to all the gigs. Shiva's last gig in the Troubadour Club, Hollywood, California had to be the one in the best location! It was arranged by John after he moved to Los Angeles and was strictly a one-off and intended to see us out with a bang. We hired a drummer, rehearsed him up for a couple of weeks, did the gig (which went down a storm) and called it a day. I've still got a ticket from it that I use as a bookmark. It was fairly ironic as we were in Tower Records on Sunset Boulevard the next day and found our album in the racks. Having never got a penny for it, this just contributed to the feeling that it was time to quit."

"I'd already left by this point," says Chris. "I was going through some changes in my life, and it all got too much. I remember I said to Andy, 'I just can't do this anymore,' much to his distress. I wasn't earning enough money to live – don't get me wrong, it was never about the money, it was the love of playing drums, but the bills had to be paid and it was a difficult time for me…"

"It was a great blow when Chris left. We were negotiating to go on tour with Iron Maiden at the time and this just blew it. It was so hard to find a replacement as he was one of the best drummers on the planet.

By the time we found Phil Jones, the momentum had slipped away and it was hard to recover. We auditioned for a new guy and went through a few drummers until we found Phil but that took quite a while. We hadn't gigged or done much promoting at all in that time so it was harder to restart. We did do a load more studio recordings and got the gigs coming again but unfortunately we had some differences with Heavy Metal Records and they consequently decided the new material wasn't 'metal' enough for them and so didn't take up the option on the second album. That was the last straw and we decided to quit."

"I should have done that second album," says Chris. "We were a hard working band and ploughed everything we made back in. It's funny, talking about it now after so long, but I do regret leaving when I did. I really do believe that if I had stayed another year – and I'm sure Andy would agree – we would have made it. Really made it. In hindsight, had I been a bit older, a bit more settled and everything, I'd have stuck it out, and we would have made it. If you think the first album was good, the second would have been absolutely brilliant."

DECONSTRUCTING FIREDANCE

If there was ever an album from the NWOBHM crying out for a remix using 21st Century technology, it's *Firedance*. Not because it's a bad record – far from it in fact: *Firedance* is a sublime offering, a tribute and testament to the band's skill and artistry, and far removed from a lot of the more straightforward metal classics of the time. As a point of reference – sorry, guys! – Shiva sounded closest to *A Farewell To Kings / Hemispheres*-period Rush when the Canadians were beginning to expand past the horizons of a traditional rock band. And so it sounds with Shiva: *Firedance* is packed with flourishes of brilliance that a small recording studio in Bristol just could not do justice to twenty-odd years ago.

"It was like three guys on a positive mission, and when we played together we were really on form," says Chris Logan. "It was hard work though, three of us plus an engineer and gear in a van, five or six nights a week. As for *Firedance*, if I had my chance I would dearly like to remix it, just to give it, I don't know, something a little extra. We worked through the nights – we did nothing to it in the day at all – which I think gave it a mystic, hard kind of feel. I think it was better working through the nights.

And John had a really weird idea – where everyone puts their cabinets on top of each other, we had them all in the four corners of the room, all facing in towards the middle, and when he was playing the sound would kind of meet in the middle of the room and funnel upwards so he had a mike up there as well, which is how we got some of the eerie kind of sounds. There were moments of brilliance in it, and there were moments that were not; it's as simple as that. The moments of brilliance, well, some of those tracks were just incredible. If we'd progressed, if we'd given it another year, because the band did carry on for a while after I left...

When the album came out I felt wonderful. I'd done recordings, but never had an album, so when *Firedance* came out and I actually had it in my hands – twenty years of age, all your mates are into rock bands and you've got this thing you've played on in your hands – it was an amazing feeling. My dad didn't like it too much," he laughs. "It wasn't Perry Como! 'What do you reckon to this, Dad?' and he's listening to it with his fingers in his ears! But he was very supportive. He'd take me anywhere, anytime. It was really exciting when the album came out, it was good fun. We had a couple of drinks that night, I can tell you!

There's some great songs on it. 'How Can I?' was also a good BBC session track. It's quite a choppy number, but it wasn't one of my personal favourites. But it was the one with the Octopan tube drums, which my girlfriend had bought me. No-one was really using those at the time; it's not something you heard, certainly on bands of this genre. 'En Cachent' on the other hand was definitely one of my favourites. That was fantastic, a beautiful song. John's guitar playing on that track is phenomenal; just lovely, nice feel, very emotional. That was the good thing about this band; you'd get something that was quite aggressive and heavy and hard, and then this lightness, almost from nowhere. That's why I enjoyed playing with Shiva so much to be honest; you'd go from 'En Cachent' to, well, 'Wild Machine', which was pure aggression, and good fun to play live. I think at the time John was just in an angry mood, and just went 'check this out!' and that was it – bang-bang-bang-bang-bang-bang! And off it went! That was always a favourite that people wanted to hear. Yeah a good, strong heavy metal song that was enjoyable to play live. 'Borderline' was another one that was full-on and fun to play. I think that was probably the oldest song we had; I think it pre-dated Andy joining the band.

Then there was 'Shiva' itself. What a strange track that was. I think 'Shiva' was basically something for us, the band, rather than for other people. There was a lot of technical things in it, weird time-changes, and the drum solo was bizarre! I mean, I had an old cymbal and I just hit it, I think with a rubber mallet or something, then we recorded it backwards, whoosh, and then there was all those little drums and stuff. You know, I still don't know what to make of it, to be honest! When I hear it now, I wonder if it's some kind of drug-crazed madness! Had we lost the plot and gone to Venus or something?! I can remember bringing a copy tape home and I played this to my friends, and after it was like 'What on earth was that!' But it was different! I've never heard a drum solo like it! And again, Andy used bows on the bass... It was a strange track, but it was something for us. A musicians' crack! A chance to show what we could do. 'Call Me In The Morning' was done in the morning! It started life as a jam, early in the morning, which was thrown in when we found we were light for the album. Because we did it about three o'clock in the morning, we were really tired, but the engineer and everyone said we needed one more track, and we put a lot of effort into it even though we were very tired by then. A beautiful song. 'Stranger Lands' was my favourite of 'em all. It had everything. It was the whole band pulling together, everybody putting everything into one track. Everything I love, and John and Andy, all of our musical tastes fell into this one song and it gelled immediately. It was my favourite song, and my favourite to play as well. It starts off nicely and then climaxes brilliantly. Yeah, that was my favourite."

Did the lyrics for 'Angel Of Mons' come from the Arthur Machen[†] story, The Bowmen? "I'm sure it probably was. John was really, really into his lyrics, and they were great. Brilliant lyrics, 'Angel Of Mons'. And of course the original single cover had the cross over the battlefield. John was a very emotional guy, very caring, lovely bloke, and it showed in his songwriting. And it seemed so natural and easy. John would, like, be eating a piece of toast and come up with something and say 'What do you think of this?' and I'd go, 'It's brilliant, John,' and he'd go 'Great, glad you like it'

[†] Arthur Machen was the author of a number of ghost or supernatural stories. The Bowmen is a short story which tells of an English company of soldiers facing certain defeat during the First World War who are saved from massacre by an army of spectral bowmen. Because of the way it is written, a number of people at the time believed it to be a true account. After this interview, I came across this in a Kerrang! interview from early 1982 by John Hall: "I'm not sure where I read about it, but on the eve of the Battle of Mons during the First World War, a vision was supposed to have appeared to the British soldiers and it was never explained."

and carry on eating! It was a lot heavier live. In fact, we actually changed it. It was slowish on the album, not so powerful. With studios, you're under pressure, you've got cans on your head, click-click-click-click and you're in, you're worried about mistakes (which is crazy really because if you're going to make mistakes you usually do 'em in live gigs), and of course when we were live we were just – wooargh!! We just loved performing live. So I would say live, 'Angel Of Mons' was much better than the album track. A great song, but better live. And it was actually a lot of people's favourite, to be honest.

"'Rendez-Vous With Death' was a strange track. Again, a good live track though. Shiva was a live band, there's no two ways about it, and when I've listened back to the album I've found songs like 'Rendez-Vous...' are always a little bit too down for me. When it's live, it's right in you, you know? We always had great gigs, we always seemed to go down well and had a good time. Difficult song to talk about, not one of my favourites, I suppose – that floppy bit in the middle," he adds humming the chorus line, "is just a bit too poppy for me. On the other hand, 'User' was great. Again, we did that for the BBC session. A good, strong song; it's what a three-piece band in a smoky club with a load of hair everywhere should be doing! We didn't use keyboards live, just drums, bass and guitars, but we did use pedals, Andy had a pedal board, again being into Rush. Most of the time though it was just raw, just the three of us as it was. Andy was a great bass player, John was full-on, and I was just crazy!

I don't think we had a song which didn't work, you know? The gigs were so energetic, and you were up there for an hour-and-a-half, and it was just adrenaline pumping through; I guess my memories really are of the songs live."

A DIAMOND IN THE ROUGH
(OR, THE ROUGH GUIDE TO DIAMOND HEAD)

Mentally google the NWOBHM and Diamond Head will be one of the first names to appear. Even now, they are one of the most revered bands of the movement, by fans and fellow musicians alike. "I had a real soft spot for Stormtrooper from Bristol – their 'Pride Before A Fall' single was a classic," recalls Sabre's Geoff Gillespie. "Also Grim Reaper, they were a great band; Angel Witch, Tygers... And of course the obvious, Diamond Head – the guvnors!" "Diamond Head: that was a great band; I still rate Diamond Head highly," says Garry Pepperd of Jaguar, and as Montalo of Witchfynde succinctly notes: "Sean's a fantastic singer, and I love Brian's playing."

1982 marked the peak of Diamond Head's career, which is bizarre really for a band so well known and respected (even my granny could hum 'Am I Evil?'; she just chose not to). In their early days the Stourbridge quartet of Sean Harris (vocals), Brian Tatler (guitars), Colin Kimberley (bass) and Duncan Scott (drums) well and truly did it their own way, self-pressing two singles, an album and two further singles before finally signing to MCA Records (too damn late, it seemed at the time), playing a special guest slot at the Reading festival in 1982 and then being slowly bled to death by the label. It's the archetypal story of the four schoolmates who made it and then had it all taken away, as Sean Harris reveals: "I guess I was about 14 when I started playing. It's all T. Rex's fault and besides, I guess I wanted to be a larger than life character. I don't think I could do a normal job, you know, I don't think I'm motivated enough! Anyway, by 1979 after writing 150 crap songs we'd started to write some decent ones, and punk had shown that any of us could do it, any of us could be in a band and make our own records. Not that I was a punk though, it was more the likes of Thin Lizzy, Deep Purple and Black Sabbath that we were listening to at the time.

There was no vision back then of what we wanted to be, it was more a togetherness, just the four of us being in a band together. It was just us working our nuts off to do something and *be* something. I mean, I wanted to carry the theme of classic rock blues forward, progress it and make it modern, but make music with roots. I didn't listen to much new stuff, and had no desire to be a cutting edge heavy metal band. *Sounds* said in a review that we were a hard rock band playing heavy metal songs – or maybe it was the other way round!," he laughs.[†] "Maybe we should have known a bit more about what we wanted the band to be?"

Diamond Head made a fairly instant impact on the press. As early as February 1980, Geoff Barton noted in *Sounds*, "this band have more great riffs in a single song than Sabbath had on their first four albums," while noting that their twenty minute set "was all it took for the dynamic

---

[†] In his review of their self-pressed album in Sounds in September 1980, Paul Suter actually called Diamond Head "an unusual contradiction in terms – a heavy metal band playing hard rock songs."

Diamond Head to disperse the clouds of depression caused by the profoundly disappointing *Metal For Muthas* album." A year later, in the same paper, Paul Suter wrote a feature entitled "Why has no-one signed this band?"

In the meantime, in August 1980, a disgruntled/confused fan wrote the following to *Sounds'* consumers affairs page 'Fair Deal': "I sent off a £4.00 postal order for a special limited edition LP by Diamond Head. The album arrived OK and I'm highly impressed with the music and quality. So what's the snag? I'm very puzzled and annoyed with the total lack of information included. The cover is just plain white, with an indecipherable scrawl across it." The information published in reply (which included track titles and running times) was avidly jotted down by the many fans who'd responded to that advert in *Sounds* and bought Diamond Head's first LP via mail order. As the review published the following month pointed out, the LP was "originally recorded as a national finished product to hawk around the majors" but with no immediate interest the band decided to sell it at gigs and through mail order. Such was its success that it was re-pressed in batches of 1,000 a number of times, although later pressings of the LP had a middle label with track information.

Diamond Head were no strangers to doing things their own way. They had already issued two singles ('Shoot Out The Lights' b/w 'Helpless' and 'Sweet And Innocent' b/w 'Streets Of Gold') prior to what became known as the *White Album*, the *White Label* album or *Lightning To The Nations* (which has been repackaged on both vinyl and CD a number of times), but were – surprisingly – finding it difficult to get interest. So they went down the potentially risky path of doing an album themselves.

"I don't think we had much choice," recalls Brian Tatler. "We were not getting any good offers so our manager Reg said he would put us in the studio to record the album himself and then hawk the album around; but even then with the *White Album* under his arm he still didn't get much interest. It was very frustrating." That said, with the album selling quite decently, the band still put out two more singles, the double-A side 'Waited Too Long' c/w 'Play It Loud' and the 12" *Diamond Lights EP* before finally signing to MCA Records.

"Desperate times call for desperate measures," laughs Sean. "It was different to the traditional demo tape approach. We'd had a bit of interest, MCA sniffed around back then, but nothing concrete so we decided to put it out mail order to help build up the fan club and merchandising. It sold out really quickly and had to be re-pressed, and this happened several times, so we'd press 1,000 at a time. So when we released *Borrowed Time* and it hit the Top 30 we weren't surprised because we already knew the fans were out there. We didn't really have much expectations for that first album, not like we did for *Canterbury*, we just put it out. We didn't think that much about it, I mean, the songs just went on it without too much thought for running order and things like that. It's not that 'Lightning To The Nations' was the obvious opener on the first album; it just had that hook, and besides, look at the length of the songs! 'Sweet And Innocent' wasn't an opener, and we figured we couldn't open with an eight-minute song! And anyway, 'Lightning To The Nations' is a classic NWOBHM song."

As for the 'indecipherable scrawl', *Sounds* offered a "surprise prize for the best and most accurate suggestion," but it was in fact simply an autograph. The first batch was divided up and each member signed 250 copies. As Colin Kimberley told *Sounds*: "Someone wrote a letter back after they'd bought one of them and it ended: 'P.S. on my album it's got Colin Kimberley's signature. Who the bloody hell is Colin Kimberley?!'"

"What did the NWOBHM mean to us?" Sean considers the question. "It meant £3.00 per diem expenses, travelling everywhere in anything from a large Cadillac to being rammed sideways in a van, gear and all, and playing everywhere from, I don't know, Neath to Sunderland. We played Genevieve's in Sheffield and there were only 12 people in the audience – and four of them were from Def Leppard! Brian wondered whether he should play with his back to the audience so they couldn't see what he was doing! It meant rehearsing in an old factory; that was fun. It was a great time. And we had some great press too. We didn't pay much attention to the other bands. We liked Def Leppard, hated Saxon but loved their production, which is probably why we hated them! Yeah, we were part of it, but had no real affinity to it or to the other bands really. Besides, we felt we were going to be the next big thing!"

MCA Records finally came sniffing around a second time, and this time Diamond Head signed up. Two singles (the *Four Cuts* EP and an edit of 'In The Heat Of The Night') preceded the release of the LP *Borrowed Time* in October 1982. The album peaked at Number 24 in the UK Albums chart but was, frankly, a disappointment. Encased in a rather nice gatefold sleeve drawn by artist of the moment Rodney Mathews (and featuring a limited edition poster of the cover) it carried too few new songs – two having been re-recorded from their self-pressed debut, two being heavily bootlegged from a BBC session and two being released as singles (and there's only seven songs on the album!). "We always saw the first album as a demo really," says Sean. "When we signed to MCA they wanted to use it as like a base which is why two songs ['Lightning To The Nations' and 'Am I Evil?'] were re-recorded for *Borrowed Time*. We should have either put out the *White Album* professionally, or started afresh with a completely new album which would have ended up being a cross between *Borrowed Time* and *Canterbury*."

> ## "The band's vocalist and sex symbol who pouted, pranced and wiggled throughout the eighty-minute set like a male Marilyn Monroe."

Prior to the album's release, Diamond Head were a last-minute addition to the Reading 1982 bill and played the special guest slot under Budgie on the Friday night.[†] They had, it seemed, finally arrived. The *Sounds* review noted that "just when it looked as though Diamond Head were going to get left behind in the record company rat race, they signed to MCA. They now have an album due for imminent release and find themselves as special guests at Reading. 'Am I Evil?' contained more riffs than the first 562 Sabbath albums (remember?) – but was spoiled by an horrendous sound. That the band have matured immensely over the last year is beyond any doubt, with new professionalism added to their youthful enthusiasm. A band with true potential."

"That was so good, that night," recalls Sean. "The crowd was great, we had a major deal, it was a good performance, and everything seemed to be going so well. Reading 1982 was about as good as it got for us. It was the

---

[†] The band due to play that night were US Metal Warriors Manowar who had been signed in a blaze of glory and ropped soon afterwards, terminating any plans they had of such a grand debut European appearance (or as Malc Macmillan puts it in the New Wave Of British Heavy Metal Encyclopedia, Diamond Head "were added to the bill of the 1982 Reading Festival…at the eleventh hour after Manowar had been stopped at customs for being too hairy, or something…").

peak of four or five years of hard work whereas Donington the following year was the start of a new band trying to be something it never could be. A contemporary band; that wasn't us, and that couldn't be us."

The band set off on a UK tour supported by Tank after Twisted Sister pulled out, and my notes from the Bristol show in November 1982 noted that "most of the limelight was stolen, as ever, by Sean Harris, the band's vocalist and sex symbol who pouted, pranced and wiggled throughout the eighty-minute set like a male Marilyn Monroe... The majority of the set was delivered as precisely as on vinyl as the band raced through their album *Borrowed Time*. But it was with the encores that Diamond Head shone. Leading the band out, Harris shouted, 'OK, from now on it's party time!' and they let themselves go, playing with less attention to detail and with more emphasis on having a good time." After the tour, "MCA just didn't seem to know what to do with us," notes Sean, "so we were sent back to the studios to record a second album for them."

Canterbury is a great album, it was a record written and recorded well before its time, but the whole thing was a complete disaster. The album title seemed to change almost daily, the band were being forced to deliver hit singles, and, to make matters worse the entire first vinyl batch was mis-pressed and so didn't play; after four copies I exchanged it for a cassette and, after scribbling a note to MCA to ask for a copy of the lyric sheet (the cassette packaging was really cheap), they sent me a whole new album from the second pressing. Diamond Head then opened the Donington Festival in September 1983, toured with the album (quite successfully from the Hammersmith show I saw) in October, did a lengthy club tour early in 1984, a handful of gigs in 1985 and imploded.

"*Canterbury* took six months of hard work," recalls Sean "MCA wanted us to make singles: we weren't a singles band, look at the length of some of our songs! That's where 'Call Me' on *Borrowed Time* came from: MCA wanted a four-minute single to promote the album and we had to go and write one, just like that. So 'Call Me' was our attempt at a 'hit' arrangement, but then was released without the album immediately following to back it up so was a missed opportunity really. 'I Need Your Love' and 'Makin' Music' were valid attempts at that lucrative promotional device, The 'Hit Single', in my opinion, along with 'Run' off *Death And Progress*. The single edit of 'In The Heat Of The Night' was a pointless attempt; the 12" remix of 'Makin' Music' was an enjoyable experience but not exactly a marketing success, so again a futile exercise.

Anyway, we couldn't write an album of singles, not to order. It just caused more friction. They wanted to shape us into something we weren't. They released 'Out Of Phase' as a single – nice picture disc, nice video – but releasing it as a single was nonsense. So there was pressure from MCA to make this particular sort of record crammed with hit singles that we couldn't possibly deliver, pressure between MCA and our management and on top of this Colin had said that he wanted to leave. You know, up to signing to MCA everything had been great – my brother-in-law, my mother and Reg our manager financed everything, and it worked. But I guess we gave the record company *carte blanche* – I mean, record companies know what they're doing, that's their job, right?," he adds sarcastically. "In hindsight, we should have kept more control. Anyway, Colin had had enough, and after he'd done the bass tracks he went. At the same time we were having trouble with the drum tracks, so much trouble getting them done, so we ended up [parting ways with] Dunc. Looking back as a mature adult, we should have carried on. We should have persuaded Colin to stay, completed the album as a band, and who knows... But that's the wonder of hindsight. We were just kids really, you know, 21, 22 years old, and very naïve about the business side of things.

That said, I like *Canterbury*. I think it's unique in that it pointed a finger forward to a modern age of music. Plus it's a very different choice and mix of songs. I hate the cover and the running order – we had no control over either – and then it was given a 'pop' mix, which meant no bass, no balls.

"After *Canterbury* we were just worn out. Brian and I had different ideas musically, the record company weren't interested. We did a club tour early 1984 and a handful of other dates but MCA didn't care and we were too tired. So we went off and did our own thing – Brian had Radio Moscow which was more 'FM' and I did the Notorious project with Robin George."

SET LIST FROM THE FEBRUARY 1984 CLUB TOUR (NOTTINGHAM ROCK CITY, FEBRUARY 18):

*'Intro' / 'Play it Loud'; 'I Need Your Love'; 'Canterbury';
'Ishmael'; 'Lightning To The Nations'; 'To Heaven From Hell';
'Sucking My Love'; 'One More Night'; 'Don't You Ever Leave
Me'; 'To The Devil His Due'; 'In The Heat Of The Night'; 'Call
Me'; 'Makin' Music'; 'Am I Evil?'; 'Shoot Out The Lights'.*

That said, Diamond Head never actually split up; the core of Harris and Tatler just subjected their fans to lengthy periods of inactivity which make three-toed sloths look like speed freaks. Sean Harris and Brian Tatler regrouped with a new line-up in June 1990 and word of a six-track mini-album soon surfaced. A limited edition single-sided 12" single 'Wild On The Streets' c/w 'Can't Help Myself' appeared as a taster in November 1991 and although the mini-album was shelved in place of a full album – *Death & Progress* released in June 1993 – it appears in most catalogues with a title, *Rising Up*, a release date of January 1992 and a track-listing. Just after *Death And Progress* was released, the new look Diamond Head opened the Milton Keynes bill for Metallica with Sean bizarrely dressed as the Grim Reaper. "That was just a reflection of how I felt at the time. *Death And Progress* didn't seem to be doing much, I don't think many of the people there knew who we were [from the crowd reaction where I was I think Sean might be doing himself an injustice there] and there was some backstage hoo-hah because I wanted to bring in a second guitarist and Brian didn't. I just thought, 'Here we go again.' What was supposed to be our big re-launch, the culmination of a lot of hard work since 1991 or so, was actually the beginning of the end."

As indeed it was, for a while at least, until Harris and Tatler began to tour in the 21st Century. "We have recorded another album but we're not sure what to do with it, how best to market and exploit it," says Sean. "Brian just wants it out and doesn't care how, but I don't want the same thing to happen as did to *Death And Progress*, where it's released and vanishes without a trace. I want to hold on to it until we get the right deal. I thought *Death And Progress* was a great record, but it seemed to sell 500 copies and vanished. I think we deserve a higher profile. Time hasn't been good to us, I don't think it's ever been favourable to us in fact. But I still want to do it at the right level. It's no good just doing eight gigs to 200 people. What we need now is a strategy with strong management, a good agent and a label firmly behind us. Also, what we lacked and what I want now is a vision, a vision all the band can share. And it would be nice for us to get a bit of recognition for what we did. Our fans believed in us and believed that we should get that recognition that we never really got. And I should know – I'm the biggest fan this band's got!"

A couple of weeks after I'd put the phone down, I emailed Sean and asked for some additional information. At the end of his response, he added: "About the band's vision – always for the music: an unshakeable faith in the power of originality to sustain the integrity of the band as an ideal." I printed the email and scribbled 'I hope this isn't an epitaph' in the margin, but news broke later in 2004 that Sean had parted ways with the band and that the Diamond Head that was Harris' soaring vocals and Tatler's evocative guitar-playing (together with their combined songwriting abilities) was to be no more. The first ever Diamond Head release without Sean Harris, an album entitled *All Will Be Revealed* was released early in 2005 to tie in with some live dates the new-look band peformed supporting Megadeth. Not so much *Death And Progress* as death or progress.

CHAPTER FOUR

BURIED ALIVE — 1983 TO 1984

"And none did frown as they laid him down
and buried him alive..."

'Buried Alive' by Blitzkrieg (p) 1981

THE US INVASION

As a sign of the times, 1982 was the last of the overtly 'metal' Reading Festivals; in fact, Reading 1982 was the subject of its own rather good compilation album of live acts from the weekend, Reading Rock Volume One (although there never was a Volume Two[†]). In 1983, the festival began to re-position itself as a more eclectic gathering of bands and musical genres so, despite the fact that the headliners that year included the only UK show ever performed by the Ian Gillan-fronted Black Sabbath, and the last-but-one show by Thin Lizzy (as well as The Stranglers on the Friday Night), there were fewer opportunities for smaller metal bands to get exposure in front of a major crowd.

[†] Reading Rock Volume One, is worth scouring the second-hand racks for, if only for the material by Stampede, Chinatown and Terraplane, who of course later re-appeared in a slightly different form as Thunder.

The Monsters Of Rock Festival at Castle Donington remained a rock/metal event, but even then, the 1983 show had more of a mainstream edge with the reborn ZZ Top following Twisted Sister, and A.O.R. O.A.F. Meat Loaf following the Texans. Of the new UK breed, Diamond Head were the sole representatives, and even they were launching their new less-metal-more-rock approach in order to prepare the way for the release of the quite different Canterbury album.

Just as movements like the NWOBHM don't really have definitive start points (forget all this May 1979 nonsense), there's never an identifiable end-point either – just a slide into obscurity as something new comes along. And as 1983 came around, the writing was appearing on the wall, and the Americans held the paintbrush.

It was obvious from the likes of *Kerrang!* and *Sounds* that the times they were a-changing. First up came an attempt at a glam rock revival spearheaded by *Sounds* ("glam metal in particular is ridding the world of the legacy of the NWOBHM, which started as an essential lifeline but soon became a jaded, half-hearted enemy of HM," wrote Dave Roberts in March 1983), followed by the UK prog rock revival, a much smaller scale event than the NWOBHM which threw up a lot of good bands if you like that sort of thing, although only Marillion really made anything out of it. The big development though was the invasion of US metal.

Again, you can't really date these things – it's not as if on July 1, 1983 loads of US bands turned up at Heathrow Airport trying to get their duty-frees through Customs. But more and more exotic looking bands with exotic names – Ratt aside – from the States were appearing in the music press. Manowar, whose *Battle Hymns* LP appeared in August 1982 could have spearheaded this; you can have an interesting argument about how things might have been different for heavy metal in general, and both Manowar and Diamond Head in particular, if the Bronzed Metal Warriors' record label hadn't lost faith in them almost immediately and dropped them, meaning that they didn't play their slot at the 1982 Reading Festival and Stourbridge's finest did. And, of course, Twisted Sister were already beginning to rattle cages with some pretty dire records but phenomenal live shows. By the end of 1984, for the second time in 40 years, the Americans (as the old wartime adage had it) were over-sexed, overpaid and over here, although this time they were bringing more than just stockings and chewing gum (Motley Crüe aside). For metal fans, 1984 was the opposite of the Orwellian nightmare – Great White toured the

UK with Whitesnake in March 1984, and Black And Blue also got to support Coverdale when two additional dates were tacked on to the end of the tour. Motley Crüe were taken round Europe by Iron Maiden (although the UK tour support was Waysted) leaving the Crüe free to play a one-off headliner at London's Dominion Theatre in November '84 as a follow-on from their explosive debut opening slot at that year's Castle Donington Monsters Of Rock festival. Bon Jovi supported Kiss on their September/October tour and weren't universally liked by the press. WASP brought their shock/rock antics over here, Queensryche supported Dio, and Metallica confirmed their growing status with a one-off headliner show at London's Lyceum with Tank and Tormé in support on December 20, 1984; for the assembled crowd Christmas had indeed come early.

A lot of the credit for the accessibility of some of the new US sounds has to go to independent record label Music For Nations, which was set up in February 1983. Whereas the label did release some NWOBHM material, in particular two albums apiece by Battleaxe and Tank and the sole long player – some might argue far-too-long-a-player – by NWOBHM glamsters Rox, MFN was far better known for the bands either signed or licensed from counterpart indie labels from overseas, and in particular from America. So releases by early US hopefuls Virgin Steele were joined by the likes of Ratt and Anthrax; Manowar were picked up, as were The Rods, another band signed to a major and then discarded, alongside Canadians Exciter, Japan's Earthshaker and Loudness, and Danish diabolists Mercyful Fate. And who was it that released W.A.S.P.'s 'Animal (Fuck Like A Beast)' single when EMI got cold feet about including it on the band's debut album? You've guessed it. The icing on the cake though was, of course, Metallica, whose first three albums, all of which appeared on Music For Nations in the UK, are classics.

"In places like Holland we are like MEGA."

All of a sudden it was almost as if the UK was being swamped by a US tidal wave. It started off with being able to read about them in the press, then you could get the records, and finally they were here, playing live. The songs were great whether you liked your metal hard-edged or overtly melodic, and either way conjured up a world far removed from dismal, wet Britain with the miners' strike, mass unemployment and extremely bleak prospects. If you really want to know why so many NWOBHM songs are fantasies either about hot chicks, sci-fi or *Omen*-style horror hack 'n' slash jobs, it's because fantasy was all many youngsters had to cling on to; something to daydream about while shuffling forward in the dole queue. To be fair, *Kerrang!* maintained a page given over to the 'Best Of British', a weekly feature on an individual UK band to keep them in the spotlight (starting with a four-band extravaganza in August 1984, with New Torpedos, Emerson, Tokyo Blade and Persian Risk, and following up with the likes of Chateaux, Lionheart, Tysondog and Limelight), but at the same time reviews of NWOBHM bands either on vinyl or live tended to be, at best, dismissive. Noting this, the letters page would carry things like "Why do you keep ramming American hype bands such as Manowar and W.A.S.P. down our throats... why not check out North-East band Avenger?" in October 1983, and "[I] find it disappointing how little space is given to young British bands, especially when you feature no-hope American outfits like W.A.S.P., Bitch etc. How about proper features on bands such as No Quarter, Saracen, Persian Risk... Shiva, Black Rose..." a couple of issues later.

"In places like Holland we are like MEGA," complained Tokyo Blade's Andy Boulton to writer Dave Reynolds in *Metal Forces*. "Gods, even. I don't mean to sound big-headed but it's just unbelievable. In this country though it's like banging your head against a brick wall. It's hard to get tours or press attention unless you happen to be in Ratt, WASP or Motley Crüe..." In a review of the same band's debut album in a previous issue, editor Bernard Doe bemoaned, "Whatever happened to the NWOBHM? To many people's ears it's truly dead and buried..."

It wasn't all doom and gloom, musically; against this backdrop came bands like Warfare whose hybrid brand of punk/metal (the emphasis being quite firmly on the punk) and couldn't-give-a-toss-about-anything attitude were about as far removed from the US material as possible. "Utterly demented... Warfare go wild in the primeval soup, heading full tilt along the sort of mindless furrow deliberately dug to pervert the course of true quality. I love it to deaf!" wrote Malcolm Dome in *Kerrang!*, reviewing the band's first album *Pure Filth* on Neat Records. Overall though, the NWOBHM sound began to change, metamorphose into something new. Newer bands springing up tried to sound as American as possible, completely missing the point that the fans didn't want bands that sounded American, they wanted American bands. "Trouble is, now is a terrible time to try and re-establish yourself as a band. It's not hard rock time any more, is it? That was 1979, 1980, let's face it," Def Leppard's Joe Elliot told Geoff Barton early in 1983. That said, although only 700 had turned out to see the band at the Edinburgh Playhouse that night, a review I wrote at the time for *Metal Rendez-Vous* noted that at Bristol there was a capacity crowd. Any fool, even this one, could tell that Def Leppard were destined for bigger things.

But Leppard were changing their sound, as were a lot of other bands. Back then, I assumed that everyone just changed because they saw it not necessarily as the stairway to the stars but at least a way to survive. Saxon's *Crusader* album was so different from its predecessors – clean, glossy, American-sounding. Girlschool too threw out baby and bathwater in one fell swoop with their fourth album. That under-produced sound so characteristic of the NWOBHM was giving way to a glossy radio-friendly sheen.

Play Dirty is a great record; make no mistake about that. But with the band's poorest showing in the charts to date, even more drastic steps were required. Signed to Polygram in the US, the band were subjected to a radical overhaul which involved bringing in a recognised freestanding vocalist who sang the newer material but remained behind a set of keyboards for the more familiar – and certainly not keyboard friendly – older songs. The singer was Jackie Bodimead who'd already broken a few hearts fronting She (the band formed by ex-Rock Goddess bassist Tracey Lamb whom I don't think actually recorded anything, rather than the act who put out one single on Neat Records) and with Kelly Johnson leaving, Cris Bonacci was recruited as lead guitarist. As a formula it sounds great especially as, for many, Bonacci was arguably a better guitarist, but the five-piece line-up simply didn't work. The band looked about as comfortable as a turkey at a Christmas fayre, half the time Jackie Bodimead didn't seem to know what to do with herself – especially as Kim McAuliffe still introduced the songs – and every reviewer and punter commented that the keyboards were at best inaudible and at worst not even plugged in. This wasn't Girlschool; no sir; not by a long way. However, they went into the studio and came out with a very pleasant album entitled *Running Wild*.

"Those older albums, you know, we were so young, we sound so young, but the records do sound exciting. But *Running Wild*... We don't ever talk about *Running Wild*, we don't talk about it at all," says Denise

Dufort. "I mean, there are some good songs on it, but when Polygram signed us in the States they tried to mould us into another Heart, you know, make us glamorous with the big hair and the radio-friendly songs. And that really wasn't us. It didn't sound like Girlschool at all. And it never even got released over here in the UK, which was probably a good thing really. It really wasn't a good time for us at all. So, like I said, although I think there are some good songs on it, we all hate *Running Wild*. *Play Dirty*, that's an album we're very proud of, and it used to be our favourite at one time. The fans didn't take to it very much unfortunately, although we did keep them; thankfully, we didn't lose our fan base."

The other reason for change though was that the musicians were evolving and in some cases finding the confines of the NWOBHM too restrictive. Some had been doing this now for five or six years, and changes in style of writing and playing are inevitable. Yes, there are bands in all genres that jump on passing bandwagons as if they were fairground rides, but nine times out of ten, changes in style are no more than personal growth and the desire to do something different. What you can't count on though, is whether your fans will come with you, as Jaguar found out.

CAN A JAGUAR CHANGE ITS SPOTS?

After two successful and very NWOBHM singles in 'Back Street Woman' and 'Axe Crazy', the songs 'Stormchild' and 'Dirty Tricks' on two different compilation albums and a great debut album *Power Games* which always reminds me of Metallica's debut (and vice versa), Jaguar suddenly veered off the NWOBHM road and turned down Evolution Highway. Unfortunately, as Garry Pepperd realises, it turned out to be a cul-de-sac. "We'd had some great times, the best for me being the Dynamo festival at Eindhoven in Holland. I mean, it's massive now, but it was born out of a club. We just went over for a long weekend and it was such an amazing show. The club was jammed to the rafters and we just weren't used to that. We were used to playing to two men and a dog normally – and the dog went home half-way through! – and I remember it so well, looking out backstage and thinking, 'Who the hell are they all here to see?' We were so naïve. 'They've come to see you!' 'OH MY GOD!!' Instant panic!" he laughs. "I've still got the photos – there's people in the audience waving clogs around! I mean, the Dutch... All the Dutch gigs we did were brilliant.

But the band started to change and it was a hell of a drastic change, and really it was all down to us growing as musicians. By this time we were 20, 21; Chris Lovell was younger, 18/19? We just discovered – I could say we discovered more chords! – we discovered we wanted to be more musical, if you like. We felt confined by the whole heavy metal tag. There were loads of outside influences coming in from the likes of U2 and Big Country, and this was bound to come out in what we were doing. We were young and were learning to be more melodic, soaking up all these influences, and they inevitably began to show in our songs.

"I remember the first song of the change of style, if you like, was 'Last Flight'. It had a real sing–along chorus and we were like, 'Wow, it's the best song we've ever written; we've got to do more like that!' And that was how the change happened really. We liked the melodic stuff so much we cast aside all that had happened before and just went for this new direction. People go 'Oh, you just went commercial for the money,' which is a load of bollocks! We never had any money and I haven't got any now! That had nothing to do with it. It was just simply four young kids discovering how to write better songs. I don't know if you've heard the album *This Time*; it is very poppy and I can see why the Metalheads didn't like it, but I'm still proud of it and although it's a pop/metal album I still really like the songs.

But we were very naïve in terms of what it would do to us, and I guess we never gave it much thought. Just four kids having a laugh, making the best songs we thought we could at the time and enjoying ourselves. Looking back at it, obviously, it was a mistake; maybe if I could go back I would change things, but it doesn't work that way, does it? Hindsight's a brilliant thing. Today we probably could have got away with such a transition, but for us back then, it was a huge mistake. That's so obvious now. It was a mistake in terms of our career, and in fact it was the death knell. But we were young and you don't think about things like that. At the time someone should have said 'You really shouldn't be doing this; it's not a good idea.' but I don't suppose we would have listened! We did what we wanted. We never gave it a thought until *This Time* came out. It did get good reviews, which was good."

Mark Putterford, reviewed *This Time* in *Kerrang!* in November 1984 and said: "Let me stick my neck out and say that you won't hear many better albums this year. Reminiscent of Foreigner at their best, Jaguar purr through each and every song with a stylish elegance that totally contradicts their relative obscurity."

"Unfortunately," continues Garry, "the fans hated it! But, having said that, since we got back together so many of those people – people I knew back then – have come back to me, and a lot of them have said (those that gave me a hard time back then) that they were wrong. They appreciate it for what it is, a pop/metal album. Some even said, 'Sorry for what we said about it at the time' – yeah, you bastards, you forced us to break up, you lot! But fair play though, a lot of them have come back and said they were wrong. I mean, I appreciate it for what it is and I think it's a good record.

"We weren't American, we didn't have perms and the tan."

At the same time we were having problems with our label, Roadrunner. Funnily enough, they actually wanted us to do another album and were desperate to keep us but we just wanted to get away from them because we'd had such problems. But they really didn't want to let us go and we had an awful battle to get away from them. I think in the end our management convinced them that we'd gone disco," he laughs, "and they let us go! But it was like, every time we complained, they upped the budget for the next record! Should we have stayed with them? Maybe... Should we have done another record? I mean, we couldn't find another label, and it all just fizzled out really. It was what, 1985, we weren't American, we didn't have perms and the tan. We did dye our hair though, and we looked bloody ridiculous! The steam went out of us, the wind went out of our sails, call it what you will. We were so skint as well, that was another factor. You don't get much money out of this, and of course in those days we refused to get 'proper' jobs – 'We're musicians, you know!' – so we're on the dole, maybe doing some odd cash-in-hand stuff here and there, but we all refused to get proper jobs and, well, you can't carry on like that forever. So, lack of money, lack of anything happening to advance the cause, as it were. We did have some people who were willing to help us, but we turned them down, so I have to say we made some really bad decisions as well. In the end, we just got fed up with it all, I suppose, we just thought, 'This is going nowhere, let's call it a day,' and we did. This was the tail end of '85; we'd done five years of it by then, maybe more, but that was enough.

That was the lowest point, when the end came. It was all rather sad, the way it ended with a whimper rather than a bang. We wasted it. In fact, I would say the low point was the fact that we know we threw it all away. At the time when we did the Dynamo Festival, Metallica was just a band with a demo tape. I'm not saying we could have been as successful as Metallica but I think if we'd stuck to our guns – our original guns – and carried on in the *Power Games* vein we could have had a reasonable career. But we threw it away. Yeah, the low point for me was the realisation that we could have had it and we chucked it away."

AFTER THE HOLOCAUST

1983 gave me two surprises one after the other. The first was a Holocaust live LP, the surprise being that I'd thought they'd split up (although it did turn out to be a posthumous release), and the other was the review the album received – 'glowing,' is the word that springs to mind.

I was resigned to never seeing Holocaust live as I didn't expect that an Edinburgh-based band on an independent label would ever raise the cash for a full UK tour, but I keenly followed their releases and their appearances in the press – such as there were – pretty much right from the off; just one hearing of the debut 'Heavy Metal Mania' single in July 1980 had me hooked. A second 12" single 'Smokin' Valves' followed, and then came 'The Big One' – their debut LP *The Nightcomers*, released in April 1981.

Whereas the two singles had a simplistic heads-down good time approach, *The Nightcomers* was an altogether darker slice of metal, with stand-out tracks 'Death Or Glory' and the title track bearing down oppressively and menacingly. Even 'Heavy Metal Mania' had been re-recorded to be less fun and more attention-grabbing. Opinion on the album though was mixed. Speaking extremely personally and as a Gillan fan, I thought *The Nightcomers* was the greatest thing since the invention of the bread slicer, and put it at Number 1 in my 1981 best album chart for the Flying V Appreciation Society – no mean feat for the band, seeing as Gillan released not one but two albums (*Future Shock* and *Double Trouble*) that year. *Sounds* – naturally – hated it. "The whole thing plods along with the ferocity of an anaesthetised porky, re-treading ground well-covered by Sabbath pre-'72," wrote Philip Bell.

"We certainly felt patronised by the press," recalls Holocaust's John Mortimer; "their attitude was, 'These youngsters are full of energy but pretty dumb.' But once the media coined the NWOBHM expression, we did feel a part of something even in Scotland because the whole movement seemed to be characterised, at least in the early days, by small, self-financed operations in unexpected places. It was like, if Saxon could emerge from Barnsley, then Holocaust could quite happily emerge from Edinburgh. Besides, the idea of moving to London didn't appeal to me or Nicky Arkless; if the other three in the band had thoughts in that direction they never said anything. I think having the record company in Edinburgh made staying in Scotland easier as well. Having said that, there was no real metal scene in terms of bands in Scotland. There were plenty of metal fans though, and heavy metal discos. In some ways we did feel isolated from the rest of the NWOBHM scene. We went to all the gigs when the English bands came up to Scotland, and as I said, there were loads of metal fans around, but let's just say Edinburgh was not Sheffield, Birmingham, London... or even Barnsley!"

For his sins, Philip Bell was despatched to Scotland to see the band live, and although he didn't seem to like 'em much ("more worn than a tramp's undies..."), his interview in *Sounds* in October 1981 revealed that the show he'd seen had been recorded both for a video and a live single. *The Live From The Raw Loud 'N' Live Tour EP* was released in October 1981 and to my mind still is one of the greatest singles from the NWOBHM. Featuring four kick-ass heavy duty songs – 'Death And Glory' off *The Nightcomers* and three others not previously available on vinyl – the EP is pretty raw around the edges but sounded like everything a young metal band should be live. As for the video, well, as mentioned earlier, it was a brave move but one well before its time really, given the price of the tapes themselves and the fact that video cassette recorders were still luxury items back then. Audio cassettes quickly appeared on the tape-trading circuit, and my copy lasted me well until the soundtrack came out on CD via Sanctuary Records in 2003. I finally got to see the gig almost 23 years after it was recorded in September 1981 via its appearance on DVD in 2004.

The 'Coming Through' 12" single appeared in April 1982, but by this time Mortimer and Arkless were gone and the band appeared as a four-piece, with vocalist Gary Lettice, guitarist Ed Dudley and bassist Robin Begg and new drummer Raymond Marciano heading down a more commercial route. As Mortimer recalls: "Myself and Nicky wanted to go further down the metal road. We wanted to increase the degree of abstraction from the hard rock roots of metal. In particular we wanted to write heavier songs and experiment with extremes of tempo. The other three guys were going in the opposite direction, towards the Van Halen and Aerosmith-type thing. So we were fighting amongst ourselves over metal and hard rock. Should it be a 'Death Or Glory'-type future or a 'Smokin' Valves'-type future? ... Phoenix Records went with Gary, Robin and Ed and 'Coming Through' and the rest is history." Things weren't that united in what remained of the Holocaust camp though and by the end of 1982 the Hologram album appeared. Using the same logo as Holocaust, and bearing a sticker 'Holocaust are now Hologram,' the band's one album *Steal The Stars* – the band, by the way, now being Dudley and Marciano plus one Gordon Band on vocals and Nelson on bass – didn't do at all well, and after a mauling in *Kerrang!* issue 30, it sank without a trace.

So, after all that, the sudden appearance of *Live (Hot Curry & Wine)* in April 1983 was a more than welcome injection of prime-time metal. The LP was edited from the tapes of the video and live EP from September 1981, although Mortimer points out that "the album actually includes bits and pieces from various gigs around Scotland at that time, although the vast majority of it was taken from the two Edinburgh Nite Club gigs, and one in particular. In those days we had no input – beyond our actual performances – to the studio process, so I'm not sure what exactly went on with the recordings."

But there is more to the Holocaust story, as Mortimer released another Holocaust album, the rather awful *No Man's Land* in 1984. "I just got the unexpected opportunity to record another Holocaust album; I had been playing with drummer Steve Cowen for a short while and so we just went into the studio and banged down some ideas very quickly. Phoenix just wanted to catch the end of the NWOBHM; it was like, 'Let's chuck something out there and see what happens.' It had to be done in a real hurry and on a tiny budget, and as the rest of the band had disintegrated by that time and the Hologram project had not sold well, Phoenix Records came to me."

After that it all went rather quiet – until Lars Ulrich heard the song 'The Small Hours' on the live album and suggested Metallica cover it, resulting in worldwide exposure and royalties which not only enabled

Mortimer to reactivate the band but also to pursue his aim of pushing metal to the extreme. Check out their later releases, including 2003's *Primal* for further proof.

WALTHAMSTOW – THE ROCK 'N' ROLL CAPITAL OF THE WORLD

At the end of September 1983, Shades, the specialist rock/metal record shop in London, started to promote a series of one-off Sunday night gigs at the Royal Standard in Walthamstow. Although not strictly a NWOBHM venture (featuring, for example, the UK debut of Canadian trio Exciter, which was both exciting and ear-splitting), it gave the perfect opportunity for such bands to come and strut their stuff in London. Jaguar were the second band up, on October 2, 1983 at a time

"Rox's lack of talent didn't seem to bother them much."

when they were beginning to change their style and which led to a mixed bag of a set with one punter shouting for 'Axe Crazy' at the end of every song until they finally relented and played it. There were a lot of highlights – Satan's first appearance being the best in my opinion (by this time the gigs had been shifted to Fridays because of their popularity, meaning the Satan gig eerily took place on Friday, January 13, 1984) – as well as some turgid under-achievers like glamsters, Rox: "Although Rox's lack of talent didn't seem to bother them much," I wrote, "it soon took its toll on the audience which thinned from a large crowd to fifteen or so people enjoying one of life's funnier moments." She were good; formed by ex-Rock Goddess bassist Tracey Lamb and featuring the delightful Jackie Bodimead who (as mentioned earlier) later jumped ship for *Running Wild*-era Girlschool; I noted at the time that She lacked confidence, "opening nervously and more shaky than an Italian government. The band's main strength lies in vocalist Jackie Bodimead who has a terrific voice to complement her stunning good looks... Tracey's bass playing seems to have improved immeasurably since I saw her in Rock Goddess ten months ago and she no longer handles the instrument as if it was a soiled nappy. By the end of the evening she was laying down some rather snappy bass lines, making me wonder if the simple songs of her previous band actually prevented her from playing to the best of her abilities… She are a talented four-piece with some catchy material and, given the breaks, vast potential." Grim Reaper did the business; Salisbury-based Tokyo Blade with original singer Alan Marsh were awesome; Savage were masterful despite being plagued by technical difficulties…The early dream–come-true, though, was seeing Hellanbach.

TOKYO BLADE SET LIST, ROYAL STANDARD, WALTHAMSTOW, DECEMBER 1983:
Power Game; Mean Streak; Break The Chains; Can't Live Without You; Liar; Death On Main Street; On Through The Night; Madame Guillotine; Tonight; The Trooper; If Heaven Is Hell; Unleash The Beast; Heaven & Hell; Sunrise In Tokyo; Attack Attack; Killer City //Highway Passion; Midnight Rendezvous; Ballroom Blitz; Dead Of The Night

SAVAGE SET LIST, ROYAL STANDARD, WALTHAMSTOW, FEBRUARY 1984:
Let It Loose; Ain't No Fit Place; We Got The Edge; White Hot; Berlin; Stevie's Vengeance; The China Run; Keep It On Ice; Cry Wolf // On The Rock'; Dirty Money

I'd already been mesmerized firstly by their contribution ('All The Way') to the Neat Records' *60 Minutes Plus Metal* compilation, and then by their debut album *Now Hear This*, which in an unpublished review for *Sounds* I'd noted "five stars just isn't enough for this album…When you've heard it your life will never be the same again." On a major label, Hellanbach would have been mega, and that's a fact. The gig itself was glorious; in spite of a dodgy sound Hellanbach were on great form that night, with bassist Kev Charlton and drummer Barry Hopper giving the band more backbone than a blue whale, aptly-named singer Jimmy Brash whipping the crowd into a frenzy and Dave Patton – all 5' 3" of him – living up to every column inch written about him being the next guitar hero. The set featured nine songs off that debut album and seven newies later to appear on the follow-up LP (bizarrely also on Neat), *The Big H.* That things weren't happy with Neat Records at the time of the gig though were fairly obvious when Brash announced a split with the label and, with regard to *Now Hear This*, told the crowd to "beg it, steal it, borrow it, tape it..." The other thing I noted at the time was his enthusiasm that we all buy a band T-shirt "as a future investment." So I did. A couple of days later I wrote to the band to get some more info for the review I was planning and, in response to some questions, received the following reply from Jimmy Brash.

"As you no doubt know, the Royal Standard gig was our first showing in London and, believe me, it won't be our last. The reception we got blew us away, we were really 'taken by surprise'! I'd like to thank you right away for coming all that way across London to see the band and I'm so glad the journey was well worth the trouble. Now as you know Hellanbach have finished with Neat Records and are now looking for a major deal with a record company who can give us the push we need to spread the Mighty H gospel around the world! The thing is, we don't know how long this will take to materialise but having been going for six years, time is of no consequence, so if you don't hear of an Hellanbach activity in that time don't worry because we will still be out there 'playing like crazy!'

Now a big thanks for buying a T-shirt because that money you gave to us is really helping us to survive. Without that kind of income we could never play outside of Newcastle. In return our manager will put in a couple of photos — it's nothing spectacular but it's as good as our finances can cover, so I hope it's OK."

What's sad is that there was a great band, with an album and EP to their name, and hardly a penny in their collective pocket. Not exactly the road to riches, eh?

Despite their differences with Neat, they ended up back on the label for their second album before succumbing to the inevitable split, with guitar player extraordinaire Dave Patton cropping up with the funkmeister Glenn Hughes sometime in the Nineties.

HELLANBACH SET LIST, ROYAL STANDARD, WALTHAMSTOW, 30 OCTOBER 1983:

Dancin'; Times Are Getting Harder; Urban Paranoia; Beaten To The Bone; Taken By Surprise; All Systems Go; Privates; Kick It Out; New Thang; All Is Said And Done; Bandits Run; Street Elite; Look At Me; Dave's solo; Let's Get This Show On The Road//Motivated; All The Way

THE UNHOLY TRINITY – BLITZKRIEG, AVENGER & SATAN

The aspirations, fears, hopes, dreams, desires and dreads of every young musician can probably be summed up in this Unholy Trinity. Blitzkrieg was the band that split well before it recognised its full potential, but ultimately reformed and became the most successful of the three. Satan changed their line-up, name, sound, image, outlook and ethos but remained forever on the edge of being the stars they should have been. And Avenger plugged away against severe criticism and ultimately toured America – surely every young heavy metal musos dream – although returned disillusioned and broke.

It was Steve who started this one off for us. He went off to university in Leicester, and sent odd snippets to Dave at Castle Records, who by this time was submitting a regular heavy metal chart to *Melody Maker*. Steve had come across a thriving rock scene and, in particular, one really good band, and duly sent a copy of their demo to Dave, who included one of their songs in his next chart.

A few days later the phone rang at the shop, and when Dave answered the caller told him that he had seen a song called 'Armageddon' by a band called Blitzkrieg in Dave's chart; "Now," the caller continued, "I too am in a band called Blitzkrieg and we also do a song called 'Armageddon', so if you can give us any details of this band I'd be grateful so we can get in touch with them 'cos one of us will have to relinquish the name."

"No problem," replied Dave, "this bunch is based in Leicester..."

"Fuck me!" exclaimed the caller [Brian Ross], "That's us!" and in his excitement he accidentally put the phone down. A couple of days later I heard this story, and this is how I first came across Blitzkrieg, in my opinion the best of all the NWOBHM bands. Most metal fans know of them, if only because of the Metallica cover version of their title track. The fact that the first incarnation of the band lasted just fifteen months and officially issued just a handful of songs is testament to their importance.

According to Jim Sieroto, when it all started "the band was called Split Image. There was me on guitar (I changed the spelling of my name to Sirotto to make things easier), Steve English on bass, Steve Abbey on drums and a singer Sarah Aldwinckle. In the first few months of 1980 we began to toughen up our sound and started writing songs like 'Armageddon' and 'Saviour'. The addition of rhythm guitarist Ian Jones cemented this direction, and with the replacement of Sarah with Brian Ross – the band really needed a male singer – the new band was complete."

"I'd moved down from Newcastle to Leicester with a band called Anvil and then promptly got sacked!" notes Brian Ross. "Well, everything happens for a reason; I went to work the next day and saw a 'Vocalist Wanted' ad in a music shop window, and that was Blitzkrieg, or Split Image as they were then. Just over a month later we were recording our first demo, featuring 'Armageddon', 'Inferno' and 'Blitzkrieg'."

Like most bands, Blitzkrieg used the demo to attract record company interest while at the same time selling it at gigs to inject some much-needed cash into the bank balance. Neat Records got to hear it and offered to release a single, and, in February 1981, a two–day session yielded 'Buried Alive' and 'Blitzkrieg' for the single, as well as a batch of one-take no-overdubs live-in-the-studio material (one of which was a re-recording of 'Inferno' which appeared on Neat's *Lead Weight* compilation in May 1981 and was well liked by the critics.

To keep the momentum going and highlight their strength as a live band, Blitzkrieg recorded and released a live six–song cassette entitled *Blitzed Alive*, also recorded in May 1981. Mick Moore replaced Steve English, John Antcliffe took over from Ian Jones, and according to Jim,

HOW ALIVE IS BLITZED ALIVE?

There has always been a degree of controversy about the 'liveness' of Blitzed Alive and certainly the audience has either been boosted in the mix or dropped in from elsewhere.

In November 1981, Brian Ross told Radio Leicester: "We did a few gigs in and around Newcastle including one supporting Trust at the Mayfair, and taped them ourselves. When we got back we played them all and realised the potential, so we mixed them, chose the best tracks and made a master reel-to-reel tape from which we could make cassettes directly."

However, "if you listen to 'Saviour' on Blitzed Alive," says Jim Sieroto, "there's a discernable thud amongst all the mayhem as I bang my Strat into the studio floor at the end of the session. Now the Neat Offices were immediately below the studio and our manager Jez Gilman was in there preparing contracts with David Wood, the boss of Neat Records. As the din comes to an end upstairs, there's the thud, followed by a gentle trickle of dust and then some plaster from the ceiling just before part of it falls on to the desk between them. The Impulse Studios were in an old Thirties cinema right in the middle of Wallsend, so some of the plasterwork must have been showing its age!"

There is no doubt that the material was recorded live, but I personally don't care whether it was live at a gig, live in the studio or live in the bathroom, it still sounds good to me. The bottom line is, does it really matter?

"this is where the band hit top gear." They pretty much now had it all – a stable line–up, a second single 'Too Wild To Tame' demoed and ready to roll and a deal with Carrere Records (home of Saxon) on the table. Then, quite unexpectedly, just when everything seemed to be falling into place, the band split up. "To be honest, we were burned out, and broke," said Jim. "The gigs seemed to be drying up, and once one of us decided to call it a day, the others soon followed…"

Brian Ross takes up the story. "December 17, 1981 was the day Jim announced he was leaving. He just said, 'Look, I'm quitting the band. I've been thinking about the offer from Carrere and I don't want to do it. I don't want to sign a deal, I don't want to do an album, I don't want to tour and I don't want to be in the band any more.' I mean, we'd got an offer of a record deal and a tour with Saxon, so the day jobs would have to go, and it was obvious that Jim had mulled this over and made his decision. And that put me in a difficult position, because I didn't want to do it without Jim. I called everyone up, I think Jez our manager went to talk to Jim but couldn't change his mind, and when they got to mine we told them that Jim wanted to call it a day. I think Steve Abbey wanted to replace Jim, as did Jez, but I didn't, and that was it.

Had we gone on, or even if we'd replaced Jim and carried on, who knows how far we might have gone. It might have been different had we known back then what we had achieved, but we didn't; not at that time anyway. It wasn't till I moved back North that I began to see Blitzkrieg being listed as people's influences and favourite bands. I wrote to everyone who mentioned us, and that's how I found out how well–liked the band had been. I found we had a huge following in the Bay Area: we only made 150 copies or so of the *Blitzed Alive* tape, but everyone seemed to have one over there! We just thought we were a Leicester band, playing – albeit to full houses – around the UK. We supported Trust at the Newcastle Mayfair and so impressed them that they asked us back four months later as headliners and we packed the place out. But a lot of bands were signing deals around that time. I think we thought that if we didn't sign then, we never would. You know, we were only together for just over a year, and 1981 was like a flash – it was over so quickly."

Meanwhile, back in Newcastle, a group of youngsters had put together the cutely-named Satan. "The origins of the band date back to when we were still at school – we had the name before we could even play the instruments!" recalls Russ Tippins. "I guess we were 16, maybe 15, at the time, and played our first gig at school. As for the name, well, we were young, into Black Sabbath and Angel Witch, and it just seemed perfect. By the beginning of 1981 we were a real band, with me, Steve and Bean [Graeme English], Trev Robinson on vocals and Andy Reed on drums and we recorded the four tracks for Guardian Records. The 'Kiss Of Death' single [b/w 'Heads Will Roll'] was released in November 1981, and 'Oppression' and 'The Executioner' appeared on the *Roxcalibur* compilation a few months later. Then we saw the chance to get a better drummer – Ian McCormack – and poached him. That lasted almost a year until he joined Battleaxe. They had a big wallet and big ideas and that was that. We'd got some Dutch dates pencilled in and had to find a drummer pretty quickly, and got Sean Taylor in. We'd seen him play in Raven days, and knew he was available. It was supposed to be a temporary arrangement but it lasted about seven years! As for Trev, well, we got the chance to get the singer Louie [Lou] Taylor. He stayed for about six months but moved to London, so then we got Swifty [Ian Swift]. We did some gigs, I remember a good one supporting Bernie Tormé, went to Holland, and in November 1982 we recorded the *Into The Fire* demo. Steve went back to Holland to do the Supersession gig – a kind of giant jam session with some of the lads from Mercyful Fate, Jaguar, etc, and Brian and Gary from Avenger were there. Steve and Brian really hit it off together, and that's where the idea came for the famous 'vocalist swap.' We [felt] Swifty wasn't the right singer for us, and it was obvious that Brian would be much better; if you get that chance, you take it. We were nothing if not opportunistic! And that was the *Court In The Act* album line-up. We were fairly well-known in Holland which led to us being signed by Dutch label Roadrunner, and we recorded the LP in August 1983. We did some more shows in

Holland, and played in London where we met Louie again who said he wouldn't mind rejoining."

As an aside, Sean Taylor volunteers: "You know, I don't really remember why I left Raven. I think in my late teens I drank too much, so probably didn't turn up for rehearsals. I really can't remember. A shame, because I enjoyed Raven and they're great lads. Mark is a bit more reserved, but John has such an infectious personality, as I'm sure most people know! In hindsight, maybe I should have stayed, but then, who knows? I had a great time with Satan."

Back with the remains of Blitzkrieg, bassist Mick Moore takes up the story: "Once Blitzkrieg had folded, Brian went home to Newcastle and I moved back to London again. I was living in Crouch End but nothing much was going on. Then Brian sent down a tape and basically asked me to join him in Newcastle in a band called Unter Den Linden. I had nothing going on and, besides, London was bloody expensive. So this was the start of Avenger, with Brian, me, Gary Young and a guitarist Malcolm. We wanted to add a second guitarist and he was opposed to it. So he left, and in September 1982 Steve Bird (who'd played with Gary before) was in, and we were Avenger."

After just two weeks together, Avenger went into Neat Records' Impulse Studios and recorded a three-track demo tape. One of the songs recorded at this session, 'Hot 'N' Heavy Express', was released by Neat on the 12" *One Take, No Dubs EP* and although it appeared in several HM Charts, it proved to be the first of many problems for the band.

"'Hot 'N' Heavy Express'," recalls Mick, "was an early song, written to score some Brownie points with Radio Metro DJ Alan Robson whose radio show of the same name was one of the rock/metal shows of the time."

Steve Bird was replaced by John Brownless, and having got some gigs under their bullet belts, Avenger went back to Neat's studios and recorded their debut single. The A-side 'Too Wild To Tame' was a reworking of the Ross/Moore song that had been demoed as Blitzkrieg's follow-up 45 to their 'Buried Alive' single, but before it could be released Avenger and Brian Ross parted company. In a bizarre twist of fate, Ross joined Satan and the singer he ousted, Ian Swift, took his place in Avenger. The press were fed a party line about an amicable agreement: "That must have looked really strange," Mick told Dave Reynolds in *Metal Forces*. "I don't think there's been any other bands who've had a straight swap of singers."

Brian Ross took over vocal duties for Satan just in time to record the band's debut album *Court In The Act*, which was pretty much an updated version of their *Into The Fire* demo. *Metal Forces* loved the album. "I always thought this album was going to be something special and indeed it's certainly lived up to my expectations," wrote Bernard Doe; "a must for any HM collection and joins Tokyo Blade as the best UK release of 1983." Despite recording such a great album and playing some outstanding gigs, in January 1984 Brian Ross and Satan parted company, shortly after the Walthamstow gig on Friday, January 13. Before the gig I'd interviewed Ross for *Metal Rendez-Vous* magazine. Things with Satan were going great, he'd said, although UK apathy was taking its toll; the night's venue was pretty empty as we spoke, and he remarked that "in Amsterdam we can play to 4,000 people and get a police escort to get us out afterwards. In Newcastle we can't get ten people." He also revealed that his long-term aim was to reform Blitzkrieg, just to record the album they'd been planning, although he was adamant that he wouldn't work with Mick Moore again.

The Satan gig that night was an absolute stormer though: "the twin guitars of Russ Tippins and Steve Ramsey cut through the dry ice," I noted, "which threatened to smother the crowd at one point. Bassist Graeme English and drummer Sean Taylor kept a tight control over the songs while Brian Ross delivered pitch-perfect vocals." The set drew largely on the *Court In The Act* album – in fact it was the LP, then more besides: 'Trial By Fire'; 'Hunt You Down'; 'No Turning Back'; 'Blades Of Steel'; 'Pull The Trigger'; 'Broken Treaties'; 'The Ritual'; 'Alone In The Dock'; and 'Break Free', encoring with the oldie-but-goldie 'Oppression'.

After tensions over the split, "it was about a year or so later that Mick and I buried the hatchet, and sat down and worked out what had really gone on," says Brian now. "I would probably have left Avenger anyway. I was happy with it in general, but not with some of the ideas. Satan and the bands like that were more akin to the Blitzkrieg sound and to what I wanted to do. So I don't regret leaving Avenger, I just regret the way it happened. And the other thing I regret is not doing a second Satan album. We had a band meeting in January 1984 to discuss the next album. We had the title – *Suspended Sentence* and the sleeve too, both of which they eventually used – and had started writing songs. So we had a band meeting, and they opened with, 'OK, we're thinking about changing the name and the sound and the overall direction.' They wanted to break through in America, and needed a more acceptable name and commercial sound. My view was that we shouldn't try to sound American, we should try and maintain our individuality, but I was up for trying to be more accessible. But changing the name seemed stupid after all the gigs and having put out such a successful album." A split was inevitable.

There were still commitments to honour, so Neat Records act Tysondog's guitarist, Alan Hunter, (who'd guested on backing vocals on *Court In The Act*) stood in, and less than six weeks later they were back at the Royal Standard. With a temporary vocalist the set had been padded out with extended solos and a cover of Priest's 'Electric Eye', and, in truth, it wasn't that good. "'Hunt You Down' in particular was awful," I wrote at the time. "Time-keeping seemed to go by the board as each member raced to get to the end of the song first."

Meantime, vocalist Lou Taylor made it be known that he wanted to rejoin Satan. Lou had formed (and then quit) a band with guitarist Kevin Heybourne – whose own Angel Witch had called it a day (albeit temporarily) – called Blind Fury. Heybourne seemed to have no use for the name, so Satan was reborn. So recalls drummer Sean (no relation) Taylor: "Steve, Bean and Russ had become very good friends with Louie, and felt the scene was changing and wanted to be more American, which didn't suit Brian's voice at all. So there was a band meeting and Brian was out. I remember thinking at the time, 'Hang on, I think we're making a big mistake here.' I didn't agree with it, but went along with it. As for Blind Fury, well, I actually quit Blind Fury during the recording of the album. The producer Steve James – son of Sid James, the comedian – was an ex-drummer and wanted the drums down-toned and simple. So eventually I just ended up playing to a click-track, which isn't me at all. I was a glorified drum machine. Me and the producer didn't see eye-to-eye at all.

Anyway, it soon became pretty apparent that Blind Fury had a limited shelf life, Russ agreed it wasn't happening and people came round to my way of thinking. In '86 we got Mick Jackson into the band and did *Into The Future*, well, it started as the old *Dirt* demo. Best drumming I ever played, I reckon; all live takes."

But again, we're getting well ahead of ourselves. Back in 1984, Blind Fury were panned in a *Kerrang!* live review in August which described their performance as "a magnificent display of songwriting ineptitude, arrangement ignorance and showmanship uncertainty... The worst live band I have witnessed in a long, long time... Maybe a name change and a complete re-think of material is in order again!" wrote Howard Johnson.

"A heavy sackful of songs full of blood, sweat and power... the musicianship can't be faulted."

Back in the Avenger camp, a second guitarist, Les Cheetham, was recruited, having already guested with the band, playing the solos on both sides of the single while still (technically!) at school. One of the truly great heavy metal singles, 'Too Wild To Tame' was eventually released on August 16, 1983, about the same time as Satan were recording the *Court In The Act* LP. A quartet once more [without John Brownless], Avenger packed their bags and set off to play dates in Holland and Belgium where the response to the single had been particularly enthusiastic. Back in Blighty, their debut album *Blood Sports* was recorded at Neat's Impulse Studios in March/April 1984, and the band officially signed to Neat Records in July with *Blood Sports* appearing in September. *Metal Forces* gave it a healthy 'eight out of ten', describing it as "a heavy sackful of songs full of blood, sweat and power...the musicianship can't be faulted." On the other hand, *Kerrang!* hated it, Malcolm Dome concluding that "they sound more pedestrian than Carnaby Street." "Yeah, well it's not as bad as Doc Doom said," replied Mick in *Forearm Smash* fanzine, "but he's probably lost us a lot of sales."

Having spent some time looking for a new venture, Brian Ross spent the second half of 1984 managing Lone Wolf. At the same time he began to think about recording the proposed Blitzkrieg album that never was, as a solo project. At first reticent, Neat eventually threw their weight behind the project and recording took place in December 1984. "I originally wanted to record *A Time Of Changes* as a solo album, keeping it as close as possible to the original Blitzkrieg sound," Brian told USA's *Metal Rendez-Vous* magazine. "I got Jim Sirotto out of retirement and Mick from Avenger agreed to help out as well." The recording line-up was completed by Mick Proctor from the Tygers Of Pan Tang and Satan's incredible powerhouse drummer, Sean Taylor. Satan's Russ Tippins played on 'Pull The Trigger' (a Satan song originally omitted from the band's

Court In The Act LP but added to the Neat Records' CD re-issue in 1997), with backing vocals added by Ian Swift.

It didn't take that long for Brian to realise how much he'd missed Blitzkrieg and the one-off studio project metamorphosed into a real live band. Mick Proctor committed to the band, and Mick Moore agreed to continue helping out during a quiet spell with Avenger, leaving the recruitment of a young guitarist Gavin Taylor and Chris Green (who had almost joined the band back in 1981) to fill the drum stool. On May 3, 1985, almost three-and-a-half years after the band originally split in 1981, Blitzkrieg appeared on stage once more, at the Royal Standard in Walthamstow; the album release was delayed and *A Time Of Changes* was actually issued a week *after* the show. It wasn't a brilliantly attended gig but it *was* a blinder all the same, the set-list drawing largely on the album with the addition of Satan's 'Blades Of Steel' which Blitzkrieg still play now and (if you want to be pedantic) 'Pull The Trigger' harking back to Satan days as well, and the frenetic 'Too Wild To Tame'.

BLITZKRIEG SET LIST, ROYAL STANDARD, WALTHAMSTOW, MAY 3, 1985

Inferno; Too Wild To Tame; Blitzkrieg; Armageddon; Take A Look Around; A Time Of Changes; Hell To Pay; Pull The Trigger; Blades Of Steel; Saviour // Buried Alive // Blitzkrieg

It's a good album, *A Time Of Changes*; Okay, the production could have been better, but this was the album many fans had waited a long time to hear and it wasn't a disappointment. But by May 1985 the NWOBHM bubble had well and truly burst, and metal fans were desperate for the hot new US bands. Brian, interviewed again in *Metal Rendez-Vous*, was typically unfazed by the odd bad reviews: "I think that some people missed the point totally. *A Time Of Changes* was meant as a solo album. It was a thanks to the kids who have seen us through. I'm very pleased with it; I've got the old songs on record at last."

Meanwhile, Avenger's *Blood Sports* had been well received in Europe and in January 1985 the band played a short tour in Holland (the only dates to promote that particular album). They reverted to a five-piece for this tour, taking out a second guitarist to beef up the sound, an unknown chap today better recognised as Ginger Wildheart. Despite being a success, the tour revealed a serious split within the band and on returning to the

UK eye-liner wearing guitarist Les Cheetham left and Mick Moore, Ian Davison-Swift and Gary Young were faced with the unenviable task of searching for a replacement with a view to capitalising on *Blood Sports* and releasing a follow-up album as quickly as possible. "We said it was the old 'musical differences' when Les 'Pup' Cheetham went, and to be fair he always had my respect as a player," says Mick.

After auditioning a number of hopefuls, the gig eventually went to Greg Reiter, an American guitarist who had placed a quarter-page ad in *Kerrang!* (and which had ironically appeared opposite a Neat Records' advert featuring the Avenger LP amongst others). Almost from the start it was obvious that Greg not only had a great deal to offer musically, but that he also fitted in on a personal level. Greg officially joined Avenger in March 1985, and the band immediately began writing and demo-ing material for their second album, *Killer Elite*, released in October 1985. Whereas *Blood Sports* had been very much in the NWOBHM mould, however, the new record was a remarkably diverse offering with traditional British metal influences rubbing shoulders with Accept-style Euro-anthems ('Face To The Ground'), US power metal ('Revenge Attack') and proto-thrash ('Sawmill'), with the guys from Warfare helping out on 'M.M.85'. And if that wasn't shock enough, the album received some very credible reviews, including top marks in *Metal Forces* and in May 1986 a surprising three-and-a-half in *Kerrang!*: "parts of it are brilliant," wrote Xavier Russell, "such as 'Steel On Steel' and the mighty fine 'Under The Hammer' with more teazin-riffin' from Mr Reiter." Such was the shock of reading a glowing *Kerrang!* review that I spent that night in intense pain and the very day my appendix burst. Heavy metal really is bad for your health, you know.

Returning to the day job after four weeks off, the first person I met as I got off the bus was Sean Taylor, who not only now lived next door to the place where I worked but whose then girlfriend now occupied the next desk to mine. Weird, eh? And the first thing I found out was that Satan was back in business.

"Brian is a good singer, there's no doubt about that, but we thought Louie was better and went for it," explains Russ. "We stayed as Satan for a while but then came the name-change. Looking back now we should have stayed with Brian and done a second album with him. But we had ideas for other songs and Brian's voice just didn't suit what we had in mind. Louie's more, I don't know, 'classically tuneful' but the whole thing, the whole ethos just wasn't right... When the end came... well, I can't actually remember too much about the end of Blind Fury. I think it was like osmosis! It was like Chinese water torture, you know, 'We liked you better when you were Satan,' drip; drip; drip; 'the Satan songs are better than the Blind Fury songs,' drip; drip; drip.'"

With a new vocalist Michael Jackson, the band recorded the *Dirt* demo, landed a deal with SPV, and, for a while at least, went from strength to strength, changing their name again to the more US friendly Pariah before ultimately hitting the buffers at the end of the Eighties. But that's a whole different story.

Back in March 1986, and about the same time as I was playing 'guess what it is' with the hospital food, Avenger were embarking on their US tour. Along with contributing some fine guitar playing and musical inspiration, Greg Reiter also knew people who knew people, and Avenger waved England's cold shores goodbye for an American tour early in 1986 where they hooked up with a number of bands including Liege Lord and the Poison Dollys. Although a relative success, the tour showed that the diversity of music on *Killer Elite* was not so much an indication of differing influences as of completely differing directions; Mick Moore was writing more melodic US sounding material, while Ian Swift was more comfortable with thrashier monsters. On their return to the UK, Avenger pretty much imploded; Greg went back to the States, Ian joined Atomkraft and Mick went into music management. After less than four years together Avenger was no more.

AVENGER SET LIST, L'AMOURS, BROOKLYN, MARCH 3, 1986

Hard Times; Run For Your Life; Under The Hammer; Night Of The Jackyl; Yesterday's Heroes; Rough Ride; Steel On Steel; Face to The Ground; Brand Of Torture // Right To Rock; Like a Tiger.

THEY THINK IT'S ALL OVER... IT IS NOW

At a time when Kerrang! was the only high street heavy metal magazine in the UK, its writers' top albums of 1984 (published in issue 84) was a complete and utter embarrassment to all concerned with just a handful of credible albums rubbing shoulders with some complete A.O.R. dross.

Prince, U2, Chequered Past, The Cars, John Waite … Cutting edge heavy metal it certainly wasn't.

Forearm Smash's Paul Miller interviewed Geoff Barton at the end of 1984 and asked him about all the British heavy metal bands that were getting squeezed out of *Kerrang!* because of the magazine's horizons being widened to include such mainstream (and potentially sales-boosting) bands. Barton replied simply, "I think the majority of young British bands are fucking awful and don't merit coverage."

The NWOBHM was dead… Long live the NWOBHM!

CHAPTER FIVE

TOO WILD TO TAME

*"Spin the wheel with nerves of steel,
the one to win the race..."*

'Too Wild To Tame' by Avenger (p) 1983

LIFE AFTER DEATH

Mick Moore reformed Avenger in 2005. "I'd always wanted to play a festival; that's the one thing I'd never done. When Satan reformed, that was the last straw really. I thought, 'I want some of that.'" Satan's classic Court In The Act line-up had reformed for a one-off gig at the Wacken Festival in 2004 to mark the album's twentieth anniversary. Russ still plays regularly anyway: "Don't laugh, it's called the Russ Tippins band! We do Seventies rock covers, and I enjoy myself. People sometimes come up and say, 'You're quite good; why don't you write some of your own stuff,' but to be honest it's too long a story to tell! During the rehearsals for the Wacken gig, Brian mentioned us all doing a second Satan album, but I just looked at my feet and avoided eye contact!"

Interest in Avenger had been stoked by the Sanctuary Records release *Too Wild To Tame – The Anthology* which rounded up the band's entire back catalogue on one double CD. Malcolm Dome, who had savaged their debut album *Blood Sports* back in 1984, noted in *Classic Rock* that "Avenger were a rather decent act to whom time has been kinder than one would expect. Not that *Too Wild To Tame* is a masterpiece – far from it – but it does suggest that those who dismissed Avenger at the time as a waste of space (including this reviewer) might have been rather unkind." Penitent words indeed but all credit to him.

With Mick hooking up with former band mates Gary Young and Ian Swift, and enlisting the help of guitarists Glenn S. Howes (who had done a stint in Blitzkrieg) and Liam Thompson, a new incarnation of Avenger was born. Although it was supposedly strictly as a one-off, contacts from days gone by led to the band supporting Y&T on their 2005 UK tour, a dream come true for Mick who had long idolised the Americans. More importantly, it was the first time the band had ever toured the UK, and although attendance for their set at the gig I saw at Dudley was sparse, overall the crowds were very good to Avenger.

AVENGER 2005 UK TOUR SET LIST:

'Run For Your Life'; 'Brand Of Torture'; 'Dangerous Games'; 'Enforcer'; 'Hard Times'; 'NOTJ'; 'Death Race 2000'; 'You'll Never take Me'; 'On The Rocks'; Revenge Attack'; 'Too Wild To Tame'

At the end of the tour, Avenger flew to Hamburg for the Headbangers Open Air Festival. German NWOBHM expert Matthias Mader reported back that he saw Gaskin (good), Weapon (decent but nothing special) and Avenger (very interesting)." "Germany was a blast!" says Mick. "I couldn't believe the response we got. And personally, I have never signed so many autographs in such a short space of time, which is very flattering!"

The demise of the NWOBHM in the UK is not the end of the story. It's not as if it packed its suitcase and moved to live in a retirement home in Weston-Super-Mare. For a movement that was supposedly over and done with twenty years ago, things are looking quite healthy for the NWOBHM at the time of writing. Firstly, many of the bands mentioned in this book have reformed and are very much alive and kicking; secondly, there is a healthy market for CD re-issues, led originally by the Neat Metal and British Steel labels, and now maintained by Sanctuary and Majestic Rock Records. And finally, whereas it's true that in the UK most

NWOBHM acts couldn't get arrested now, those band that have got (it) back together can pull healthy crowds at gigs and on the festival circuit particularly in Europe, America and Japan.

In terms of milestones, *Kerrang!* published a tenth anniversary supplement in 1989 which was swiftly followed by the first decent post-NWOBHM compilation (as opposed to cheapo cash-ins that had been cobbled together on cheap labels over the years). *New Wave Of British Heavy Metal '79 Revisited* was co-compiled by Lars Ulrich and Geoff Barton and boasts an impressive selection of tracks. Ex-Sabre and Snowblind bassist Geoff Gillespie, who by this time had swapped life on the road for a cosy life in the office, remembers it well:

"The bill for the artwork alone came to £7,000 – no wonder the bloody album never made any money!"

"When I became PR man at Phonogram records in early 1989, it fell into my lap to co-ordinate the putting together of the *NWOBHM '79 Revisited* album. I had known Lars since the early 1980s, but we argued about what tracks should be included – though I don't know why I bothered, he was always going to get his way! – and I then sourced the masters, had them compiled and sent out to him to listen to. I also went over to the *Kerrang!* office where there was a large, though sadly incomplete, collection of *Sounds* from the period in question, photocopied all the relevant bits I could find and then took them to the art company to put the sleeve together. And that's where the fun started!" Arguments ensued between bands about the size of their respective photos. "With [that] sorted we finally had a finished sleeve – only for the marketing director to say, 'You can't use that image, that's a rapist's mask' when he saw Samson's Thunderstick on the sleeve! The bill for the artwork alone came to £7,000 – no wonder the bloody album never made any money!"

On stage, the NWOBHM lived on, most healthily in Europe where, for example, the first outdoor Eindhoven festival, held in the club's car park in 1986, played host to the reformed Michael J. Jackson-led Satan, Angel Witch, Chariot and Paul Di'Anno's Battlezone among its seven-band line-up. NWOBHM bands have become a feature at festivals like Wacken in Germany with the likes of Blitzkrieg and Tygers Of Pan Tang putting in recent appearances. As noted above, the *Court In The Act*-era Satan played their first gig together at the 2004 Wacken festival since Brian Ross left 20 years ago; only Sean Taylor, possibly the greatest drummer of the NWOBHM, declined to get involved. And back in 1999, Tokyo hosted a NWOBHM extravaganza, with Geoff Gillespie's assistance: "In February 1999, I was contacted by a friend at Pony Canyon Records in Tokyo asking if I would be able to help them contact some bands that they were trying to track down with a view to them playing a one-off event in Tokyo. 1999 was, of course, the twentieth anniversary. Little did I know how manic the following few months would turn out to be."

Top of the list for the *Metal Crusade* (they do like their daft titles out here!) were Diamond Head and Angel Witch but, of course, they wanted the original line-ups. It was quickly explained to them that this wasn't going be possible, so it was back to the drawing board. After much rumination and consultation, and with the original line-up of Praying Mantis booked to headline – Mantis having remained active in Japan over the years – a supporting bill of Samson (reuniting Chris Aylmer and Thunderstick with Paul as per the pre-Bruce power trio days), Tank and Suffolk's finest, Trespass, was agreed upon. It's worth pointing out here that the events Tokyo-based organiser – DJ, journalist and TV personality extraordinaire Masa Itoh – had wanted the Brabbs, Brabbs & Ward line-up of Tank. This time, when told this just wasn't going to be possible, he actually relented.

What followed was a feverish round of trips to the Japanese embassy, endless forms, piles of passports and passport photos, a continuous stream of faxes back and forward containing equipment requests, stage layouts etc. During all of this, I took a short trip out to Tokyo to meet with the event's promoters Club Citta and to see the proposed venue, Hibiya outdoor auditorium. Thunder had recently played there, and I must say it looked great. Everything was now set for August 1.

On the morning of July 30, everybody met at Heathrow for the flight to Tokyo's Narita Airport. Upon arrival in the sweltering heat – and believe me, Tokyo is hot in the depths of summer – we were driven back to the hotel to be greeted with the sight of the Mantis guys luxuriating in the hotel pool, and went straight into a production meeting! I nearly had a mutiny on my hands until I explained to everybody that, with the show the next day, it was important that this was done now. After that, the next 18 hours were theirs to enjoy in any way they saw fit.

Following a busy afternoon, the evening and late night involved record stores, the Hard Rock Cafe and a succession of young ladies following us all back to the hotel (don't ask...). The morning of the great day arrived: in typically efficient Japanese style, the bands were ferried out to the venue at their allotted sound-check time and then went back stage to the dressing room area until their show time. Just prior to taking the stage, each band was shepherded into a side room for a few photos and a quick interview for Masa Itoh's TV show. Trespass took the stage at 2pm and played a spirited set. It was so obvious that they were just pleased to be there, having more or less re-formed just to play the show. The cheer that greeted the opening chords of 'One Of The Days' sent shivers down my spine.

By the time Samson took the stage, the event had found some momentum. Paul, God bless him, was a star that day, having to fill a large stage with only a three piece, he threw himself into proceedings with serious gusto. My personal highlight would have to be the day's renditions of 'Hammerhead' and 'Vice Versa'. Although nobody knew it, for many of us that was to be the last time we'd ever see Paul perform. R.I.P., mate...

Tank literally exploded on to the stage; 'Shellshock' never sounded more brutal. In truth, Tank were the real revelation of the day, pure unadulterated heavy metal that hit you hard in the diaphragm and left little room for subtleties, and Algy Ward in particular held the audience in some kind of awestruck trance. The legend that was and possibly still is Tank has endured over the years in Japan, and this was amazingly their first chance to see the band. They were not disappointed, and neither was I...

Headliners Praying Mantis didn't have to do much to win the crowd over. Having remained popular in Japan over the years, the opportunity to see the *Time Tells No Lies* line-up was a real treat for the Japanese crowd. By their own admission, the band under-performed that night, but it scarcely seemed to matter. It was all about the occasion, the camaraderie of the event and a celebration of a special time and some very special music. With everybody trooping back on stage for a chaotic but nonetheless enjoyable romp through 'Roll Over Beethoven' the evening drew to a close."

In 2003 the respected and knowledgeable Canadian writer Martin Popoff published *The Top 500 Heavy Metal Songs Of All Time* based on points accrued in a poll. It's a fascinating labour of love and an extremely interesting read. Even more interesting is that his Top 500 contains numerous NWOBHM entries (as well as quotes from many musicians citing the NWOBHM as an influence). Even knocking out Def Leppard's MTV fodder (6 entries), Saxon's equal number of chart placings (although there's nothing post-*Power And The Glory* so realistically they can all be seen as good ol'-fashioned NWOBHM songs), and Iron Maiden's massive 28 titles (17 of which come from the first 4 albums), there are still 8 other NWOBHM toons in this Top 500. Add the lot together, in fact, and arguably almost 10% of a 21 [st] Century poll of the most-liked 500 heavy metal songs are NWOBHM related.

The songs that made it into the poll are:

Venom	*Black Metal*	Number 75
Diamond Head	*Am I Evil*	Number 141
Angel Witch	*Angel Witch*	Number 237
Angel Witch	*Angel Of Death*	Number 367
Holocaust	*Death Or Glory*	Number 398
Witchfinder General	*Witchfinder General*	Number 416
Venom	*In League With Satan*	Number 420
Tygers Of Pan Tang	*Gangland*	Number 493

That's not a bad showing for a musical corpse. Angel Witch, in fact turn up again in Ian Christe's book *Sound Of The Beast* where their self-titled debut album, so hated by the critics on its release, turns up alongside Iron Maiden's second album *Killers* and Saxon's *The Eagle Has Landed* in the writer's 'Best 25 Heavy Metal Albums Of All Time'.

Even in *Kerrang!*'s 2004 feature '666 Songs You Must Own – the Ultimate Playlist' in November 2004, three NWOBHM songs ('Run To The Hills' by Iron Maiden, 'Am I Evil?' by Diamond Head and 'Wheels Of Steel' by Saxon) popped up in the heavy metal Top 20 section. Of 'Am I Evil?', *Kerrang!* noted: "The young Lars Ulrich loved Stourbridge's Diamond Head so much he went and stayed with them on an early visit to the UK – and this hulking slab of classic metal would become the cornerstone of Metallica's live set for years to come. No 'Am I Evil?', no 'Tallica."

NEW DISCOVERIES

The second issue of *Kerrang!*, in August 1981 carried an interview with Aragorn, a band only known for their one Neat Records single. Written by Mick Middles, the feature revealed that (a) Middles didn't like the band's name and (b) there existed a new three-track cassette, with a track entitled 'Tickets On The Wall'.

"It was planned," says drummer Mike Ellis, "to be an EP and also the next step in getting enough material recorded for an album; with the EP sessions we would have had half an album (nearly!). We did the recording when 'Black Ice' was released so spirits were high, we were getting supports with a lot of bands who were on their way to greater things and we thought we were on the way too. We spent 1981 gigging and after a few months we sort of 'realised' the EP hadn't been released. Neat weren't being very communicative and by the end of the year they called us in and said 'That's it – bye!' They suggested we weren't stable enough as [there'd been some personnel changes and then the band were dropped]. I recall Bronze Records showed some interest, but I think they were after a Twisted Sister-type band and we just weren't up for that! The EP remained in the Neat vaults for twenty-plus years. A few bootlegs escaped during that time but apart from the unreleased album, there were no more Aragorn recordings.

Neat dropping us was probably the lowest point in our career. Chris and Jon came to see me to tell me that Chris had quit, and did I want to carry on? It was like all the effort, work and passion had been whipped out from under my feet. We decided to carry on and struggled for another 18 months, but we never really regained the momentum, and when the band finally did split I wasn't sad, just kind of relieved really – but I still wish we'd achieved more. Jon wanted to carry on regardless, Chris Dunne was disenchanted – he'd found religion and his life priorities were changing along with the musical direction he wanted to take. I was starting to get a lot of session work in Manchester, so there was still the glimmer of work on the horizon. But the total lack of interest from the business combined with the feeling that metal was moving into sanitised, commercial territory, made us less enthusiastic to work against it. We finished recording the album in February 1983, but it was clear during the sessions that all was not well and much of the album was recorded without even seeing each other. We had a few gigs booked up to April, and called it a day at the end of the month."

In the booklet notes for the CD *Noonday – The Anthology*, Ellis told Malcolm Dome that he had "always kept an eye out for any mention of Aragorn. One day I saw an advert for Sanctuary Records' Neat Compilation *The Flame Burns On* and our magnum opus 'Black Ice' was included. This pricked my curiosity as to whether there was any interest in the band. I found a couple of websites listing basic details of the band, but what intrigued me was a site I later found out to be run by Phil Lentz in the USA." It transpires that Lentz had a copy of the demo that was to be the follow-up EP to 'Black Ice', which Ellis himself didn't even have. Rooting through his own collection, Ellis found some demos and rehearsal tapes, and a cassette containing a copy of what was to have been the band's debut album. The result is the aforementioned CD, featuring the original Neat single, the supposed follow-up EP, the twelve songs of the LP and some demos: a rather smart and instant collection.

The point of this story is that, even now, discoveries are still being made and there is a wealth of great material yet to see the light of day. The discovery of the lost Mythra album proved that, as does, for example, the amount of high-quality demo material unearthed by Trespass for their *The Works* and *The Works 2* CDs, finally collected up for the band's Sanctuary Records anthology release *One Of These Days*. And top of the pile for me is Shiva's *Continuance* CD, a collection of demos which came to light after I'd interviewed Andy Skuse and prompted him to rummage in his attic to find some unreleased material he'd alluded to, and which Majestic Rock Records issued in 2004. There's a lot of great stuff still out there somewhere. And that's before you start mining the BBC archives to see what sessions recorded for *The Friday Rock Show* can be unearthed...

THE REFORMATION

As mentioned earlier, Blitzkrieg got their split and reformation out of the way quite early on, although it's only in recent years that releases from them have become regular occurrences. Trespass seem to go through periods of wild abandon when something happens and then get lost in sleepy Suffolk once more. I interviewed them in December 2003 and Dave Crawte noted at the time: "Last night was, what, the first rehearsal, the three of us for what, four years? And we just sort of busked our way through loads of old Trespass stuff and it all came straight back to us as we were doing it. It just all came flooding back – it was brilliant." Unfortunately, nothing much has happened since though. As for other bands, the word 'reformation' followed by a question mark elicits quite interesting responses.

"We never split up and nobody fell out; we just didn't bother to meet up for, well, about twenty years!"

"Well, we never really split up,' replies Montalo of Witchfynde. "Everyone asks us this – it was just that after the *Lords Of Sin* LP, I think we all got very disillusioned. We spent about a year in the studio doing *Lords Of Sin*. Phil Chilton, our producer – well, he was more than that really, more our mentor – bought his own studio in London and put the deal together with Mausoleum Records. As it was his own studio, we just kind of moved in. We spent the first week making up bunk beds and kitting out the kitchen!† We weren't paying for it so the album just took its time really; it took as long as it needed to get it right. *Lords Of Sin* finally came out at the end of 1984 and Mausoleum promptly went out of business. The only way we could do anything would be to record yet another album, and we were all too tired, to be honest. We came back to Derbyshire and rented a place – an undertaker's workshop, as it happens, we had the room above where the corpses were laid out – and worked on three or four songs there. One of them was 'The Other Side' which came out on *The Witching Hour*, although I don't think it was called that then. But the energy was gone. So we never split up and nobody fell out; we just didn't bother to meet up for, well, about twenty years! But Gra [Scoresby] and I, who I guess were the main creative force back in those

---

†1 In the booklet notes to the CD re-issue of Snowblind's one and only self-titled album, bassist Geoff Gillespie remembers The Yard slightly differently: "We had to wait for Witchfynde to vacate the studio – they were finishing their Lords Of Sin album. The studio was in a suburb to the south-west of London called Southall and was called The Yard... Let me just tell you a bit about the conditions under which this album was made. We all five of us were sharing a room with bunk beds, and it was cold. Being resident at the studio, sessions would run 18 hours or more at a time. It was hard work, I can tell you..."

days, certainly in the early days, we thought we couldn't pull anything more out at that time. So it wasn't that we fell out or split up; we just went our separate ways for a long time!

Cloak And Dagger is available of course through the website, and *Lords Of Sin* did come out on CD; we were asked if we had any objections to it coming out and thought that as it was going to come out anyway we might as well go along with it, and asked for some [help] to go out and promote it. But we never heard any more.

But we did *The Witching Hour* in 2001, and we're working on a new album, we're in the middle of it at the moment, but we've done some shows in the meantime and so have been recording new stuff off and on, doing it in pieces rather than in one long session. Nowdays the music we're writing seems to be going more towards the original feel. I think there's two reasons for that. One is that we're not working with Phil Chilton, who, I think, and this is no disrespect to him, tried to help us write 'proper' songs or create a song that says something with a structure. In the early days, you see, we just wrote as it came. The other is that our vocalist Harry likes the earlier stuff. He's a fair bit younger than the rest of us and was a real heavy metal freak kid. The sort of songs we were writing in the early days was what really turned him on to us. He'd tattooed himself with the band's logo before he joined us – he had photos of us playing with him down the front and said he knew one day he'd sing for us. Back with Luther Beltz singing, it got a lot more aggressive – macho aggressive as opposed to stage excitement; when Harry joined he just said he didn't think that lent itself to what we were and what we were trying to do."

For Aragorn's Mike Ellis the thought of a reformation is a bit of a non-starter. "In a word – no! I can't see us reforming. I spoke with Chris Dunne at the end of 2002 about this, he seemed quite keen, but after talking it over with Jon, they decided to decline the offer I'd had to play a rather large, well-known metal festival. I have been in touch with Dale Lee, the original bass player, and he is keen to do something, but whether or not the metal-going public would be happy to see a 'half' Aragorn perform is something I couldn't answer. I have plenty of volunteers for the vocals and guitar positions, but I'm undecided if it would be regarded as a cynical move or a genuine attempt to put on a reproduction of the old Aragorn show. I'd love to do it, but not if I am going to look daft."

Chris Logan and Andy Skuse of Shiva see things quite differently. "I would love to do a big one-off gig," says Chris, "just for the fun of it, and for fans and friends who might never have seen us before. But only with John and Andy. I don't even know where John is; I believe he got very religious and went travelling round the world. I think we would be better than we were before – my style hasn't changed but I've got a lot more subtleties in my playing now. But it would have to be 'we three'. That's the line-up people know, that's the line-up that did the album – it would have to be us. OK, me and Andy didn't see eye to eye all the time, you can't, but when you're playing, to have someone like Andy, this school-teacher-type but looking the perfect rock star, grinning away... it was fantastic." For Andy though, the answer is a definite "No; there's no chance of us reforming. I haven't played since the split and John is now living in Tennessee. It's not going to happen."

Soldier have successfully reformed, as Garry Phillips points out. "Both Steve Barlow and myself completely gave up with the music business when we left Soldier. Ian Dick spent time on his own project, Fret, and concentrated on his business and building his studio, Ian Astrop kept on drumming with a Commitments-type band (which he still does). Steve Taylor is still drumming I think, and Nick Lashley is living in L.A. and plays session with a few names. Nick Bicknell is not playing anymore though he did come to a rehearsal a few weeks ago! The reformation just kind of happened. I had spent some time looking for anything about Soldier on the internet and a chance signing of a guest book brought an email from a guy in Poland called Bart Gabriel. He had been in touch with Steve Taylor and gave me his email address. Steve said he wanted to do the *Infantrycide* album just to put Soldier to bed for good, he got in touch with Steve Barlow who then got in touch with me (they all thought I was dead for some reason!) and oddly that was the last I ever heard from Steve Taylor. Steve Barlow contacted Ian Dick and Ian Astrop, we arranged a rehearsal and just clicked after all these years. There have been other people involved in our reformation along with all the die-hard fans that have contacted us since I raised my head. We hadn't realised we were so well-known. At the moment the band are writing new material and recording tracks for inclusion on the *Sins Of The Warrior* album and rehearsing for live shows. This is taking longer than anticipated due to the fact that we all have 'proper jobs' now and the fact that I live quite a way from the rest of the band, which means we can only rehearse as a full band once a month.

But it is coming together. One thing I want to do is get our sound properly recorded; we could never get our live sound on record."

Another band who have successfully got back together is Jaguar. "We got back together in '98," recalls Garry Pepperd. "I was in a covers band, earning decent money, having a laugh, and I got a letter out of the blue from Jess Cox at Neat via the Performing Rights Society. He said he was planning to re-release *Power Games*, and would I contact him. So, he explained he was going to put it out with extra tracks and did we want to be involved in the booklet, the artwork and so on. Well, I figured it was going to come out whether I liked it or not, you know, so it's better to have a bit of input, so I got together some pieces of memorabilia, lyrics, the whole thing really. A bit later Jess rang up and said something like '*Power Games* is doing OK. Would you consider doing a new album?' Well, I hadn't regularly seen any of the other guys since I can't remember when, but he told me to think about it and said he would finance it and put it out. I found Jeff Cox through a friend of a friend, and sat down and thought, 'Yeah, we'll see what we can do with this.' Couldn't find Chris Lovell, and Paul Merrell said he wasn't interested, which I respected; he said he hadn't sung rock music for many years and didn't want to do that any more. We got Nathan Cox in – yeah, there's a lot of Cox in this band! You can't join unless your name is Cox! – on drums, and after trying out several singers, Nathan remembered Jamie Manton who fitted in nicely. But it wouldn't have happened without Jess. It was an idea that had never occurred to me. I'd never thought about it, and neither had Jeff."

THE 'NEW WAVE' OF THE NEW WAVE OF BRITISH HEAVY METAL

As Lemmy noted, when labels try to manufacture something it's "the kiss of death. The bands they pick are always the wrong ones!" Which is probably where *Metal Hammer* magazine went wrong with its April 1987 freebie single, presumably designed to promote British interest in a market increasingly dominated by American bands and, God help us all, Europe's 'The Final Countdown' single. The *Metal Hammer* 7" entitled 'The 2nd Wave Of New British Metal' featured Paul Samson's Empire, who had supported Maiden on their 1986 *Somewhere In Time* tour; Heavy Pettin, whose stint with Polydor was pretty much in decline; Chariot, who were past their sell-by date; and Strangeways who never even had a sell-by date. As a collectable, it's well worth having – there's precious little material kicking about from Empire, and this was Chariot's last vinyl release, for example – but the single did nothing to re-position British heavy metal at the top of the tree. The wrong bands indeed.

Fast-forward fifteen-plus years and in 2003, Communique Records released a CD entitled *The Second Wave: 25 Years of NWOBHM*, featuring Oliver/Dawson Saxon, Girlschool and Tygers Of Tang Pang. This release was to tie in with a tour by the three bands in 2003, but unfortunately the tour never got off the ground. OK, so this release wasn't really an attempt to launch anything new, but rather to ensure that the bands could still get their music out while the major record labels kept their blinkers on, and in fact the album itself received surprisingly good reviews. Geoff Barton, the man who wrote off the NWOBHM over twenty years earlier and was now at *Classic Rock*, wrote: "I approached this album, which commemorates the 25th anniversary of the New Wave Of British Heavy Metal, with enormous trepidation. But I was astonished to discover a massively refreshing celebration of all that was (and indeed still is) good about the ground-breaking late Seventies rock explosion. Amazingly, *The Second Wave...* crackles and fizzes with all the gleefully naïve, upfront and unpremeditated enthusiasm that made the NWOBHM so great in the first place." Further praise came from Glenn Butler, writing in *Powerplay* magazine, who called it "an impressive compilation...*The Second Wave* showcases three bands who were fundamental in starting the NWOBHM and therefore shaping the very nature of metal today. A very impressive release and essential listening for people who want to see where modern metal originated."

THE NEW BLOOD

Possibly the most famous band doing the rounds at the time of writing with the most obvious nod towards the NWOBHM is Blaze, the band fronted by ex-Wolfsbane and Iron Maiden singer Blaze Bailey. "I started becoming aware of music about the time of the Sex Pistols and stuff like that in the charts. The thing about punk was that it made you feel that anyone could do it, anyone could be in a band. That got me into music with guitars and attitude, and then I started to become a bit more serious about it. I wasn't allowed to have a record player or stereo when I was a kid so I went round to my mate's house and listened to Led Zeppelin's *The Song Remains The Same*, which is a huge album; when you're just getting into music it's so magical and exciting. And then I heard the first Sabbath album. It was horrific, ghastly; it really felt like the devil was coming out of the speakers. And that was it, then. Musically, that was the way I was going to go!

When I was growing up it was a great time musically, if your tastes went that way. There was the *In Concert* programme on Saturday evenings where they'd play a live gig – Rory Gallagher one week, Gillan the next, so you could tape a live gig and check out bands you didn't know as well. And living in Birmingham at that time, all the big touring bands played the Birmingham Odeon. The 'Life Changing Moment' for me was seeing Ronnie James Dio there – I was spellbound by his voice, and that was what made me want to be a singer.

We'd go and see anybody and everybody back then – there was a great club called Edwards No. 8 where the smaller bands would play; great place to see bands. It was a great time, and it was OK to like the music back then. It was acceptable, if you like, and it was great to be part of a scene. We hated the New Romantics with a vengeance! Obviously I saw Iron Maiden a number of times. I thought they were great, I was a big fan. I bought the odd NWOBHM single, but I was never a great collector of singles at all. But what I do now is pretty much a direct link back to those great days of British metal, as that was when my ideas of the kind of band I wanted and the sort of music I wanted to play came together."

Up-and-coming band UK band Intense play 21st century power metal with very direct references to the NWOBHM. "To be honest, I had quite a late induction to heavy metal courtesy of a friend of mine when I first started work," says frontman Sean Hetherington. "I'd been listening to a bit of Status Quo – had been since school really – and he said 'Try this… and this… and this' and I started borrowing a lot of albums. I was drawn to mainstream metal I guess, you know, Maiden, Whitesnake, Warlock and then came Def Leppard and many American bands like Tesla, Dio and Skid Row. I became so engrossed in the music, I bought a guitar, started singing and thought I should be in a band and hey presto… I went and did it! I liked the heavy metal attitude of not caring what people thought about you and doing what *you* wanted; the whole rebellion thing I guess. I liked to be different and I never believed being into metal was a fashion statement; it was a lifestyle and I still believe that today.

"Intense was started by myself and a group of friends when we were pretty young. Everyone lived in Basingstoke and it was kind of like, 'Let's start a band...' We did the usual demos, played gigs etc and then the band became a serious going-concern. In 1997 we self financed a six-track CD *Dark Season* and I put it out through my own label Full Volume Records. It was very successful for a self-financed release and got distribution as far as Japan. After that the old chestnut of musical differences came up and I rebuilt the band to the line-up we have today. Our first full length album *Second Sight* was released in 2004 when we also played our first European shows plus our first UK festival appearance at Bloodstock.

At the time of the NWOBHM, I was alive and kicking but hadn't discovered metal. But I can appreciate that the NWOBHM was a very important period for metal music and set a precedent for many bands. It influenced bands all over the world as well as, of course, later British bands and I don't think we would have the scene we have now without it. Iron Maiden and Saxon are still holding true. I saw Maiden at Earls Court in 2003 and was surprised at how strong they have become once again – it's a joy to see such 'masters of their trade' back at work. I also got to see Saxon at Wacken and they were superb also. I had a friend of mine introduce me to Rock Goddess years ago so I do have a soft spot for them; they had some great songs. But if you look at a list of the bands included in the NWOBHM listing, there are loads of them and, to be truthful, there's plenty of them I've never heard of. As with all scenes some rise above the rest and succeed.

I wouldn't have said we were overtly influenced by the NWOBHM, but then I don't really analyse our sound too much anyway. I think we as a band are conscious of the elements that make up our sound but if we started worrying about those elements too much, we'd be too paranoid to write anything. But I have no problem whatsoever with comparisons to the NWOBHM; I believe it's quite a compliment actually."

Surprisingly, goth metal band Liquid Sky see themselves as very much NWOBHM influenced. "I feel that the NWOBHM was absolutely essential to the development of metal music and that there is probably not a single metal band playing today that doesn't owe *something* to one NWOBHM band or another," says guitarist Jon Craven. "I'd suggest that without bands like Iron Maiden and Diamond Head, much of the sound of many of the heavier bands of the Eighties and Nineties (Metallica, Slayer, etc) would never have come about. Likewise, I think that Def

Leppard's success suddenly showed record companies that the American market was ripe for the taking if presented with the right formula of attitude and stadium-friendly songs, as played later by the likes of Bon Jovi and Guns N' Roses.

Although I hate to risk pigeon-holing ourselves, if forced I would probably best describe our sound as 'dark metal' – not to be confused or classified with death or black metal by any means. It just takes into account some of our influences from bands that are gothically-tinged and also refers to the general 'dark' sound and lyrical content of much of our work. Our sound incorporates elements from many different facets of the rock and metal genre, as well as hints of other musical styles as well, and we draw influences from bands such as Lacuna Coil, Dream Theater, Paradise Lost, Soilwork and Type O Negative. However, the band's sound has been changing and evolving steadily and constantly over the past four to five years to the point where we now actually have very obvious nods to our NWOBHM forebears in much of our music. From my earliest NWOBHM influences – Iron Maiden and Def Leppard – I probably gained several traits that are fundamental to the band's sound today: the heaviness, the love of guitar solos, and the epic scale similar to many of Maiden's songs and the irresistible melodies and hooks similar to those that are intrinsic to much of Def Leppard's music.

Of all the NWOBHM bands, though, Iron Maiden is the one means the most to me. I think it is very easy to underestimate the impact and influence that this band has had on individuals, bands, heavy metal and the music scene in general since their formation. And I do have a bit of a soft spot for Def Leppard as well! 'Photograph' has one of the best hooks ever in a song and can 17 million people be wrong when it comes to the *Hysteria* album?"

IT IS THE MUSIC THAT MATTERS

"We should have hung on to the NWOBHM more really, and sort of cherished it," says Sean Harris. "When you look at what came after, the next generation of bands from America, it was all a direct result of the NWOBHM. It should be more celebrated than it is, if for no other reason than its place in the evolution of heavy metal." And he's right. It is the past that informs the present and creates the future – or at least creates the environment in which the future can develop. The NWOBHM is what it was (and I make no apologies for that); a snapshot in time, a particular era in the development of the loud 'n' heavy music that many people at least flirt with during their teens. Certainly it's flawed by today's standards: the production is pretty raw (but was good for the time's analogue sixteen or twenty-four track studios), the playing on some records is 25% talent and 75% enthusiasm, and some of the lyrics... Well, I wrote once that the bands were in general fuelled by "first pints, first shags and first horror films" and their lyrics rolled everything into one big youthful fantasy. What else was there to write about? Nothing curtails aspirations and experiences like the increasingly high rates of unemployment that characterised the end of the Seventies in the UK.

But the NWOBHM was also a link to what was to follow and, in that respect, it was the progenitor that spawned the global rise of heavy metal and turned it into an acceptable music form for the masses for a healthy chunk of the Eighties. Furthermore, it led to the rise of speed metal, thrash metal, black metal and so on, all of which are no more than sub-genres of what was just heavy metal, pure and simple, but all related to the NWOBHM.

Celebrate the movement and, above all, enjoy the music. As the late, great Tommy Vance used to say, "it's the music that matters," and you know what? He was spot on.

CHAPTER SIX

IT'S THE MUSIC THAT MATTERS ...

T here's no point in having the Flying V, the bullet belt, the studded wristband, arse-length hair, bike jacket and spray-on spandex pants if you haven't got the songs to back it up. At the end of the day, the only thing that's important is the music, and the fact that it's still of interest to fans now is a testament to its quality and power.

THE SONGS THEMSELVES...

"My motivation for my songwriting and recording is to have been part of writing something classic; and you can't know if it's classic because it has to seep into the consciousness of the rock community," Blaze Bailey told me. "It has to be there for a long time, it has to be one of those songs that's pulled out and played again and again, and played in twenty years' time. So a lot of that motivation is to come up with a song that screams 'This is a classic!'"

Every time I interviewed someone, I asked them to pick one of their own songs and to tell me how it came about, or what it means to them.

These are all classics.

'A TIME OF CHANGES' BY BLITZKRIEG

'A Time Of Changes' was always ear-marked as the title track of the album that never was, and when Brian Ross finally decided to record the songs that would have made up that original album in 1984 (with ex-'Krieg members Jim Sirotto, as he then spelled his name, and Mick Moore alongside Satan's drummer Sean Taylor and guitarist Mick Procter) the song rightfully took pride of place. The one-off turned into a permanent reformation which has led to countless line-up changes and a number of releases over the years, the latest being 2005's *Sins And Greed* CD. A slow start, the fast section, twin guitar solos; everything you need in a NWOBHM song. Like 'Hell To Pay' later on, the original rough demo version can also be found on the 2003 Sanctuary Records double CD *A Time Of Changes – The Anthology*. The demo version is slower, and, as befits its epic status, two minutes longer.

Brian Ross: "My favourite Blitzkrieg song is 'A Time Of Changes' – always has been and it always will be – both because I like the song itself and am proud of the lyrics, and because it was a bit of a challenge to write. Jim came up with the music which we thought sounded kind of Eastern rhythmically, but I didn't know enough at that time about Eastern religions and mythology to write anything meaningful in that vein. Then I came up with the idea for 'A Time Of Changes': I thought, let's take the Sermon On The Mount and change it to 'blessed are the meek for they have had nothing, the doors of the world have been slammed in their faces...' It was based on what I thought Jesus would say if he came back today, and it gave me a chance to say what I wanted to say. I am quite a religious person in my own way, and it's a part of my life that means a lot to me.

But it is a song of hope, believe it or not. The world is changing, and so there is always hope. If you believe Jesus is going to come back, this is what he's going to see and it must change. I don't mean necessarily as in the Apocalypse of The Book of Revelations, but I think it would change for the better. Jim really loved what I'd written. He'd written rough ideas for the lyrics for 'Saviour' – 'the man in the shroud spoke to the crowd, and His name was hallowed, Believer!' – so the two songs complemented each other and made a great run-off to the album when I finally recorded it at the end of 1984. So we sat down with his music and tweaked it to fit the pattern of the lyrics and that was that.

The voice-over I added a lot later. When I finally came to record the album I thought, 'How the hell am I going to start this song off? How am

I going to make it a bit different?' So I went back to the Sermon On The Mount itself and recorded the voice over – then bang! – straight into the main riff.

We don't play it live, largely because it's quite difficult to pull off, although I remember we did it back in 1985 when I first reformed the band. There are probably better Blitzkrieg songs, in fact I know there are, but this is the one that means the most to me."

'AM I EVIL?' BY DIAMOND HEAD

Diamond Head – the band much beloved by Metallica who recorded cover versions of 'Helpless', 'The Prince', and this, Diamond Head's epic of epics. Originally released on the band's self-financed untitled *White Label* or *White Album* in 1980 and subsequently re-recorded for the band's debut album for MCA *Borrowed Time* in 1982, 'Am I Evil?' must be one of the most instantly recognisable songs of all time; the 'Mars' intro, through the main riff to the fast middle section, the inspirational guitar solo and the main riff revisited for the outro. It's a prime example of a song written and performed by a band who knew that for eight minutes they held the world by its balls. Ah, what might have been...

Brian Tatler: "We started taping stuff while we were looking for a singer, and found we learned a lot by taping every new song and analysing the structures. That's how we learned and improved our songwriting.

I think 'Am I Evil?' will always be the most important song to me; it's certainly become our most famous and made the most money. I think it started with my riff and Sean and Colin both liked it straight away – I personally like the way it's the same riff over and over again for about two-and-a-half minutes with just the key of it and the drum pattern changing. We linked it to the fast section later which was probably another song we had in the pipeline, and then the intro was added on which of course was inspired by 'Mars' from the *Planet Suite*. And finally came the guitar solo which I didn't finish until we were in the studio, just in the nick of time! I was and still am very pleased with the finished song; it must have taken about 18 months on and off to write. Actually, I wanted to write a song heavier than Sabbath's 'Symptom Of The Universe' – that was my original goal! The rest of the band were up for it, but then why shouldn't they be? If there was something several us of didn't like, we would always change it."

'AXE CRAZY' BY JAGUAR

Thrash metal started at Neat Records with Raven and Jaguar. Jaguar's first single 'Back Street Woman' lacked finesse, and decent vocals come to that, but then along came its successor 'Axe Crazy' and the world was never quite the same again. 'War Machine' on the flip-side showed that 'Axe Crazy' was no fluke, with numerous time changes and a heavy riff, reminiscent of early Iron Maiden. The band cut three songs at the session, the out-take being 'Dirty Tricks' which appeared on Neat Records' *60 Minutes Plus Heavy Metal Compilation* cassette.

"It was just about us being axe crazy, guitar crazy."

Garry Pepperd: "'Axe Crazy' is all tongue-in-cheek, like a lot of our stuff was, and came about because at the time we just loved playing fast. Basically we came up with the bones of the song and thought, 'Wow! This is great fun!' you know, double bass going ten-to-the-dozen, so we came up with the rough song and thought 'This is brilliant, this is really fast, and we can really bang our heads to it, so we've really got to make a song out of it!' It was born from that really. The title 'Axe Crazy' is actually a reference to guitars, not 'axe' as in the tool as some people later misunderstood; it was a reference to playing guitars fast, a kind of an homage really, I suppose, and it was just about us being axe crazy, guitar crazy, about getting a guitar and saying 'See you in two minutes, see you at the other end!' I guess the connection would have been explained a little bit better by the original artwork; we've got these photographs of us with as many guitars as we could find – it sounds really silly now! – we found guitars and bits of guitars and we had this shot where we just sat there with bits of guitars everywhere. Neat rejected the artwork and so sadly a little bit of the meaning got lost. There's a bit of paying homage to certain favourite songs in there as well, I would say. It was just so brilliant to play so fast. So 'Axe Crazy' is just that; a song of joy to fast guitar playing!

We put 'War Machine' on the B-side because, as I recall, we picked what we thought were the best two songs we had available, and besides, as much as we loved playing fast we did try to vary things a bit, so it was good to have a fast one and a slower one. Light and shade, as

Jimmy Page would say. But we didn't think the single was going to do as well as it did. We didn't give it any thought, we just recorded it and let it go. We weren't that 'deep' about it, if you like, we just did it. It was great fun, you know? 'Wow, it's going to come out as a single!' And yeah, I was quite surprised that it did so well. Again, I look back and think, 'the production, oh God!' But that was the sound of the time; it's a good example of the genre, you know from the second wave of the NWOBHM.

I wouldn't say it was an albatross at all, we play whatever people want to hear – you know, give them what they want. If people shout for a particular song then we'll play it. When you're rehearsing a song that old it can be a bit, 'Oh no, not again,' but we still play it now. It's just that I'm knocking on a bit now and it's a bit of an effort to play it these days! The drummer's like, 'Are you ready?' and I'm like – [takes three long, deep breaths] – 'OK, go!' I have to psyche myself up for it these days, even though it's only two-and-a-half minutes long! But yeah, we still do it, we're happy to do it, and on the Continent we really have to play it, like we have to play 'Back Street Woman' and 'War Machine' too. They're the ones people shout for."

'CRY TO THE WIND' BY SABRE

For a long time only three recordings existed of Sabre, the two sides of the single 'Miracle Man' and 'Cry To The Wind', recorded at the same time and issued on the Neat Records' *60 Minute Plus Heavy Metal Compilation* cassette album in November 1982. Recently *Roar To The Core*, a CD of demos and rehearsal material, has been released, but this is the one that does it for me, a perfect example of how to do classy melodic rock. File under 'what might have been…' (again).

Geoff Gillespie: "'Cry To The Wind' was, in all fairness, about as heavy as Sabre got, and I think grew out of a desire to show to ourselves as much as anyone else that we could play in a heavier vein. Even then, it ended up being melodic, and none the worse for that. The bulk of the material that remains unrecorded is much more Thin Lizzy in feel, with much use of the twin guitars. With 'Cry To The Wind', Allan Angold the drummer and I wanted a track that was very rhythm-section led, and I think we achieved just that. Early rehearsal versions that I have on tape are sometimes on the verge of coming off the rails completely – total mayhem! The tempo and overall pace of the song made it hard at times to fit the lyrics in! I had written some old cobblers about Vikings and Valhalla, and it all got a bit wordy.

I feel immensely proud of what we as a band had achieved, and with that one track I felt we came of age to some degree. As I said earlier, it wasn't particularly representative of what we did, but it did show what we were capable of. With more time to record the track – the Neat session had us tacking the track on at the end of the last day in what little time remained – it could have been pretty damn special. That being said, I am not a revisionist. It is what it is, warts 'n' all.

As for what came next, well, the single was actually received pretty well, and even to this day seems to be reasonably well regarded. I can remember Howard Johnson's Kerrang! review, which was very kind indeed. I have seen signed copies in Japan that have sold for £20 and upwards… it's a sick world, you know!"

'DON'T TOUCH ME THERE' BY TYGERS OF PAN TANG

The song that launched both Tygers Of Pan Tang and Neat Records in one fell swoop. Originally released as the A-side of the band's debut single (backed by 'Burnin' Up' and 'Bad Times') on Neat Records in 1979, and subsequently re-recorded for the band's debut album *Wild Cat*. OK, the production is poor, but crank it up and hear the Tyger roar! They did write better songs, but for the vibe, and for what was to follow, things didn't get much better than this.

Jess Cox: "I was playing rhythm guitar in another band and Brian Robb and Rocky were doing covers, stuff like Ted Nugent. I went along a few nights later and thought, 'Yeah, OK,' but it was still just covers. But they had this one original song with no lyrics, so I put some lyrics to it – just hummed along at first to get a melody line, put some words together, and that was it – 'Don't Touch Me There'. I'd never actually written any lyrics before. It was all a bit tongue-in-cheek. I'd been a lifeguard on Whitley Bay beach – 'went down the beach, a little girl there, hey babe I could make you care…,' a kind of role reversal thing really, she's making all the moves and he's saying 'don't touch me there…'

We didn't have any gigs at the time, we were just rehearsing and rehearsing at first. Our first gig was at the club where I'd met Robb. The barmaid fancied Robb so we sent him in with the idea of getting a gig by getting to the management through her. We played all these covers with 'Don't Touch Me There' tagged on. The local bike fraternity had turned up and we ended up as the resident band there. That must have been late '78. In January '79 we went into Neat's studios just as punters to record a demo tape. I think that's when we decided it should be the first single. We'd begun to write quite quickly; even though 'Don't Touch Me There' didn't come out till the end of '79, a year later, by the time we'd come to record it (which would have been sometime that summer) we had more than an album's worth of songs written, but we still chose that one, and backed it with 'Bad Times' and 'Burnin' Up'. I mean, when you're doing these things as kids you just do it, you really don't pontificate about it.

The reaction to the single was fantastic. It's funny; it's so difficult to explain to people now because there was no mass media, no internet, just *Sounds* and *The Friday Rock Show* on Radio One. So I mean, for us to be in the local paper was a really big deal. Then we had a good review followed by a big feature in *Sounds*. The single really propelled us. From that MCA signed us and then re-released 'Don't Touch Me There' on MCA. We were signed on the strength of that single – so, really, it was everything. As a song, 'Don't Touch Me There' made the band.

"A good song's a good song – and we had some good songs. That's one of the things about the New Wave Of British Heavy Metal; there were some great songs written – great hooks, melodies – and they have stood the test of time. A lot of later bands did sound the same – Anthrax, Megadeth, you know. But that's another thing about the New Wave thing: at least everyone sounded different, distinctive. Iron Maiden didn't sound like Def Leppard, Def Leppard didn't sound like us, we didn't sound like, I don't know, Saxon... Well, we did a bit I suppose," he laughs. "I think that's why the interest is still there though, because the songs have stood the test of time."

'EN CACHENT' BY SHIVA

A beautiful, well-crafted, well-played song by one of the most under-rated bands of all time, originally released on the only album they put out in their lifetime, *Firedance,* on Heavy Metal Records in 1982.

Andy Skuse: "Getting *Firedance* finished was a real struggle; we were gigging all over the place, had no money and had to work extra to make ends meet by renting and manning our PA system for other bands and doing delivery runs using the band-mobile. The record company paid for the recording time of course, but we were such perfectionists we soon spent up all the time we'd been allocated. Step in our friends at Cave

Studios, Bristol, once more! Stuff like the extended middle section of 'Shiva' were made up as we went along and involved some unusual improvisations using whatever came to hand; Chris could make percussion out of anything, including potato peelers and steel tubes! I still feel *Firedance* is a really good effort, and we did have better in the pipeline too before it all came unstuck...

As for a favourite song...? Okay, this is a purely personal choice, but my favourite song on the album has to be 'En Cachent', hence its appearance on *Heavy Metal Heroes II*. This was one of John's songs, although the music was always a joint effort to some extent or other. I've only got a vague idea as to what it's about lyrically but the melody and particularly the guitar solo still do it for me even now – amazing. The original track was demoed with the previous line-up and there were some obvious flaws but I felt that the solo was something really special so we had John try and duplicate it for the album. Usually he just went with the flow so making a copy of a previous solo was a little more tricky, but it worked. We had great fun adding various effects during the recording, especially the waves and seagulls courtesy of a BBC sound effects record! We always liked to add different instruments to the mix if we could, in this case a grand piano played by John.

I think it's my favourite because I have always gone for songs with a lot of light and dark, both lyrically and in intensity. Songs which start off light and burst into full-blast guitar crescendos have so much more impact that those which are all on a level. The lyrics are also typically Shiva; you need to make up your own mind what it's all about. Knowing John it's been inspired by a book he's read at some point but I never wanted to ask him and spoil the secret. I can tell you though that the title means 'in hiding', by the way."

'GIVE 'EM HELL' BY WITCHFYNDE

I have a real soft spot for Witchfynde, as I saw them on the 1980 Def Leppard tour and thought they really were the business, but they never got the breaks they deserved. They had the unfortunate habit of ending up on record labels that went bust – Rondelet, Expulsion and finally Mausoleum – which fairly obviously did their career no favours at all. And after their initial, very positive, press (around the time of the first album and the Def Leppard tour), both *Sounds* and later *Kerrang!* seemed to revel in having fun at the band's expense and completely missed the point that Witchfynde were writing some of the most interesting and exciting songs of the NWOBHM. 'Give 'Em Hell' was originally released as a single on Rondelet Records in February 1980, taken from the album of the same name, released a few months later. A live version appeared on a bonus 12" single that came with the first pressing of their 1984 LP *Lords Of Sin*, the band's last album for the best part of twenty years. They re-appeared in 2001 with *The Witching Hour*, a CD which featured a new singer, three new songs and re-recordings of six older favourites including this one.

Montalo: "'Give 'Em Hell' is what started everything off for us and has become a trademark for us and a bit of a catch-phrase. It encompasses everything there is about the band, and is a very basic, a very raw song. It was not the first thing we'd written, we'd done loads of songs before it, but this is the one where we said, 'we're going to record this and put it out ourselves.' And then came the deal with Rondelet. So it's a song that's very important to us as a band, and still relevant to us to this day. We still use it to round off the set, and is probably the favourite song of all of us."

'HEAVY METAL MANIA' BY HOLOCAUST

The band's first single, subsequently re-recorded for their debut album *The Nightcomers* with a different opening passage, 'Heavy Metal Mania' is the ultimate heavy metal anthem, the perfect introduction to Holocaust, and the first step in John Mortimer's quest to combine heavy metal and power to the *n*th degree and take them to the ultimate extreme. A lot of people didn't get it then and don't get it now – but then, that's their loss.

John Mortimer: "'Heavy Metal Mania' was the second song I ever wrote ('It Don't Matter To Me' was the first). It all came to be in about ten minutes in my bedroom after school one day, all the parts in the right order, virtually all the lyrics in their final form. I've never written anything so spontaneously since. I'd only had my guitar for about two weeks and I still didn't have an amp, so I just had to imagine the distorted sound!

Ed Dudley and I were the first to the practice session at which I first presented the song, and the two of us just kind of got that instrumental intro piece together, based on the middle/solo section riff. Everyone else thought it would be cool to have it at the start of the song, but John Mayer, owner of Phoenix Records, reckoned it didn't suit the single concept. To be honest, I think he was right; we just got excited about an instrumental part like that because it was the first one we'd ever tried. Personally, I prefer the song without it; having said that, it is surprising how many fans complain about us not doing the intro live!

Anyway, when I said virtually all the lyrics were in their final form, the lines, 'rock 'n' roll was far too slow / so the adrenaline does not flow' were originally 'rock 'n' roll was far too slow / punk... it's as bad as soul' but John Mayer asked us to change that because he said he could see 'hundreds of £5 notes flying away out of the window.' He reckoned a lot of punks would like the song.

As to what influenced the song, I would sum it up by saying it was a

"What similarity is there between Eddie Cochrane's 'Summertime Blues' and, say, 'Overkill'?"

very special feeling... A feeling that I wanted to dedicate my entire life to this music I had found. I always insisted on the expression 'heavy metal' rather than 'heavy rock', because at that time I disliked the rock 'n' roll roots of the bands we all adored and I wanted to see a more abstract, purer form of heaviness distilled out from all the blues and rock 'n' roll of the past. It used to really irritate me when Lemmy would say something like, 'Motörhead is just a rock 'n' roll band...' and I would think, 'You're kidding, man... what similarity is there between Eddie Cochrane's 'Summertime Blues' and, say, 'Overkill'?' I've got to say, I can see what he means now, but back then it seemed like a daft statement. Anyway, I could see the possibilities for the future of metal if it developed onwards and upwards, away from its rock and blues roots. I just felt like I had a foretaste of what it would be like in the future, and it was glorious!"

'HELL TO PAY' BY BLITZKRIEG

A fast 'n' furious slice of metal, but not a straight-forward sprint to this finish; 'Hell To Pay' takes a few diversions along the way to keep headbangers and drummers on their toes. The album version on *A Time Of Changes* was augmented by a phoney crowd track as an in-joke. "We did the *Blitzed Alive* tape totally live," Brian Ross once told me, "but dropped in some audience noise to beef the crowd up a bit; unfortunately, we overdid it, and people assumed the tape was fake. So, with 'Hell To Pay' we dropped the crowd in from a Queen album onto the studio track, but this time everyone thought it was real!" The band's original demo version can be found on the 2003 Sanctuary Records CD *A Time Of Changes – Phase 1*.

Jim Sieroto: "We had a song, 'Vikings', which was intended to be a concept piece taking up at least one side of an album. As it was, only Part One was ever realised, and finally made it onto vinyl on the *A Time Of Changes* LP. The ending of the third part was recycled as the ending of 'Hell To Pay', influenced by Mott The Hoople's 'Thunderbuck Ram'. The main riff was original, but the drop down by a semi-tone at the end of each line I got from 'Better By You, Better Than Me' by Spooky Tooth (recently covered at the time by Judas Priest). The original demo was improvised in one take, with an Akai tape deck linked up to a stereo cassette deck so that I could produce demos in stereo.

The chorus 'there's gonna be hell to pay' just sounded great from the start but I had trouble with the rest of the lyrics; I was stuck for lyrics for the verses but found that Ozzy's lyrics to 'Black Sabbath' fitted so sang these on the demo. I remember the 'if we don't stop it now' bit came very naturally though and seem to recall that the band's finances were very dodgy and as I was bankrolling it, it was a cry from the heart! But checking back on my records I saw that 'Hell To Pay' was first played in front of an audience at Leicester University on May 1, 1981, so relatively early in the band's first incarnation. I would think that my mood was very optimistic at this time and that the dramatic lyrics were probably just me using artistic licence. I would just hear stuff in my head and transcribe it onto tape as best as I could – whatever it was, I could always 'hear' complete performances of it by the band. Most of my songs I just heard in my head. Having the overdubbing facilities of my tape deck was great, as it meant I could play the finished thing back to everybody. Often I'd just scribble things down on paper at the oddest times – the chorus to 'Take A Look Around' came to me just as I was getting into bed one night!

Blitzkrieg later recorded the song at the local Q Studios, and it is this version that appears on the Sanctuary release, with heavy metal verse lyrics written by Brian. I always thought 'Hell To Pay' was a great name for a heavy metal track and it's my favourite track from that era."

INTO THE FUTURE BY SATAN

I got to know Satan pretty well about the time of their re-birth and was pretty much blown away when they played me the fruits of a day in the studio – the *Dirt* demo. I remember listening to it on a Walkman with the guys sat around in Sean Taylor's flat waiting to see what I'd say. It retained a lot of the old *Court In The Act*-era sound, but with an obvious nod to the direction Metallica were heading in and an edge so hard it could have been a Soho nightclub bouncer. SPV Records signed the band on the strength of the demo and pressed it up as the *Into The Future EP*, featuring all four songs ('Key To Oblivion', 'Hear Evil, See Evil, Speak Evil', 'Fuck You' and 'The Ice Man') from the tape. A welcome return for the band after the bad career move that had been Blind Fury.

Russ Tippins: "My favourite song? Well, it's not a song, as I'd have to choose the *Into The Future EP*. That's the best thing we ever did, in my opinion. It was also the first thing we did with the new singer Mick Jackson, and I think it's his best ever performance too.

The whole thing was recorded and mixed in a day – well, 28 hours actually; we arrived at the studio at 10 o'clock and left 2 o'clock the following day. The session went well, we went in and bang! bang! bang!, it was done, just like that. It was the first time we'd used Roy Rowland too as a producer rather than as an engineer – he'd been the engineer on the Blind Fury *Out Of Reach* LP, and I think the results speak for themselves. We only recorded it at first as a demo – the *Dirt* demo – but it was through that demo that we got the record deal with SPV, and of course the first thing they did was press it up and release it as the *Into The Future EP*.

We always wrote the same way – either Bean, Steve or I would bring in a new idea and then see if anyone could add anything or do anything with it. I still think that's the best thing we've done. It did actually come out on CD through Steamhammer USA with *Suspended Sentence*, the album that followed it, on the same CD. Personally, I prefer the sound on the original vinyl though; you know, a 12" EP with big grooves, it sounds pretty fantastic; well, it does on my system anyway!"

'NOONDAY' BY ARAGORN

A bit of an odd song really, and not straight-down-the-line metal but a quirky-punky hybrid. Originally released as one side of the double A-sided single by the band (c/w 'Black Ice') on Neat Records in 1981, the song was subsequently included on the Neat Records compilation cassette *Lead*

Weight. As an aside, 'Black Ice' on the other side was one of two songs (Angel Witch's 'Extermination Day' being the other) that Celtic Frost used in their early days when they were short of material for their formative live set.

Mike Ellis: "We'd recorded a demo in October 1980 and one evening Chris Dunne took it to a local metal DJ, Chris Tetley. He wasn't at all keen on 'yet another' demo but he gave it a listen, liked it, made a call or three and a month later we were trundling up the A1 to Wallsend to record 'Black Ice' and 'Noonday'. I was particularly pleased as another drummer friend of mine had called me round to his place earlier in the year to hear this 'great new band' who turned out to be Raven. I loved it, so I was really chuffed that Aragorn were going to be the next release on Neat. As soon as we'd finished recording 'Noonday', everyone felt that it was the stronger of the two tracks, although personally I still favour 'Black Ice'. All the radio stations picked up on 'Noonday' although officially the single was actually a double A–side. "

'ONE OF THESE DAYS' BY TRESPASS

THAT intro, followed by THAT riff. Like Mark Sutcliffe, when I did this interview I hadn't heard the BBC version since it was broadcast way back when, and like Lars Ulrich I prefer the *Metal For Muthas Volume II* version. The original single cut sneaks up and mugs you from behind, whereas the re-recorded version punches you full in the face – BAM! TKO! – and leaves you sprawled on the canvas with a halo of cartoon stars and tweeting birds. All the versions were eventually corralled up and included on the Sanctuary Records' *One Of These Days – The Anthology* double CD.

Mark Sutcliffe & Dave Crawte: "'One Of These Days' was one of our first songs, and certainly one of the first lyrics that I ever wrote," says Mark. "We did the song with my cousin on bass to start with, with a completely different riff, and then I bought this bashed about old synthesiser and wrote some of the intro parts on that to start with – it made the most godawful noises; it would suddenly go wrong and just go 'bleuuur'!! It was an interesting gadget, to say the least! I suppose the intro... well, I don't know where it came from; my brother says it's a rip-off of 'Love To Love' by UFO – although that's in E! But I guess there is a definite similarity. It's in the slide down, I think, and it's because you *do* pick up influences – you know, 'I like that, it turns me on, therefore I want to do it as well.' That's what music's all about. And I was very much into Lizzy – that kind of choppy riff in the verse, that's very much a Lizzy kind of thing. But Dave and I had a way of playing – the rhythm guitar work we did together was very solid, almost like one guitar, you know, and I think that helps the song along.

It was actually written about a girl that I pursued but was never actually able to get my hands on... Ahh, another love lost! The way I see it, music can be throwaway pop or you can try and make it mean something. You don't have to make it mean something with the lyrics, there's plenty of music out there with no lyrics, going back to classical music – the emotion is conveyed by the music, there are no words, you know? But as soon as you put words on something it conveys a different meaning because those lyrics take over everything. So I find it quite difficult to write imaginings and things like that; it's easier to write about real life."

"I think one of the reasons that people picked up on 'One Of These Days' is that a good intro makes a good song – and it is a good intro," adds Dave. "The version of the song on *Metal For Muthas II* is a lot heavier, which is a reflection of the direction we were starting to move in," notes Mark. "For a start, the gear had changed. On the early stuff we had combos and basic guitars; by the time we recorded that we had Marshall stacks and we were really cranking it, really rockin' by then. But for me, the definitive version would have to be the original 45. I know Lars Ulrich prefers the *Metal For Muthas II* version. I mean, I know it's better recorded, but for me, it's got to be the single – that's the one. As for *The Friday Rock Show* session, I don't think I've heard it since pretty much when we recorded it!"

'RUNNING FREE' BY IRON MAIDEN

The first single for EMI in a collectable picture sleeve and a live performance on *Top Of The Pops* that made everyone stop and stare for three minutes (the *TOTP* version was an edit). The story goes that when the single was released the band refused to mime, but no-one at EMI cared because metal bands didn't have hit singles anyway. Then 'Running Free' charted in its first week and the label had a problem. The compromise solution was that the band would only appear if they could play live and, surprisingly, the BBC agreed. From such small acorns, as the saying goes...

Paul Di'Anno: "We always had a belief in ourselves. Even when we did the *Soundhouse Tapes* we thought we were heading straight for the big time, but it was also wishful thinking to a degree; but when it really did start to take off we all wanted to take credit for our individual foresight! I think we knew, though. Quite frankly, most of the other bands at the time were just part-timers and they came across that way. We had a definite magic to us, and I think we became so big so quickly because we were a young band that kids could actually relate to.

We did the BBC session which actually was quite boring to do although the outcome was great, the two songs for the *Metal For Muthas* album which, as far as we were concerned, was the first step to the big time, and then 'Running Free' on *Top Of The Pops*. 'Running Free' is probably my favourite song from that time. It was more or less my song ...After that performance I became a more arrogant bastard than I already was, if that was possible!" [The song is credited on the sleeve to Di'Anno/Steve Harris]

'SILVER SCREEN TEASER' BY SOLDIER

The band that Heavy Metal Records' Paul Birch regrets never doing an album with. First time round, Soldier's legacy – just the excellent 'Sheralee' 7" and a track ('Storm Of Steel') on the *Heavy Metal Heroes* compilation album – just didn't do the band justice (like Blitzkrieg, there was also a live cassette album entitled *Live Forces*, but Garry Phillips reckoned that it was a very limited release), but when they effectively called it a day at the beginning of 1983 that appeared to be the end of things. The band reformed twenty years later and recorded the *Infantrycide* CD EP, and now appear to be well and truly back in business. The original version of this song (and the rest of the demo) is now available on a CD entitled *Heavy Metal Force*, along with some live material and a 2003 demo of 'I'm Taken In'.

Garry Phillips: "I've always written weird lyrics, it's just what comes to me really. We were never a band to do the 'traditional' heavy metal stuff – you know, death, doom, Satan, black sabbaths, that sort of stuff. A lot of what we do is either very tongue-in-cheek or political. The band went into the studios to record their first demo where we recorded 'Silver Screen Teaser', 'Magician', 'Circuit Breaker' and...there was another, I'm sure of it. All the rest had lyrics apart from 'Silver Screen Teaser'. Now I'd only heard it a couple of times and was watching TV in my flat and there was a programme about Marlene Dietrich (at least, I think it was her; I really can't remember now!). But the programme was about her being gay or bisexual, so I wrote these lyrics about not needing a man, or not needing a man all the time anyway. I visualised it with a big theatrical ending, you know, violins, the works! First lyrics I had ever written, as well. When we reformed and recorded the *Infantrycide* EP, it was an obvious choice.

I remember that after my first audition-stroke-rehearsal, I went back to Ian's where his wife cooked this wonderful fry-up. Now, remember, I didn't really know this guy from Adam, I'd only met him earlier that day. I shook a bottle of ketchup and completely redecorated their kitchen. I was always breaking things; the band used to call me Crusher!"

'STRANGERS ON THE SHORE' BY BITCHES SIN

Bitches Sin were criminally under-rated by the mainstream and the severe kicking of their debut album in *Kerrang!* hit them hard. That said, they had a loyal cult following and wrote a number of short 'n' snappy well-constructed songs. 'Strangers On The Shore' is to my mind the best of the bunch, especially in its original form where it is probably *the* stand-out track on the *Heavy Metal Heroes* compilation. It was subsequently re-recorded for the band's debut album *Predator*.

Ian and Pete Toomey: "'Strangers On The Shore' is a favourite of mine, and a very good example of what Bitches Sin is about. Pete wrote the song and it was his interpretation of the Acker Bilk classic of the same name. Inspired!" notes Ian.

"The truth about 'Strangers On The Shore' if I remember rightly," adds Pete, "was that it was meant to be a total contrast to the Acker Bilk classic and I guess in that I succeeded! The inspiration came from Queen's 'Brighton Rock' and the Gillan sound of the Seventies, kind of, with a manic guitar and the stomp beat verse (like John McCoy's bass playing). The lyrics were just an interpretation of a dream which I think at the time had been inspired by watching *The Hitchhikers Guide To The Galaxy* on TV, the episode where they watched the purple sea going backwards instead of forwards on the beach.

The thought of Acker Bilk in his waistcoat and bowler hat doing a rendition of the song is certainly a surreal thought but I must say it has crossed my mind on many occasions. I think what makes the song a personal favourite of mine is the way the three musical segments – although different in their own way – still manage to capture a mood and element of excitement, and to me it is one of the definitive Bitches Sin songs. In total, from memory, I think it took about thirty minutes to write;

if something works that immediately you can normally feel assured that the song has some quality to it. I think it's about the same time it took Black Sabbath to write 'Paranoid'."

"I think that at that time 'Strangers On The Shore' and 'Down The Road' were very much what Bitches Sin was about," notes Ian, "with 'Ice Angels' on the other side of the coin. Pete and I were naturally quite competitive, but when it came to who played what solo, it always came down to who had the best feel for the song. So for 'Strangers On The Shore', Pete does the opening arpeggio, then I do the opening solo, Pete the central guitar solo and I do the run out solo. Originally, in fact, there was only going to be one guitar solo in the middle of the song but on the day at the studio I played a guitar solo at the start and finish just to warm up and the guys said 'You must keep that in!' so that's why 'Strangers On The Shore' has three guitar solos!"

'SUZIE SMILED' BY TYGERS OF PAN TANG

Life Changing Moments Number One: the day the Tygers played at Torquay Town Hall and strolled down the High Street before the gig. The word 'cool' was redefined as far as I was concerned. The four Tygers personified cool. They were ultra-cool, uber-cool, cooler than a pack of polar bears at the ice cap. These were ROCK STARS, in Torquay for God's sake, all shaggy manes and bike jackets, and they looked so damned cool. Seeing them made me want to join a band. In fact I did join a band, *and* I had the shaggy mane *and* I had the bike jacket, but I was still never cool. That's life, I guess. As for this song (the band's third single from August 1980, a pointlessly edited version of a track from the band's debut album *Wild Cat* released the following month), well, I named a book after it. I think that just about says it all...

Robb Weir: "We recorded the album *Wild Cat* very quickly because by the time we came to record it we'd been playing the songs for over a year on the road. The whole experience was new to us though in as much as we were recording in a big London studio with a real producer. It all went very smoothly, as I do remember, with producer Chris Tsangarides.

My favourite old song from those days is 'Suzie Smiled'. I just love that song. As for an insight, well, remembering that I wrote the song twenty-five years ago, I'll do my best! The title came about because my sister June had just had a baby girl who she called Suzie. Now as far as I can remember I only titled the song; it was Jess who wrote the main lyrics.

In those days I would write all the music and some of the words but leave the melody up to the singer. 'Suzie…' has always been a top favourite of mine just because it rocks! And I think it stands up musically to anything you care to compare it to. When we recorded it with Chris 'Tangledgaragekeys' the first time around in Morgan Studios in 1980, he gave the guitars a bigger feel on my insistence, gave them more of an edge. I was really pleased with the finished product at the time, but I still wish my guitar sound was stronger and bigger.

Throughout the years, 'Suzie Smiled' has always been a crowd pleaser and a pleasure to play. We have given it a face-lift recently, reworked it a little with some more twin guitars and a modern half time section. I now sing it live as well; you can check it out on the live album *Live In The Roar*.

It also reminds me of what was a very special time in the late Seventies/early Eighties when I was living in London. The whole place just had a friendly 'let's-get-together, mine's-a-pint, who-are-we-off-to-see-tonight?' feel about it. Guess you had to be there…"

'TAKE CONTROL' BY RAVEN

By the time of their third album *All For One*, released on Neat Records (their last recorded for the label) in 1983, Raven began to trade speed for power – witness 'Break The Chain', the single drawn from it, as a taster of what was to come. The sound of a band maturing and discovering new musical territories.

John Gallagher: "'Take Control' is one of my favourites – some killer riffs from Mark, and Rob Hunter's drums really have a great groove on this. As a song, it introduces the whole 'power' thing we wanted to explore on the album. We wanted to break from the routine and go with a 'real' producer in a 'real' studio. We loved Accept's *Breaker* album and found out the guy who got the sounds was Mike Wagener, who was working with Udo Dirkschneider, Accept's singer as a production team. So we did the *All For One* album in a small London studio over a two-week period. It was an amazing experience; I died laughing every day, we worked our arses off and came up with a great album.

Anyway, the song's in the key of A, which for us is more exciting and brighter than E, and usually means I get to sing *really* high. The lyrics are totally autobiographical – we were taking control of what we wanted to do, we were fed up of being pushed around and being forced to do things on the cheap all the time. Technically we did some weird stuff – Mark played about four guitar tracks on this, on two of them Mike slowed the tape a tiny amount to create a subtle phasing sound that just fattened everything up. And the guitar solo actually has Rob sliding a bottleneck up the strings just before Mark plays... and on some of those signature pick slides, Mark was using a razor blade!!"

'TOO WILD TO TAME' BY AVENGER

Originally released as the A-side of the band's debut single on Neat Records in 1983 (although previously demoed by Blitzkrieg and released in this form in 2003 on the Blitzkrieg anthology *A Time Of Changes – Phase 1*), this is one of those songs that qualifies for the definitive NWOBHM workout: a killer riff, a solo to die for, the rhythm section working out like a Japanese bullet train and through-and-through heavy metal lyrics sung with passion and verve – and the whole thing is done and dusted in less than three minutes.

> *"The definitive NWOBHM workout:*
> *a killer riff, a solo to die for,*
> *the rhythm section working out like*
> *a Japanese bullet train."*

Mick Moore: "The funny thing about 'Too Wild To Tame' is that it came about while I was watching *Coronation Street* on TV – there was Hilda Ogden cleaning up at the Rover's Return while I was strumming away at what was to become the first proper song I'd written.

At that time, there was talk of Carrere signing the band, they already had Saxon on their books of course, so I was trying to write something catchy. I knew it was a cracking riff. I wasn't bothered about taking it to the band because I knew it was a great song... I thought this would make a good single; we were looking for a new single because it was about time that we did a follow-up to 'Buried Alive'. We demoed it and played the demo during an interview with Radio Leicester in November 1981, I think Jim introduced it as the rough mix of the new single, and then the band split up in December, and that was that.

I remember Brian saying that as I had given it a title he had to come up with lyrics to fit, rather than having a free hand. I usually did that though; when I wrote a piece I would give it a title because it gave it some form of identity. If you listen to a piece of music it should conjure up some kind of image or emotion; that's what music does.

Anyway, after Blitzkrieg split and Brian Ross and I decided to form Avenger, 'Too Wild To Tame' was still the obvious choice for a single. Some of the lyrics were re-written... I think I preferred the original lyrics but I think Brian co-wrote them, maybe with Jim, and re-writing them made the song more Avenger, kind of severed the links between the song and Blitzkrieg. Then of course Brian left, and Swifty came in in-between the recording of the single and its release.

'Too Wild To Tame' didn't appear on the album because I'm never very happy buying a single then finding it on the following album; I wouldn't have bothered wasting my money on the single had I known it was going to be on the LP. That said, when we recorded *Blood Sports* we found we were a bit short of material so we had to re-record the B-side 'On The Rocks'. I think the album version is slightly different, but it's been so long since I played it, I really can't remember!"

'TOTAL METAL' BY ATOMKRAFT

The brainchild of bassist/vocalist Tony 'Demolition' Dolan, Atomkraft was another one of the bands that formed the bridge between the NWOBHM and the speed metal boom – between what was and what was to come. A number of different versions of the band existed before a stable line-up with Rob Mathew and Ged Wolf gelled and landed a deal with Neat Records, and it was apt that this incarnation made its live debut opening for Slayer at The Marquee in 1985. Original Atomkraft guitarist Steve White went on to form War Machine, who issued one album *Unknown Soldier* on Neat Records in 1986. As for Atomkraft's gig at The Marquee supporting Slayer on June 24, 1985, Paul Miller, of *Forearm Smash*, reviewed it for Neat's *Lead Weight* magazine for me.

'Total Metal' was originally released on the band's debut album *Future Warriors* on Neat Records in 1985. The original demo version (as well as its demo companion 'Death Valley') can be found on the Sanctuary Records CD *Total Metal – The Neat Anthology* which features the entire officially-released Atomkraft back catalogue.

Tony Dolan: 'Total Metal,' I suppose, is *the* song, if I had to pick one of my songs, that means the most to me. It was the first track on the 1983 Atomkraft demo and when we were signed by Neat Records in 1985, albeit with a completely different line-up, it featured on our debut album, *Future Warriors*.

Originally, way back in 1982, we were planning on the album title being *Total Metal*, should we ever get lucky enough to be signed, and myself and Steve White were writing material and I was trying to fit lyrics to certain tracks in the hope of finding the title track. Nothing seemed to fit or work exactly, then one day in a rehearsal Steve came up with this riff (well, two new riffs actually) which we played around with for a week or so as instrumentals, then we booked some studio time to record. Time was restricted because of lack of money (we were unemployed at the time!) so we thought we'd concentrate on just two numbers in the recording session. We already had one backing track – minus lyrics – chosen and needed a second. The night before the session I listened to the three tracks we'd narrowed down and wrote lyrics to the first – that was 'Death Valley'. Then I spent the rest of the night trying to figure out lyrics for one of the other two songs. I couldn't find or chose lyrics that fitted so I gave up and went to bed. I got up again at 3am and wrote the other set of lyrics that we needed, and that was 'Total Metal'.

"I wanted to express what we as Kraftmen were and what we wanted to deliver as a musical entity. 'Total Metal' is an angry song. It's about not compromising at a time of conforming music. Punk was all but over and the NWOBHM had taken its place. Musically we had taken the heaviest stance but lyrically I guess I was finding it hard to let go of that punk aggression. Almost every song I have ever written since has been themed but 'Total Metal' is something real and from our hearts. I love lines like, 'at total metal, we're the best, 'coz we're the fucking dirtiest!' No greater meaning other than the fact that between myself and Steve, we *were* actually probably the dirtiest. I recall Steve actually pulling his old jeans out of a washing basket and spraying them with furniture polish to rid them of their soiled smell before we headed off for one of our shows! Now, that's dirty! I think Paul Spillet our original drummer was probably the cleanest of the three of us.

By the time we recorded the debut Atomkraft album, Venom had already released *Black Metal* and some comparisons had already been made between our heaviness and theirs, so I thought it prudent to title the album differently, again picking a themed title! But the song sums Atomkraft up: 'total' being our belief in ourselves and conviction in what we were doing and 'metal' because that's what we were all about! Just let the music tell you what it wants to say, I guess!"

'TO THE DEVIL HIS DUE' BY DIAMOND HEAD

One of the highlights of, and one of the heavier songs on the band's second 'torture-to-make-but-pleasure-to-listen-to' *Canterbury* album, 'To The Devil His Due' is another Diamond Head masterpiece, a song that maps out an epic journey and takes you there, one pace at a time.

Sean Harris: "My favourite song is actually on the new album, a song called 'Real Woman'. It's a ballad, the first real ballad I've ever written, and is more like The Eagles than heavy metal as we know it. It's just taken nine years to actually write it, but I'm very pleased with it. There's another one on the new album called 'Medusa's Gaze' which has taken me a long time to write, and is kind of classic pop/metal; I guess that's really what I want to do – I like metal with a pop edge rather than pop with a metal edge.

"As for my favourite older song... [after a long pause and much deliberation]... 'To The Devil His Due'; I guess that would be it. It took a long time to do. We'd played it live but re-arranged it before it finally appeared on *Canterbury*. I think it just got the production values I thought it needed, and when we finally got it on record it came pretty close to what I thought it should sound like."

[Unfortunately, following the split between Sean Harris and Brian Tatler, it may be that no-one ever hears either 'Real Woman' or 'Medusa's Gaze'.]

'WHEELS OF STEEL' BY SAXON

Saxon always write evocative songs – almost every lyric tells a story. My only request to Biff was not to talk about '747 (Strangers In The Night)' or 'Princess Of The Night' as everyone knows what they're about already. So he opted for 'Wheels Of Steel', possibly one of the greatest anthems of the NWOBHM and the title track of the album which set them on the path to fame and fortune.

Biff Byford: "When I'm writing lyrics, generally I'll come up with a title first (or at least I like to come up with a title first). Some people come up with certain lines and then work around that, but with me it's a strong title; as soon as I have that I have the first bit of the song written in my head already. For 'Wheels Of Steel' the original idea was actually about a steam train but I also had another idea about a steam train called 'Princess

Of The Night' which of course wasn't used until later. And at the time of 'Wheels Of Steel' we always used to have American cars, either a Pontiac Towncar or an Oldsmobile Cutlass because you could get six people in and they were quick and comfortable and cheap. And we liked the idea of having American cars. So basically I turned 'Wheels Of Steel' into a song about the American car we used to have at the time; well, actually the song is half about the car and half about racing cars, really. So it's just a general song about the car we had – 'she's got wheels of steel'," he sings, "a love affair with a car really. Lyrically, it's a '68 Chevy we have in the song, but it was in fact an Oldsmobile Cutlass." He starts to sing again: "'I've got an Oldsmobile Cutlass...' No, doesn't sound half as good as a '68 Chevy, does it! I changed it for artistic content," he laughs. "But 'Wheels Of Steel' could easily have been 'Princess Of The Night'; in fact, I'm not so sure if anyone knows what 'Princess Of The Night' is about anyway!"

A HANDFUL OF PERSONAL
NWOBHM OBSERVATIONS

I was mistaken for Duncan Scott at the Diamond Head gig at the Colston Hall in Bristol in 1982. At the time I did resemble (slightly) the drummer's photo on the sleeve of the *Borrowed Time* LP, so it was an easy mistake for any partially sighted fan to make. The guy was adamant though, and really wanted my autograph.

It's 100% true that the manager of HMV in Swansea refused to sell me Venom's *Welcome To Hell* LP. He called it "an abomination" and said he was going to send it back as faulty, claiming that when he first played the opening track he thought the stylus had missed the record and hit the edge of the turntable instead (ask your parents to explain, kids). It's also completely true that I wrote the second half of the 1985 Hammersmith Odeon Venom gig review in *Lead Weight* without actually seeing that part of the show, but needs must, as they say. No-one ever seems to have noticed, and I'm sure worse things have been done in the name of rock 'n' roll.

A band I had a soft spot for was Warfare, the brainchild of drummer/vocalist Evo whom I regard as a very clever and talented individual utterly committed to what he was trying to do. I lost touch with them after a stunt they played outside Metallica's Hammersmith Odeon gig in 1986 – they wanted to be on the bill and weren't, so played off the back of a flat-bed lorry outside until they got chased away and arrested. Their later albums displayed an almost *avant-garde* Celtic Frost approach; check out the Sanctuary Records 2002 compilation *Metal Anarchy: The Best Of Warfare*. Incidentally, the best 'get well soon' card I received while in hospital was from Evo, who scrawled across the inside: "Give me back my appendix, you cunts!!"

As a piece of complete trivia (which, I guess, is why you're reading this) I once spent a lengthy bus ride in London sitting behind Jackie Bodimead and guitarist Kat Burbella of She, who, like the bus, were on the point of going places. But I couldn't pluck up the courage to speak to them. A wasted opportunity; some journalist, eh? It was the Number 37 bus, by the way.

I am not the John Tucker of White Heat, who cut one rather good single 'Soldier Of Fortune' (b/w 'Lovemaker') in 1984, as I am sure said bassist is a far more talented individual than I. We did have a laugh over our shared name when we corresponded for a while though. Well, I did; he probably thought, 'Bugger, why do I always get the nutters?' Tell you what though; had I been in the band, this one-and-only single would not have been released in a pink picture sleeve!

Probably the most obscure NWOBHM band I ever saw would be Iona, a Welsh five-piece whose one single, the double A-side 'Don't Cry For The Innocent' c/w 'You Ain't A Lady' is listed in Malc Macmillan's *Encyclopaedia* as a "highly-prized item which should be on every serious NWOBHM wants list." A cracking night at a small pub just outside of Swansea, the gig was played as though the band were at Hammersmith Odeon; tight band, great sound, obligatory NWOBHM Flying V. Macmillan also notes that the single even made "the Number 2 position (a remarkable achievement for such a little-known outfit) in the *Melody Maker* heavy metal chart." Said chart was of course the work of Dave of Castle Records.

The weirdest record of the NWOBHM in my opinion is Severed Head's one-off 7" of 1983, 'Heavy Metal', produced by *The Friday Rock Show* producer Tony Wilson (apparently, the band wangled a session on the show, then managed to get two tracks from it put out as a single). It's so odd, it's a masterpiece! The A-side features the immortal line "Country & western, I don't like/except for Dolly Parton I could play with her all night." On the flip is 'Killing The Kidz', which is kind of a Hawkwindy, spacey thing, I think (the band, a four-piece, had a couple of backing singers/dancers too, to further the space ritual). Truth be told though, I can't be bothered to drag it out and play it.

I do regret not seeing Venom's first UK date, at the Hammersmith Odeon on June 1, 1984 on the seventh and final date of the *Seven Dates Of Hell* European tour, just for the spectacle really. I know everyone else claims to have been there, but from what I can remember of reports of the night, the upstairs of the Odeon wasn't actually open, limiting the numbers somewhat. Anyway, I was watching Kevin Heybourne's reformed Angel Witch that night at the Royal Standard, Walthamstow, which was certainly musically more interesting. In *Classic Rock* in June 2004, Geoff Barton credits Venom for introducing Metallica to Europe for the first time on that 1984 tour, but failed to mention that the support act for the UK date was joke rock 'n' blues outfit Dumpy's Rusty Nuts.

Worst NWOBHM song? My nomination would be Nightime Flyer's 'Heavy Metal Rules', the flip-side of their 'Out With A Vengeance' single, released in 1980. It's quite a collectable record, and the A-side actually isn't that bad, but if you want a real laugh, flip it over…

Neat Records' biggest gaff was their one – awful – compilation video *Metal City*. Originally titled *Metal Bitch* (which accounts for the horrendous cover), it featured Avenger, Saracen, Venom and Warfare, all getting three cuts apiece, with some of the worst link footage known to man. Avenger's 'Under The Hammer' featured the band playing in a scrapyard, while Saracen's sublime 'We Have Arrived' showed the band getting lost en route to a gig and being chased by women whose embarrassment at being videoed topless probably was nothing to how they must have felt when they saw the finished video. After that, it just gets worse…

Very little personified the NWOBHM better (aside from the under-produced sound and generally dodgy lyrics, that is; oh, and bullet belts, stripey strides, and studs; lots of studs) than the Gibson Flying V guitar. Popularised by the Schenker brothers, but used by members of Diamond Head, AIIZ, Bitches Sin, Witchfynde, Blitzkrieg, Iona etc, etc, the Gibson Flying V was as much a trademark of the NWOBHM as the studded belt or the patched denim jacket. In *Kerrang!* issue 53, Max Kay wrote: "…perhaps the ultimate in heavy metal headbanging hardware, the Gibson Flying V is one of the few really sexy instruments still available to the self-respecting poser. A distinctly firm favourite with the leather lads of Brum, it's still a high-image guitar. In fact, if you're wearing one of these, it doesn't even matter if you can't play." Perhaps that's over-egging it a bit, but it is a gorgeous guitar to look at and throw shapes with and, in an interview in *Powerplay* in June 2004, Rudolf Schenker admitted that he had over 130 Flying Vs in his collection. According to the guys at Gibson, the guitar was first introduced in 1958 and is currently still offered today, although there have been several different models or variations of the Flying V over the years.

Finally, I started writing this book in August 2003. Having finished it, the one thing that comes across to me now is the sheer naïvety of the youngsters who made the music back in the NWOBHM's glory days. How they made such good music when they were ripped off, messed around, twisted, manipulated and generally shafted by The Record Business defies belief. The heroes of *Suzie Smiled…*, I salute you!

ABOUT THE NWOBHM BANDS
IN THE BOOK...

For detailed information on each band, check out Malc Macmillan's
The New Wave Of British Heavy Metal Encyclopedia.

ARAGORN
Check out www.aragorntheband.co.uk
Recommended listening: *Noonday – The Anthology* (Sanctuary, CMRCD808)
which wraps up everything they recorded on one CD.

ATOMKRAFT
Still playing in one form or another under Tony Dolan's expert hand.
Check out www.tonydolan.net
Recommended listening: Everything's on *Total Metal – The Neat Anthology*
(Sanctuary, CMDDD994) including the entire *Future Warriors* LP, the *Kerrang!*
review of which noted (completely off the mark, by the way) that "...there's less
here than meets the eye. The retarded team of Rob Mathew (possibly guitar),
Ged Wolf (probably drums) and Tony 'Demolition' Dolan (general noize) is so
narrow-minded they could probably all look through a key-hole with both eyes
at once..." Incidentally, there is no rhyme or reason to the way the anthology is
sequenced; according to Tony Dolan, "I just messed around with the tracks so
there was no linear order. It wasn't to fuck anyone up, just a kind of preference
of tracks, really." So now you know!

AVENGER
No official website at the time of writing, although as the band reformed in the
Summer of 2005, who knows what might happen next.
Recommended listening: Everything's collected together on the Sanctuary
Records double CD *Too Wild To Tame – The Anthology* (CMDDD571).

BITCHES SIN
Reformed around 2003 and have been active ever since, co-sharing the limelight
with Ian Toomey's other project, Flashpoint.
Check out: www.bitchessin.co.uk
Recommended listening: Second album *Invaders* is available through their website
as are both Flashpoint albums and, at the time of writing, an entire CD's worth
of demo material entitled *Your Place Or Mine* can be downloaded for free. *The*

First Temptation (Majestic Rock MAJCD038) contains their first demo and BBC session on one CD, and is a cracker.

BLITZKRIEG

Got the split and reformation out of the way quite early on, and have been recording and gigging ever since.

Check out: www.absolute-blitzkrieg.com

Recommended listening: *A Time Of Changes – Phase 1* (Sanctuary Records CMDDD523) is a double CD which rounds up all the early material (including the *A Time Of Changes* album and *Blitzed Alive*), and *Absolutely Live* (Metal Nation MNR001) of which Malcolm Dome said in *Classic Rock* in August 2004, "…it's decent… thoroughly decent. Recorded in the 'North East of England' during May and June last year, this isn't exactly state of the art. No exotic overdubs here; when the band say this is 'absolutely live' they aren't kidding. Mistakes a go-go, notes that go AWOL in battle, vocals from Brian Ross (the only original member left) that sometimes miss their mark in a way that would lose any penalty shoot-out. However, the basic, raw attitude of Blitzkrieg triumphs. 'Inferno', 'The Wraith' and 'Metalizer' prove they've got more than one song… *Absolutely Live* is something of a vindication."

DIAMOND HEAD

Now up and running with just guitarist Brian Tatler remaining from the original line-up. Vocalist Sean Harris and Tatler had recorded an album that was ready to go, apparently, but their split seems to imply that it will never see the light of day.

Check out: www.diamond-head.net

Recommended listening: Anything. Everything. Sanctuary Records re-issued the first album on CD with a handful of singles tacked on in 2001 (*Diamond Head*, CMRCD239) which is a good start, but there's no such thing as a bad Diamond Head song. Trust me.

GIRLSCHOOL

Girlschool remain one of the most hard-working, hard partying and immensely likeable metal bands ever. They have never split up and despite some rather iffy moments as the Eighties unfolded, they're as good now as they were all those years ago.

Check out: www.girlschool.co.uk

Recommended listening: I've always had a soft spot for their 1980 debut album *Demolition* and the fourth album *Play Dirty* (Sanctuary Records released the first four albums with bonus tracks in 2004). 2004's *Believe* (Communique Records CMGCD027) isn't half bad either. I also really like *Running Wild* which cost me an arm and a leg on import when it came out, but I don't think I'm allowed to talk about it!

HELLANBACH

Great band who just never got the breaks. Fantastic guitarist in Dave Patton, and bucketloads of attitude.

Recommended listening: The entire Hellanbach back (bach?) catalogue – both LPs (*Now Hear This* and *The Big H*), their *Out To Get You EP*, and two Neat compilation tracks – was pulled together on CD and issued as *The Big H: The Hellanbach Anthology* by Sanctuary Records in 2002.

HOLOCAUST

John Mortimer continues to lead a terrifically underrated band who are a very different proposition to the NWOBHM youngsters who cut 'Heavy Metal Mania' all those years ago, as they continue to push the boundaries of metal with some extreme compositions.

Check out: www.holocaustmetal.com

Recommended listening: *The Nightcomers* and the posthumous live album *Live (Hot Curry And Wine)* for the purposes of the NWOBHM, both of which have been re-issued by Sanctuary (CMDDD780 and 812 respectively) with bonus tracks. Otherwise, have a shot at *Primal* (Edgy Records, EDGY 114). *The Live From The Raw, Loud And Live Tour* video footage was released on DVD in 2004 by Metal Print MTL001DVD. It's worth picking up because of its historical value. Yeah, the film quality isn't great; it has, after all, been kicking around for over twenty years, but it's great to *see* the NWOBHM rather than just hear it.

JAGUAR

Still going strong under the watchful eye of guitarist Garry Pepperd.

Check out: www.jaguar-online.com

Recommended listening: Most of what you need is on the Sanctuary Records release *Power Games – The Anthology* (CMDDD413), but the 2003 release *Run Ragged* (Angel Air SJPCD150) maintains the power and speed of some of their early material.

RAVEN

John Gallagher (bass/vocals) and brother Mark (guitars) are still going strong and notched up a homecoming UK gig at Bloodstock in 2005.

Check out: www.ravenlunatics.com

Recommended listening: Debut album *Rock Until You Drop* and third LP *All For One,* again both re-issued by Sanctuary with bonus tracks (CMRCD492 and CMRCD494 respectively). *For The Future,* a four-track live video EP shot in 1982 or thereabouts was issued on DVD by Metal Print in 2004 (MTL002DVD). Tracks are 'Rock Until You Drop', 'Crash, Bang, Wallop', 'For The Future' and 'Chainsaw'.

SABRE

Bassist Geoff Gillespie recently issued a compilation of Sabre material through his own label, Majestic Rock Records, which sweeps up everything of note by his band (*Roar To The Core,* MAJCD061).

Check out: www.majesticrock.com

SAXON

Had good times and bad times and eventually split into two distinct camps. Biff Byford and Paul Quinn continue to front Saxon, and Graham Oliver and Steve Dawson lead Oliver/Dawson Saxon, which also features Nigel Durham (who played bass on the *Destiny* album), singer John Ward who had a stint with Shy amongst others and Hadyn Conway, who played guitar for Saracen on their Neat Records *Change Of Heart* LP.

Check out: www.saxon747.com and www.oliver-dawson-saxon.com

SATAN

The classic line-up (minus drummer Sean Taylor) reformed for a one-off at the Wacken festival in Germany in August, 2004. "I personally thought we could've played better but I don't think we could've gone down any better. An amazing response. It was good for what it was. As you might expect though, immediately afterwards there was talk of another tour, another album, another this and that. I managed to avoid getting drawn into it by suddenly noticing as many distracting things going on around us as possible!" Russ Tippins told me.

A really, really good band.

Recommended listening: *Court In The Act* (Neat Metal NM019), and the *Into The Future* mini-LP is pretty damn good as well. They have released *Live In The Act,* a recording of a Dutch show from 1983 (Metal Nations Records

MNR003) which is a bit rough 'n' ready, but gives you an idea of the power of this band live.

SHIVA

Called it a day over twenty years ago, but demos for the second album Continuance were located in 2004.

Check out: myweb.tiscali.co.uk.amskuse/

Recommended listening: The 1996 CD re-issue of *Firedance* (British Steel Records, CD METAL 8) features the whole album and the band's first single 'Rock Lives On' (the second was two tracks taken directly off the album). An instant and well-worth-having Shiva collection in one purchase. The *Continuance* material (along with some older demos) was released in 2004 by Majestic Rock Records under the same name (MAJCD051)

SOLDIER

Back in business after a long time out in the cold.

Check out: www.soldierstormtroopers.com

Recommended listening: The 'Sheralee' 7" on Heavy Metal Records is a fine single of the genre and takes some beating, and obscurists can enjoy the *Live Forces* cassette album. It's all on *Heavy Metal Force,* a collection of material released on Hellion Records (HELO228) in 2005.

TRESPASS

When I interviewed them in December 2003, they were positive about the future, but nothing's been heard of them since.

Check out: www.trespass-alienegg.co.uk

Recommended listening: *One Of These Days – The Anthology* (Sanctuary Records CMQDD 957) – everything they did, aside from three lost tracks ('Look Alive', 'Doctor Roco' and an alternative version of 'Midnight Hour'), on one double CD.

TYGERS OF PAN TANG

Where it all started for Neat Records. Jess Cox and Robb Weir fronted an ersatz Tygers at the Wacken festival in 1999 after which Weir put a full-time band back together.

Check out: www.tygersofpantang.com

Recommended listening: Debut album *Wild Cat* (Edgy Records EDGY101), and *First Kill* (Metal Nation MNR002) which is a collection of the original band demos.

WITCHFYNDE

Released their fifth album *The Witching Hour* in 2001, just 17 years after its predecessor *Lords Of Sin*. Vastly under-rated band; it's great to have them back, really. Check out: www.witchfynde.com

Recommended listening: The third album *Cloak And Dagger* is available from their website (as is *The Witching Hour*), but my personal favourite is *Lords Of Sin* (Mausoleum 251012). First and second albums *Give 'Em Hell* and *Stagefright* are now available on Lemon Recordings (CDLEM 51 and CDLEM 61).

AND FINALLY, LAST, AND BY ALL MEANS LEAST, TARSUS

Dave Cogan (drums), John Cruttenden (guitars), Chris Hole (guitars), Simon Mulvay (bass), John Tucker (vocals).

The best band to rehearse in the Unitarian Hall, The Strand, Torquay. Spent forever trying to find the definitive NWOBHM name, and ended up with a great moniker but just two songs. Preceded the speed metal boom by a good two years by playing Status Quo's 'Caroline' so fast they shaved a minute off its original length; it's just a shame that they all didn't shave the same minute off. Despite the fact that the core of the band existed long before Tucker joined, Tarsus folded shortly after he quit to go to university, meaning that the 48 minute version of 'Nothing To Lose' and potential cult classic 'Driller Killer' remain unrecorded. Probably for the best really.

SOME NWOBHM 'CHARTS'

TEN PERSONAL NWOBHM-RELATED MOMENTS (IN CHRONOLOGICAL ORDER)

Iron Maiden's gig at Routes, Exeter, December 1979

Iron Maiden performing 'Running Free' live on *Top Of The Pops,* February 1980

The Saxon/Tygers Of Pan Tang tour at Torquay Town Hall, June 1980 (and the Budgie/Vardis tour the following month)

The release of the Neat Records' compilation cassette *Lead Weight* in May 1981

The Angel Witch/Vardis/Geddes Axe/Raven four-band NWOBHM Metalfest at the Lyceum, May 1981

Blitzkrieg's reformation gig at Walthamstow Royal Standard, May 1985

Back in business once more, Satan opening the first Eindhoven Open Air Festival, August 1986

The reformation of Diamond Head's original line-up for ten minutes at Metallica's show at the Birmingham NEC, November 1992

The release of Shiva's *Continuance* CD (a collection of demos lost for almost twenty years) on October 2004.

The reformation of Avenger and their UK tour supporting Y&T, June 2005

TEN GREAT CD RE-ISSUES OF ORIGINAL NWOBHM CLASSICS

ANGEL WITCH - *Angel Witch*

(25th Anniversary Expanded Edition – Sanctuary CMQCD1157)

The original album with almost all the singles, the BBC session and 'Baphomet' from the *Metal For Muthas* compilation. All it needs now is the original EMI single version of the song 'Sweet Danger' to make it complete. While you're at it, have a look at *Sinister History* (Zoom Club Records ZCRCD21), some early demos and live tracks.

AVENGER – *Too Wild To Tame – The Anthology*

(Sanctuary Records CMDDD571)

Both albums and three single cuts on one CD; an instant Avenger collection.

DIAMOND HEAD

(Sanctuary CMRCD239)

The original debut white label album, with a handful of bonus single tracks. The artwork cleverly recreates the original album with band autographs.

HOLOCAUST – *The Nightcomers*
(Sanctuary Records CMDDD780)
or *Live (Hot Curry And Wine)* (Sanctuary Records CMDDD812)
Couldn't decide whether to include the storming debut album (complete with a bonus disc containing all of the band's singles) or the posthumous live album with the bonus disc featuring the live video soundtrack. You choose.

SATAN – *Court In The Act*
(Neat Metal NM019)
Complete with the three tracks that would have been the *Hunt You Down* EP if they hadn't decided to do their Blind Fury thing instead.

SHIVA – *Firedance*
(British Steel CD METAL 8)
"It's got a bit more punch than the original vinyl as they've obviously done a bit of EQ-ing to the bottom end." So says Andy Skuse, so now you know too. Contains the whole album and the non-album single tracks 'Rock Lives On' and 'Sympathy'.

TYGERS OF PAN TANG – *Wild Cat*
(Edgy Records EDGY101)
What a debut! The CD comes with all the appropriate singles and B-sides. Also have a look at the CD of early demos, *First Kill* (Metal Nation MNR002)

TYTAN – *Rough Justice*
(Majestic Rock Records MAJCD022)
No bonus tracks, but still a great album.

VARIOUS – *Lead Weight*
(Sanctuary Records CMUCD456)
Neat Records' first compilation, and probably the best NWOBHM compilation ever released.

VARIOUS – *Metal For Muthas*
(Sanctuary CMRCD 142)
Where it all started really, all those years ago.

CLASSIC ROCK'S 'THE NEW WAVE OF BRITISH HEAVY METAL – THE 20 HOTTEST BANDS' ("IN AN A-Z FORMAT TO AVOID ACCUSATIONS OF FAVOURITISM") BY GEOFF BARTON:

Angel Witch	Rox
Def Leppard	Samson
Diamond Head	Saxon
Fist	Silverwing
Girl	Sledgehammer
Iron Maiden	Tygers Of Pan Tang
Mythra	Vardis
Praying Mantis	Venom
Raven	Witchfynde
Rock Goddess	Wrathchild

"So, just which was the most important band to emerge from the New Wave Of British Heavy Metal after it kicked off all of 25 years ago?" wrote Geoff Barton in *Classic Rock* in June 2004. "Iron Maiden, perhaps? Def Leppard, maybe? Nope. The most influential group of the era were Venom, the Geordie devil-worshippers who unwittingly invented at least one, and more likely several, brand-new musical genres." [Surely some mistake, Geoff?]

TERRORIZER'S SILVER BULLETS – CELEBRATING 25 YEARS OF THE NEW WAVE OF BRITISH HEAVY METAL (PUBLISHED IN *TERRORIZER* ISSUE 119, MAY 2004)

Chris Chantler's Best Albums…

Iron Maiden	*Iron Maiden*
Angel Witch	*Angel Witch*
Elixir	*Son Of Odin*
Witchfinder General	*Death Penalty*
Venom	*Black Metal*
Diamond Head	*Lightning To The Nations*
Saxon	*Wheels Of Steel*
Desolation Angels	*Desolation Angels*
Satan	*Court In The Act*
Holocaust	*The Nightcomers*

...and Singles

Ricochet	*'Midas Light'*
Arc	*'War Of The Ring'*
Fist	*'Name, Rank And Serial Number'*
Trespass	*'One Of These Days'*
Virtue	*'We Stand To Fight'*
Hell	*'Save Us From Those Who Would Save Us'*
Reincarnate	*'Take It Or Leave It'*
Blitzkrieg	*'Buried Alive'*
Tyrant	*'Hold Back The Lightning'*
Requiem	*'Sacrificial Wanderer'*

THE SUZIE SMILED... TOP TEN

I asked everyone I know for their ten favourite NWOBHM songs and came up with the following chart. I guess it's not that representative, because there was a lot of vote-splitting; for example, everyone voted for Diamond Head but almost everyone picked a different song. So, this was not a particularly scientific exercise, and just remember, don't blame me; I didn't vote, I just counted 'em...

1. Def Leppard – *'Getcha Rocks Off'*
2. Trespass – *'One Of These Days'*
3. Tygers Of Pan Tang – *'Hellbound'*
4. AIIZ – *'No Fun After Midnight'*
5. Iron Maiden – *'Running Free'*
6. Diamond Head – *'Am I Evil?'*
7. Praying Mantis – *'Cheated'*
8. Raven – *'Don't Need Your Money'*
9. Angel Witch – *'Angel Witch'*
10. Samson – *'Take It Like A Man'*

TEN GREAT (AND NOT SO GREAT) NWOBHM COVERS...

'20th Century Boy' – Girlschool

Girlschool weren't ashamed to cover songs – 'Fox On The Run', 'Tiger Feet' and 'Live With Me' spring immediately to mind. Then there was 'I'm The Leader Of The Gang (I Am)', although that was co-recorded with Gazza himself so maybe more of a tribute than a cover. Headgirl's 'Please Don't Touch' was more Motörhead's idea, and '1 2 3 4 Rock 'N' Roll' had to be completed by session players when the band decided it was just too awful for words and walked. But '20th Century Boy' is probably the best NWOBHM cover version. A great rendition of a great song.

'I Got The Fire' – Iron Maiden

Maiden covered this Montrose song twice. Originally it cropped up as a live B-side to 'Sanctuary' with Paul Di'Anno singing, and then it was recorded in the studio with Brucie for the flip to 'Flight Of Icarus'. The live version is better.

'Love Potion #9' – Tygers Of Pan Tang

Whoa! Just pipped at the post by '20th Century Boy' as the numero uno NWOBHM cover, the Tygers' update of this old classic has it all: it's fun, it's lively, and what a solo. A great single, unfortunately it's the only good song on an otherwise poor album.

'Tush' – Girlschool/Tygers Of Pan Tang

Two single B-sides, to 'Hit And Run' (10" version) and 'Suzie Smiled' respectively. The girls do it justice with a fun and funky version, the boys turn it into the sonic equivalent of putting your head in a blender.

'Women In Uniform' – Iron Maiden

There was a kid I went to school with who had no redeeming qualities whatsoever. Just like this cover (and single) from October 1980. "It was actually Steve Harris's idea, and at the time I also thought it was a winner," recalls Paul Di'Anno. The 12" added a live version of 'Phantom Of The Opera' which was good, and a retread of 'Invasion' from the *Soundhouse Tapes EP* which wasn't.

'The Wanderer' – Fist

Now I like this; I like it a lot. Unfortunately, no-one else did. Two years after it came out, Status Quo recorded a lacklustre version of the same song and it got to Number 7 in the UK Singles Charts. Go figure.

'Everybody Wants To Be A Cat' – Hellanbach
Inspired. There's no other word for this album closer on the band's debut LP *Now Hear This*. A spin on the song from *The Aristocats* with a booming double-bass, a kick-ass middle section and a humalong outro. That's the way to do it.

'Do You Love Me?' – Girl
Perennial live favourite on stage, poor filler on an otherwise great album on vinyl. The word 'Why?' springs to mind.

'Silver Machine' – Vardis
Up there with 'Jeepster' and 'Jumping Jack Flash' in the Vardis catalogue of bad ideas. The concept of a chestnut is to leave it in the fire until it's hot and then devour it – not stick it back in for another ten years and drag it out when it's completely overdone. The lead single off their second album *The World's Insane*, it failed to chart. I wonder why.

'I Didn't Know I Loved You (Till I Saw You Rock And Roll)'
– Rock Goddess
What is it with girls and Gary Glitter? Alongside Girlschool's version of '...Leader' and Joan Jett doing almost everything else, comes this rather good version of the second single I ever bought. Although they don't actually add much to it, it's still very pleasant to listen to, in a lightweight sort of way. Nice.

THE SOUNDTRACK OF THE FILM
OF THE BOOK...

These days, it seems the only reason for writing a book is to get a Hollywood blockbuster movie made from it. And then of course, there's the obligatory soundtrack album. So, as a precursor to the movie (with Johnny Depp playing the handsome West Country heavy metal author hero, if he can get to grips with the accent), and because I didn't 'vote' in the above listings, let's wrap things up with *Suzie Smiled...The Ultimate Soundtrack CD*:

'*Inferno*' – Blitzkrieg (from *Lead Weight* compilation album)
'*Blades Of Steel*' – Satan (from *Court In The Act*)
'*Suzie Smiled*' – Tygers Of Pan Tang (from *Wild Cat*)
'*Sanctuary*' – Iron Maiden (from *Metal For Muthas*
          compilation album)
'*Break The Chain*' – Raven (from *All For One*)
'*Shoot Out The Lights*' – Diamond Head (7" A-side)
'*Stab In The Back*' – Witchfynde (from *Lords Of Sin*)
'*Name, Rank And Serial Number*' – Fist (7" A-side)
'*Baphomet*' – Angel Witch (from *Metal For Muthas*
          compilation album)
'*Ain't Life A Bitch*' – Bitches Sin (from *Invaders*)
'*Take It All Away*' – Girlschool (from *Demolition*)
'*The Duel*' – Trespass (from *Bright Lights EP*)
'*Angel Of Mons*' – Shiva (from *Firedance*)
'*Angel Dust*' – Venom (from *Lead Weight* compilation album)
'*Death Or Glory*' – Holocaust (from *The Nightcomers*)
'*All The Way*' – Hellanbach (from *60 Minutes
          Plus Heavy Metal Compilation* album)
'*Axe Crazy*' – Jaguar (7" A-side)
'*Soldiers Of War*' – Satan's Empire (from *Lead Weight*
          compilation album)

THE LAST WORD

"Originality is running low, but I've accepted that heavy metal bases its values in traditions and power and I'm fully prepared to judge it on that level. Heavy metal has apparently no desire to change the world, I accept that lack of responsibility."
– So you don't like it, then? Mick Middles talking bollocks while reviewing the Heavy Metal Barndance, in *Sounds,* August 1980).

"We took out some great bands. As well as Saxon, and Girlschool, there was Tank – they were great for a while, then they fucked up. They were great on our tour though. Who else was it? Sword. And Anvil… They all did OK with us but fucked it up afterwards. You see, you can give 'em the baton, but it's not my fault if they fuckin' drop it!" – Lemmy, Motörhead.

"On February Friday 13, 1981 we were playing a gig in Burton-on-Trent. That night Tommy Vance was broadcasting the session we had recorded for *The Friday Rock Show* so we sat outside in the car to listen to it on the radio. The time came for the session, Tommy Vance announced it and there was complete silence. The machinery just wouldn't play the songs no matter what Tommy Vance did. He announced that it had never happened before. We then went onstage. Firstly the PA blew up, then the lighting rig blew and finally my amps blew up. The deities were obviously having a laugh that night." – Montalo, Witchfynde.

"I knew nothing about the band before I joined, although coincidentally, I had worked with the outgoing drummer Chris Dadson a few years earlier – we both had paper rounds at the same newsagents!" – Mike Ellis, Aragorn.

"Much abuse has been hurled my way because of a recent flirtation with some of the better exponents of, for God's sake, heavy metal. This I understand because HM is still the most regressive, posey, stupid, naïve, ridiculously pompous music on this planet." – So you still don't like it, then? It's Mick Middles talking bollocks again, this time in the introduction to a review of a batch of metal singles in Sounds.

"Getting signed to MCA gave us the chance to compete with all the other bands that were premier division rock. We had money to update our gear, get some clothes, and buy some petrol for the van instead of siphoning it out of other cars in car parks!" – Robb Weir, Tygers Of Pan Tang.

"We've done a deal with Ian Toomey and Bitches Sin for their original demos and BBC session which we've called *The First Temptation* and it'll be housed in an out-take photo from the 'Always Ready (For Love)' single photo session – you remember, blonde in suspender belt with her legs wrapped around a Flying-V? Now how's *that* for NWOBHM!" – Geoff Gillespie, Majestic Rock Records.

"We've done quite a few gigs since we got back together, mainly one-offs and festivals and stuff like that, but I guess we tend to be a bit more choosy now. People talk big and offer us stuff but it often never comes off, you know? One thing I'm not going to do is get in the back of a van and go up and down the motorway for weeks on end, not for anyone. For one thing, my back just wouldn't take it! Honestly, I'll have you in tears in a minute! Get the violins out! Fucked up old git!"

– Garry Pepperd, Jaguar.

"One of the consequences of setting up the website to coincide with the release of *Continuance* was a request from a university lecturer in Venezuela who wanted a copy of *Firedance* for her students who are studying the history of rock music (she being herself a 'female musicologist with a PhD in rock and pop music'), I had to send her a copy of course – even though I guess it means we're officially history now!" – Andy Skuse, Shiva.

"Headlining Reading was brilliant. Again, I was really nervous before we went on. I mean it was massive, thousands of people, but it was brilliant too, all our families were there. We turned up in a pink open-top Cadillac that our management had hired for us. As we were driving towards Reading, a load of bikers spotted us and waved, and then formed an escort in front and behind the car and escorted us all the way to Reading! Apparently the car was Jayne Mansfield's – but I didn't want to ask if it's the one she got killed in!" – Denise Dufort, Girlschool.

AND FINALLY...

"...A gentleman named John Tucker wrote the liner notes for the CD. As I read his words, I can picture him in his suit and tie sitting behind a desk at the Sanctuary offices, wondering how he got stuck with an assignment to write liner notes for this Holocaust band..." – Holocaust's Ron Levine rightly lets off steam following the release of the Smokin' Valves anthology on Sanctuary Records.

We both had a good laugh about it later, but to be fair to him, there were a few glaring errors in the liner notes, not the least of which being my constant misspelling of band leader John Mortimer's name. The most annoying thing about the cock-ups is that getting the Holocaust material out was my ruddy idea in the first place, the moral being, if you are going to screw up, you might as well do it big time! But a "suit and tie"? The last time I wore a suit and tie was when I got married; still got the wife, but the clothes went in the bin years ago...

REFERENCES AND NOTES

Apart from living the NWOBHM, I collected a vast array of cuttings, magazines and books from that era, a lot of which I read and re-read while writing *Suzie Smiled...* I am very grateful to the writers and publishers of non-original material that I've quoted from in this book.

INTERVIEWS

Mike Ellis, Aragorn, *November 2003*
Tony Dolan, Atomkraft, *October 2004 and ongoing correspondence*
Mick Moore, Avenger, *ongoing correspondence since 1984*
Ian Toomey, Bitches Sin, *ongoing correspondence since January 2004*
Pete Toomey, Bitches Sin, *June 2004*
Sharalee, The Bitches Sin Girl, *July 2004*
Blaze Bailey, Blaze, *March 2004*
Brian Ross, Blitzkrieg, *ongoing correspondence since 1985*
Jim Sieroto, Blitzkrieg, *February 2004*
Sean Harris, Diamond Head, *June 2004 and September 2004*
Brian Tatler, Diamond Head, *June 2004*
Denise Dufort, Girlschool, *March and August 2004*
Paul Birch, Heavy Metal Records, *June 2004*
John Mortimer, Holocaust, *December 2003 and ongoing correspondence*
Sean Hetherington, Intense, *November 2004*
Paul Di'Anno, Iron Maiden, *September 2005*
Garry Pepperd, Jaguar, *November 2003*
Jon Craven, Liquid Sky, *November 2004*
Lemmy, Motörhead, *October 2003*
David Wood, Neat Records, *from material collected from 1984 to 1986.*
John Gallagher, Raven, *March 2004*
Geoff Gillespie, Sabre, Snowblind and Majestic Rock Records,
March 2004 and ongoing correspondence
Sean Taylor and Russ Tippins, Satan, *ongoing correspondence since 1985*
Biff Byford, *April 2004 and October 2005*
Andy Skuse, Shiva, *April 2004 and ongoing correspondence*
Chris Logan, Shiva, *April 2004*
Garry Phillips, Soldier, *April and June 2004*
Mark Sutcliffe and Dave Crawte, Trespass, *December 2003*
Jess Cox, Tygers Of Pan Tang, *November 2003*

Robb Weir, Tygers Of Pan Tang, *February 2004*
Montalo, Witchfynde, *July 2004 and ongoing correspondence*

An extra special thanx goes to Sean Hetherington of Intense, (check out the 2004 release *Second Sight* on Nothing To Say Records via www.intense-uk.com) and Jon Craven of Liquid Sky (whose album *Bloodline* is available from www.liquid-sky.co.uk) for taking things forward for the next generation.

QUOTED BOOKS

The best A-Z on the NWOBHM is Malc Macmillan's excellent *The New Wave Of British Heavy Metal Encyclopedia*, first published 2001 (ISBN 3-931624-16-1), which contains (I believe, although I've never counted them) write-ups on some 500 bands. Very informative and a great read.

All chart positions are taken from *The Great Metal Discography From Hard Rock To Hardcore* by M.C. Strong, Mojo Books, second edition published 2001 (ISBN 1-84195-185-4).

Garry Bushell, *Running Free – The Official Story of Iron Maiden*, Zomba Books, first published 1984 (ISBN 0-946391-50-5).

Paul Di'Anno's autobiography *The Beast*, John Blake Publishing, first published 2002 (ISBN 1-904034-03-9).

David Fricke, *Animal Instinct – The Def Leppard Story*, Zomba Books, first published 1987 (ISBN 0-946391-55-6).

Joel McIver, *Justice For All: The Truth About Metallica*, Omnibus Press, first published 2004 (ISBN 0-7119-9600-8).

Ian Christe, *Sound Of The Beast – The Complete Headbanging History Of Heavy Metal*, HarperCollins, first published 2003 (ISBN 0-06-052362-X).

Martin Popoff, *The Top 500 Heavy Metal Songs Of All Time*, ECW Press first published 2003 (ISBN 1-55022-530-8).

Martin Popoff, *The New Wave Of British Heavy Metal Singles*, Scrap Metal Records first published 2005 (ISBN 0-9762133-0-3).

In addition, there were numerous books written when metal became big in the early Eighties. One such was Brian Harrigan and Malcolm Dome's *Encyclopedia Metallica - The Bible Of Heavy Metal* (Omnibus Press, ISBN 0-86001-805-9) which was really just a rush-job in my opinion. It's got a snappy title though, and some rather good NWOBHM pictures. Finally, the information that Celtic Frost played both Aragorn's 'Black Ice' and Angel Witch's 'Extermination Day' was confirmed in Tom Gabriel Fischer's autobiography *Are You Morbid – Into The Pandemonium Of Celtic Frost* (Sanctuary, first published 2000, ISBN 1-86074-310-2).

Credit is due to Geoff Barton, who obviously wrote about the NWOBHM widely and his articles in *Kerrang!* and other publications are essential reading; I'd also like to thank *Kerrang!* and *Sounds* magazines.

INTERNET SOURCES

Just scratching the surface on the internet, there's Grinder's Old School Metal Show and more at www.nwobhm.net, loads of information at www.nwobhm.com, and the Iron Pages website (the organisation behind a number of books including *The New Wave Of British Heavy Metal Encyclopedia*) www.iron-pages.de is extremely informative). It's all there, believe me.